CW00968698

CURRENT RESEARCH IN EGYPTOLOGY 2008

Proceedings of the Ninth Annual Symposium

which took place at
The KNH Centre for Biomedical Egyptology
University of Manchester
January 2008

Edited by
Vicky Gashe and Jacky Finch

Rutherford Press Limited

Published by Rutherford Press Limited for CRE. Edited by Vicky Gashe and Jacky Finch.

All rights reserved: no part of this publication may be reproduced by any means, electronic, mechanical, photocopying or otherwise, without the prior permission of the publisher.

First published in Great Britain in 2008

Rutherford Press Limited, 37 Rutherford Drive, Bolton, BL5 1DJ
Registered Office: 52 Chorley New Road, Bolton, BL1 4AP

www.rutherfordpress.co.uk

Copyright © CRE and the individual authors

A CIP catalogue record of this book is available from the British Library

ISBN 10: 0-9547622-5-8
ISBN 13: 978-0-9547622-5-4

Printed by the MPG Books Group in the UK

CONTENTS

ACKNOWLEDGEMENTS

To organise a postgraduate conference of such international standing, whilst also continuing our own research at the KNH Centre, required a great deal of support and effort from many people. On behalf of us both our special thanks must firstly go to Professor Rosalie David for her initial suggestion that we bid to host CRE IX, and for her continuous advice in the planning and delivery of the conference. We would also like to thank Roland Enmarch, Karen Exell, Ken Griffin, Bob Partridge, Kathryn Piquette, Peter Robinson, Alice Stevenson, Angela Thomas, Keith White and Penny Wilson for their help and advice during our time as CRE organisers and editors.

The publication of this volume would not have been possible without the help and support of Joyce Tyldesley and Steven Snape at Rutherford Press Limited, whose editorial advice has been gratefully received.

We are grateful to all of the staff at the Michael Smith Building and at The Manchester Museum who were involved in hosting the conference and the evening reception, but particular thanks must go to Karen Reeson, Ian Miller, Bob Bird, Anna Davey and Nick Merriman. Many of our colleagues at the KNH Centre helped to run the conference – chairing the sessions, manning the registration desks, meeting and greeting, providing a friendly welcome to visitors and sustaining the usual CRE camaraderie – but we are particularly grateful to Ryan Metcalfe and Jenefer Cockitt in this regard, and also to Tim Finch (who became an unofficial member of the KNH Centre for those three days!).

CRE is funded entirely by each host institution, the costs usually being met by fundraising activities on the part of the students involved in the organisation of the conference. Financial support this year has been most generous. Special thanks must go to the KNH Centre, J. H. Davidson, A. Parker, the Egypt Exploration Society, *Ancient Egypt Magazine*, Poynton Egypt Group, Manchester Ancient Egypt Society, Archaeopress, Shire Publications, Rutherford Press Limited, and to the KNH students (Lidija McKnight, Mervyn Harris, Gillian Riley and Jo Roberts) who wrote articles on their work for *Ancient Egypt Magazine* and donated their fee to the CRE fund.

Finally we must acknowledge the tremendous effort of all those speakers who provided such a stimulating three days of presentations, and to all the authors who have contributed to this volume. May we take this opportunity to thank you all for making CRE IX such an inspiring experience. We wish you all every success for your continuing research and careers.

ILLUSTRATION CREDITS

Cover illustration, the funeral of Kyky from Theban tomb TT409 (after M. Abdel-Qader Muhammed (1966) 'Two Theban Tombs: Kyky and Bak-en-Amun', *Annales du Service des Antiquités de l'Égypte* 59, 159–84, pl. 87; adapted by S. Snape).

Individual authors are responsible for the use of images within their papers. The editors, the KNH Centre, and Rutherford Press Limited are not responsible for the obtaining of copyright permission for these images.

SYMPOSIUM PAPERS NOT INCLUDED IN THIS VOLUME

A Study on a Title
Rehab Assem - University of Helwan, Cairo

Specialisation in Predynastic Pottery: Standardised Straw-Tempered Ware
at Hierakonpolis
Masahiro Baba - University of Cardiff

Climatic Change in the Early Pharaonic Period: A Re-evaluation of the Evidence
Jenefer Cockitt - University of Manchester

Cocaine and Nicotine in Ancient Egypt?
David Counsell - University of Manchester

Walk Like an Egyptian: Religious Ritual or the Dawn of Prosthetic Medicine?
Jacky Finch - University of Manchester

Evidence for Predynastic and Old Kingdom Burial Practices: An Assessment of
the Use of Early Excavation Reports
Vicky Gashe - University of Manchester

A Curious Female Figurine in the Egypt Centre Collection, Swansea
Kenneth Griffin - University of Swansea

The Historiography of Asasif and a Changing Focus
Meg Gundlach - University of Swansea

The God and Goddesses of the Central Hall
Amr Gaber - University of Durham

Kings' Crowns in Ancient Egypt
Sarah Jackman - University of Swansea

A Study of Ivory in Predynastic Egypt
Sarah-Jane Langley - University of Liverpool

Experiencing the Eastern Desert Rock Art
Francis Lankester - University of Durham

Identifying the Great Overlords of the Nome
Steven J. Larkman - Mount Royal College, Calgary

Reconsidering the Problem of Bes and the Seated Goddess
Adrienn Nagy - Eötvös Loránd University, Hungary

Horses of a Different Colour
Pauline Norris - Independent Scholar

Agency and Materiality in Late Period Non-Royal Statuary
Campbell Price - University of Liverpool

POSTER PRESENTATIONS

INTRODUCTION

The ninth Current Research in Egyptology Symposium was hosted by the KNH Centre for Biomedical Egyptology, University of Manchester, in January 2008. The KNH Centre, which was founded in 2003, is the culmination of over thirty years of multidisciplinary research into ancient Egyptian artefacts (most notably mummies) at Manchester, under the direction of Professor Rosalie David OBE. This work builds on an even longer tradition of mummy studies at Manchester, stretching back just over a century to 1907, when Dr. Margaret Murray unwrapped the mummies of the two Twelfth Dynasty 'brothers' housed at The Manchester Museum.

The staff and students of the KNH Centre were proud to host CRE IX in 2008, and to welcome our colleagues from across the world to our city and university. The conference, hosted each year by and for graduate-level researchers in all fields of Egyptology, has gone from strength to strength over the last few years. The 2008 meeting was no exception, attracting a record ninety-eight delegates from twelve countries. Amongst the delegates were representatives of eighteen universities, along with a number of independent scholars. In total, some thirty-seven papers were presented over the three days, and our new 'poster session' – an alternative format to the presentation of a full paper – allowed the work of students in the early stages of their research to be represented.

Aside from those presenting their work, it was particularly gratifying to welcome to the audience a large contingent from local Egyptology societies, showing the high level of interest in and support for all things Egyptological for which the North-West of England is renowned, and which the KNH Centre is pleased to be a part of.

One of the recurring themes at previous CRE meetings has been the discussion of how we might include more of our colleagues from Egypt, who are carrying out vital research but who may not be able to participate in a UK-based conference. There were some innovations at CRE IX in this regard. During the first two days, the UK delegates linked up with Egyptian students and researchers at the National Research Centre in Cairo and the Bibliotheca Alexandrina in Alexandria via video link, which enabled the Egyptian students to hear and see each of the speakers in the UK, and to participate in the question and answer sessions. We also tested the possibility of using the video link to allow papers to be presented to the UK from Egypt, and Essam el-Saeed from the University of Alexandria took part in a question and answer session on his paper on the location of the land of Punt (the contents of which are reproduced in this volume). The idea of the video link may eventually allow CRE to widen its audience across the world, but we remain conscious that the greatest benefit from such an event is to enable students to meet their fellow researchers and to share ideas. We are therefore also pleased to announce that the idea of a CRE Bursary (to help with the cost of travel to CRE for an Egyptian student) has been realised for the first time this year thanks to generous donations from our supporters, and that the first recipient will present their work at CRE X in Liverpool.

The work presented at CRE IX covered a vast array of topics, and shows the diversity of study categorised within Egyptology today. The selection of papers published in this book give some idea of this variety.

The study of ancient Egyptian artefacts is represented by a paper from Arnaud Quertin-mont, who discusses his newly-developed technique for the dating of New Kingdom statues of canine deities, based on their morphology and method of construction. Kathryn Piquette's paper shows us how we can interpret items associated with writing in a way other than by translating their scripts, by focussing on the materiality of Early Dynastic ivory labels – a concept often overlooked in the discussion of early writing, but which is, as Kathryn shows, of great importance for our understanding of the use of these items.

Within the field of linguistic studies, Henning Franzmeier looks at the definitions of several words often used to describe wells and cisterns in ancient Egyptian literature, and using the *emic* versus *etic* approach, attempts to show us what these different words tell us of the contexts in which they were used. Patricia Berg takes her focus away from the study of individual words, looking rather at examples of pieces of literature (and particularly letters) from Deir el-Medina, and examining what they can tell us about Egyptian attitudes to travel and foreign lands.

Examination of ancient Egyptian architecture is the theme of Kate Liszka's work on water basins in Middle Kingdom Egypt. Her study places these features into context within the particular buildings in which they are found, showing a relationship between the structure and function of numerous examples, and helping us to visualise the 'everyday life' of these buildings as she does so. Szymon Zdzieblowski looks at the mudbrick architecture of the Predynastic period, and discusses how studying the development of this particular style of architecture might tell us more about other long-standing questions in this period, such as state formation in early Egypt.

Tomb art is used as the basis for two papers, but each analyses it in a different way. Kim Ridealgh gives an example of the use of imagery in Eighteenth Dynasty tomb art to convey an abstract concept (in this case masculinity), using the tomb of Rekhmire as her main case study. Nico Staring's paper brings a quantitative approach to the study of tomb scenes – here, the position of Old Kingdom scenes themed around desert animals is discussed, and a statistical approach employed to discover whether the use and positioning of such scenes within the tomb followed a pattern, and what this pattern might suggest about the function of the scenes.

Research into aspects of Egyptian society is represented by Dan Boatright's paper, which focuses on what an Egyptian soldier might have faced during battle – as the author points out, this may have been somewhat different from the version of 'battle' seen in artistic representations.

Lucile Haguet's paper represents a study not of ancient Egypt, but of the western concept of Egypt during the sixteenth, seventeenth and eighteenth centuries, and in particular how our idea of Egypt was represented in various ways, particularly through the cartography of the period. She discusses the differences between this concept of Egypt (termed *Aegyptus*) and reality.

Finally, the application of science within Egyptology – the specialism of the KNH Centre - is demonstrated by three papers, each showing the use of a different technique. Lidija McKnight shows how science can give us vital information on ancient Egyptian artefacts, as she describes her use of radiography to look more closely at three unusual museum items, which at first glance appear to be mummies. Natalie McCreesh uses the molecular analysis of the coatings of a mummy of the Third Intermediate Period, and its associated shabti box, to discover more about the composition of these coatings, and relates her findings to the creation, decoration and use of the objects. Ryan Metcalfe shows the importance of the development of a clear methodology, designed using modern samples, in the study of ancient artefacts, which are a finite resource. His paper demonstrates this using the case study of his own research, which looks at the preservation of tissues at the molecular level afforded by ancient Egyptian mummification techniques.

These papers collectively show the huge variety of research being carried out by graduate students at universities across the world, and the innovative methods being employed to look at various problems within Egyptology. Sharing work, developing ideas and making new contacts has always been an important part of CRE, and we hope that this volume expresses the enthusiasm and talent that we saw during our three-day conference. This book represents the culmination of the KNH Centre's role as hosts of CRE IX, and we now pass the baton on to the University of Liverpool, who we know will organise a great meeting for CRE X in January 2009.

Vicky Gashe and Jacky Finch
Manchester, September 2008

Perspectives on Travelling
in the Texts from Deir el-Medina

Patricia Berg
Helsinki University

Introduction

This paper forms a part of my PhD thesis, with the provisional title 'Perspectives on travelling in non-literary and literary texts from the New Kingdom'. The research is being done at Helsinki University, Institute for Asian and African Studies, Department of Egyptology under the supervision of Associate Professor Dr. Jaana Toivari-Viitala (University of Helsinki, Finland) and Professor Dr. Antonio Loprieno (University of Basel, Switzerland).

The purpose of my thesis is to examine perspectives on travelling during the New Kingdom embedded in the textual material preserved from this period. My aim is to present a picture of the Egyptians' attitudes to travelling and the foreign and to look at the Egyptians' ideas behind and conceptions of going away and returning home. In a broader perspective the attitudes recorded in the written discourse could give an insight into the Egyptians' idea of themselves, their families and the society they lived in, i.e. the contemporary cultural norms and social opinion.

Some preliminary findings regarding perspectives on travelling stemming from my study of texts from Deir el-Medina are presented below. Hundreds of literary as well as non-literary texts, which include references to travelling and journeys, have been found from this workmen's village (e.g. Černý 1939; Gasse 1990; Gasse 2005; Janssen 1991a; Posener 1938; Posener 1951; Posener 1952; Posener 1972; Posener 1977; Posener 1978; Posener 1980). The literary texts including such references are for example well-known stories like Sinuhe (Koch 1990) and didactic texts like Menna's Letter to his Son (Fischer-Elfert 2006, 87–92; Guglielmi 1983, 147–166). The non-literary texts with references to journeys are mainly private letters written by villagers away from home, and letters written by people at home to someone on a journey (e.g. Allam 1973; McDowell 1999; Wente 1967; Wente 1990).

When one compares references to travelling presented in literary texts with references in non-literary texts from Deir el-Medina, the literary texts reflect a shared cultural knowledge and awareness at Deir el-Medina; that is to say, they represent the kinds of fictional journey-related issues the villagers were acquainted with. On the other hand, non-literary texts, especially private letters, convey real life knowledge and attitudes towards travelling and the foreign. This may differ, at least occasionally, from what is presented in the literary media.

As conceptions of travelling have varied throughout pharaonic history a short overview of different perspectives on the issue is called for and thus presented below.

References to travelling in Egyptian texts

References to travelling both within the borders of Egypt and to foreign countries occur in textual material during the whole pharaonic period. Autobiographies composed on the walls of Old Kingdom noble tombs provide evidence of how the elite took part in various military and administrative excursions (Loprieno 2003, 34). These autobiographies have been shown to include the main features adapted by later Egyptian literary compositions, such as concern for moral behaviour and a narration of individual achievements (Gnirs 1996, 191–241), and in the end, the Old Kingdom autobiographic texts became predominately fictional, and thus more like literary texts. The excursions mentioned in autobiographies were undertaken by direct order of the pharaoh, so travelling was therefore part of fulfilling the duties of the elite towards the central government (Baines 2004, 10). In these texts there are few or no mentions of crossing a border or entering a foreign country. Travelling is here presented as a matter of pure economical or political concern (Loprieno 2003, 36).

Autobiographies continue to be written throughout the pharaonic period, but from the early Middle Kingdom onwards a far wider range of other literary texts were produced as well. The Middle Kingdom is therefore generally considered to be the high era of ancient Egyptian literature and many of the stories which are well-known today, as well as didactic texts, were written during this period (Parkinson 2002, 4). In some of these Middle Kingdom literary tales the main plot centres around a journey made by the protagonist. Compared to the autobiographies from Old Kingdom noble tombs these literary tales offer a new perspective on travelling. Travelling is here usually not undertaken merely for the purpose of fulfilling duties to the central government, nor does it have a strict economical or political concern. The contrast between Egypt and 'the other' has become more prominent and the protagonist needs to struggle to overcome the border rather than just pass it (Loprieno 2003, 40).

The New Kingdom is one of the most international periods of pharaonic history during which Egypt's contact with the outside world increased (Shaw 2000, 308–23). This fact is reflected in the literary compositions of the period, such as the so-called Late Egyptian Stories (Gardiner 1932). As in the Middle Kingdom tales, the protagonist is here often performing some kind of journey. The nature of the journey is now, however, of an even more personal character and without a clear connection to the central government. Thus the Late Egyptian Stories offer yet another new perspective of travelling in the ancient Egyptian textual discourse.

Thus one could state that in general many of the ancient Egyptian literary texts appear to have a protagonist performing some kind of journey. The journeys or journeying forms a part of the main plot, yet the nature of and the perspective on the journey conveyed in the texts changes through time (on journeys in Egyptian literature see for example Galán 2005; Moers 1999; Moers 2001; Posener 1956).

Defining Egyptian literature

Several serious attempts to define ancient Egyptian literature have been published during the last decades (e.g. Assman 1974; Fech 1990; Foster 1980). Assman suggested (1974;

1996; 1999) the Egyptian texts were to be divided into functional non-literary texts and non-functional literary texts. Based on Assman's definition, Loprieno (1988; 1996) built his theories on literature, generally accepted and used among scholars today. Perhaps the most significant of Loprieno's work (1988) is his theory on how to define Egyptian literary texts by introducing the theoretical concepts of *topos* and *mimesis*. The large group of diverse didactical texts, like instructions and lamentations, is, according to Loprieno, assembled under the term *topos*. These texts function as transmitters of the ideological expectations of the society, i.e. they instruct the officials on how an ideal member of the Egyptian state should act. *Mimesis*, the narrative literature, on the other hand represents the individual response to these social expectations (Loprieno 1988, 10–13). Most of the Egyptian literary texts include both of these elements and cannot be submitted to just one of the groups, e.g. autobiographies from the Old Kingdom onwards express clearly the tension between social expectations, *topos*, and individual reactions to them, *mimesis* (Loprieno 1996, 46).

A decade later Loprieno (1996, 43) introduced a group of other concepts from the field of literary theory in order to define ancient Egyptian literature. They are fictionality, intertextuality and reception. Fictionality means that there is a mutual understanding between the author and reader that the text does not need to coincide with the real world, but can do it. This agreement is generated through the form and style of the text. Thus ancient Egyptian literary texts cannot be used as historical documents that provide solid data about real occurrences, yet they may serve as mirrors that reflect the contemporary political and social situation.

Moers (1999; 2001) established a theory on travelling in ancient Egyptian literary texts based on the concept of fictionality. According to Moers, travelling and journeying motifs are the ultimate forms of fictionality. Travelling represents a transition, as do the literary texts in general; a 'crossing of a border' from the real world into a fictional one. Therefore travelling and journeys were used as motifs in the Egyptian literary tales as a way to express and emphasise this transition, where the home environment represents the real world and a distant foreign region the fictional world. Further, fictional travel-literature is the only group of literary texts preserved from ancient Egypt where the dichotomy between *topos* and *mimesis* is openly discussed, i.e. the problematic interface of cultural and individual identity (Moers 1999, 58). When a protagonist in a literary text is crossing the border of Egypt and entering a foreign country, he is also crossing the Egyptian socially defined boundaries. Therefore, when Sinuhe is leaving Egypt and travelling over Sinai to Syro-Palestine he is not only entering the fictional, chaotic world but also revolting against the role he is assigned by Egyptian society (Moers 1999, 53).

References to travelling in the texts from Deir el-Medina

A notable amount of the literary Deir el-Medina texts are trial pieces copied by students practicing to become writers. Usually the same texts have been copied over and over again. Thus we have thousands of fragments of varying sizes of literary texts found at Deir el-Medina (Gasse 1992, 51–2). The following well-known texts have, for example, been found in the village: the Story of Sinuhe, the Satire of the Trades, the Prophecy of Neferti, the Loyalist Instruction, the Book of Kemit, the Instruction of Ptahhotep, the Instruction of Djedefhor, the Instruction of Ani, the Instruction of Amenemhat I and Papyrus Anastasi I (Gasse 1990; Gasse 2005; Posener 1938; Posener 1951; Posener 1952; Posener 1972; Posener 1978; Posener 1980).

In these literary texts the above-mentioned theory by Moers (2001) is indeed applicable. Egypt or the hometown represents the real world, whereas foreign countries and regions outside the home area represent the chaotic world, the fictional one. Not surprisingly, therefore, journeys and travelling are usually combined with negative expressions and sometimes even physical pain. The general assumption in Egyptology that Egyptians preferred to stay within the borders of their familiar environment is in tune with ideas voiced in these literary texts.

However, Moers' theory appears only applicable to literary texts since non-literary texts include few or no aspects of fictionality. The literary texts reflect on shared cultural knowledge at Deir el-Medina, i.e. on what kind of fictional journey-related issues the villagers were acquainted with. Non-literary texts on the other hand convey real life knowledge and attitudes to travelling and the foreign. Thus, the reason why travelling and journeys are mentioned in non-literary texts should differ to some extent from the way this motif was used in literary texts.

Among the non-literary texts from Deir el-Medina private letters form the most likely type of texts to include references to journeys and travelling. Hundreds of letters have been found in the village, some are copies of real letters that were written by writer-students, the so-called model letters, but many of them are genuine ones (Bakir 1970, 2; Janssen 1992, 87–91). The latter were written by villagers who for some reason spent time away from the village and while away received letters, which they brought back home to Deir el-Medina on their return.

Scholars such as Baines and Eyre (e.g. 1989), and Sweeney (2001, 6) have drawn our attention to the fact that there probably existed a noteworthy oral tradition in ancient Egypt. Thus we can assume that the communication between the villagers of Deir el-Medina was predominantly oral rather than written (Janssen 1992, 89). If so, the written letters preserved until today only form a very small part of the whole communication system in the village, but they can still give us an indication of which topics were the common subject of communication (Sweeney 1993, 523–9).

Definitions

Travelling, and how long a person should travel in order to make a journey, have not, as far as I am aware, been defined in Egyptology. Since we are dealing here with Deir el-Medina, a workmen's village in the desert on the West Bank of Thebes, I have included in my definition of a journey any references for going across the Nile to the East Bank of Thebes. The definition for a journey in this paper thus includes various lengths of journeys from going across the Nile to Eastern Thebes to journeys to foreign countries.

Another question which needs to be addressed is where the difference between a literary and a non-literary text should be drawn. As mentioned before, the main group of non-literary texts with references to travelling and journeys are private letters. These are generally considered to be non-literary. But there are also letters found at Deir el-Medina which are not as clearly defined as literary or non-literary. For example the abovementioned Mennas's letter to his son has been discussed by Fischer-Elfert (2006, 87–92) and McDowell (1999, 48), who seem to disagree on whether the letter is a genuine or a literary, model one.

Sweeney (2001, 3) suggests that the line between a real-life non-literary letter and a fictional literary one could be drawn on the basis of intentionality. According to Sweeney real-life letters are written in order to achieve a certain purpose, even though this purpose is only to maintain personal contact. Literary letters on the other hand are written in order to entertain or teach a larger group of people. I find this definition problematic since it requires us to identify the intention of a letter. The intention is rarely mentioned in the text itself and thus we would have to rely on our own secondary opinion. Sweeney further states that real-life letters usually discuss matters with someone who knows them fairly well and can refer to them elliptically. Literary composed letters take their public into consideration and provide at least some amount of background information (Sweeney 2001, 4).

Non-literary letters from Deir el-Medina

An important group of letters among the source material for my study is the corpus of Late Ramesside Letters, published by Černý in 1939. The group of 51 letters in the aforementioned publication has been augmented by Janssen's publication of nine additional letters in his Late Ramesside Letters and Communications in 1991 and a letter published by the same scholar in the *Journal of Egyptian Archaeology* (Janssen 1991b, 79–94, pl. 4, 2). These letters were written during the Twentieth Dynasty, but since only very few are dated it is difficult to put them in chronological order (Wente 1967, 1). None of the letters have been found in modern excavations. Rather, they have been part of private and museum collections for numerous decades. According to Černý (1939, 15-17) the letters originate from Deir el-Medina and most of them were probably found by local people during their pillaging of the necropolis in 1817 and 1818, and then passed on to collectors in the early 1820s.

The structures of the Late Ramesside Letters follow a quite similar or standard pattern. The letters begin with an epistolary formula including address and blessings – thus, an introductory formula (Sweeney 2001, 16). A complimentary preamble and then, the actual message or topic of the letter follow the introductory section while further blessings and formulae end the letter, thus constituting a terminal formula. This is the model structure for a regular complete and real letter. In reality, however, all parts do not necessarily occur in most letters (Bakir 1970, 31), although the introductory and terminal formulae are coherent and sometimes even exact copies of each other.

About half of the Late Ramesside Letters are written by Djehutymose, the well-known scribe from Deir el-Medina (Černý 1973, 360–1). Djehutymose went on at least two journeys, one to the south and one to the north of Thebes. He followed expeditions that were organised by the central government – the journey Djehutymose made to the south is probably identical with the Nubian campaign led by the army commander and high priest Payankh (Haring 1992, 77–8). During Djehutymose's absence his son Butehamon took over the position as scribe at Deir el-Medina. Son and father wrote to each other about daily life, their family and their property, but also about administrative matters. In addition to the correspondence between these two the Late Ramesside Letters corpus also includes letters written by other persons, some of whom remain anonymous, but all in some way associated with the Deir el-Medina community.

References to travelling in non-literary Deir el-Medina texts

Having studied groups of private letters from Deir el-Medina, I have collected a database of the text passages where journeys or travelling are mentioned. So far about 200 letters have been processed. I have also made a separate list of the relevant text passages found in the letters. The latter number 250 in all. The transliterations and translations presented below are based on the work by Černý (1939), Černý and Groll (1993) and Wente (1967, 1990). The more or less standard introductory formula at the beginning of private letters appears almost always to include some negative notion about going away and being away from home, such as:

P. BM EA 10326/P. Salt 1821-155, rt. 4
imi in wi imn nsty tꜣ.wy pꜣy=i nb iw=i ꜥnḫ.kwi
Let Amon of the thrones of the two lands, my lord, bring me back alive.

P. BN 197, IV, rt. 6
ḏd n imn in=i iw=i wḏꜣ.kwi yꜥr pꜣ nty tw=i im ḫꜣꜥ[.tw]
Tell Amon to bring me back sound [from] Yar the place where I am abandoned.

Similar negative expressions can also be seen in the letters written by people back home to somebody on a journey. Such as:

P. BN 197, VI, rt. 2–3
in tw iw šd=k mi ḥty nb r nty m pꜣ tꜣ ḥry r nty tw=k [..] im=f
To bring you back saved from all danger, which is in the land above in which you are [..].

P. Geneva D 407, rt. 6
mtw imn in=k iw=k wḏꜣ.ti
May Amon bring you back sound.

P. Turin 2026, rt. 10–11
[in=i] iw=i wḏꜣ.kwi imi tw pḥ=i r ḥry kmt m pꜣ tꜣ wꜣ nty tw=i [im=f]
[Bring] him back sound and let him reach down [to] Egypt from the far-off land [in] which [he is].

In the main body of the letter, after the introductory formula, where the actual subject or message is written, the correspondents usually write about travelling and being away in a much more neutral way. Such as:

P. Berlin P 10494/P. Suffrin, rt. 5
sḏm= <n> i.ḏḏ.tw=k ìì.ti pḥ=k r niwt pȝ dmy
We have heard what has been said about you that you have returned having reached the town of Ne.

O. DeM 114, rt. 8
ḥr iw=ì r šmt m ḫdi
Now I will be travelling to the north.

P. BN 197, V, vs. 2–3
tw=k rḫ.tw pȝy mšꜥ nty tw=ì m nꜥy r irt=f
You know about this journey, which I am going to make.

P. BM EA 10284/P. Salt 1821-239, rt. 8–9
ḥr bwpwy=f irt nȝ m š.wꜥ nty sw im.w ꜥn
He has never made the journey in which he is (now) engaged.

P. Turin Cat. 1972, rt. 8
ḥr tw.n mni.tw r ȝbw
Now we are moored at Elephantine.

O. DeM 446, vs. 4–7
yȝ sw m ḫdi r pȝ ḥbsd
See, he is travelling north to the royal jubilee.

Sometimes slightly anxious or sometimes clearly positive comments are written about a foreign place or about travelling and making a journey in itself. Such as:

P. Geneva D 407, vs. 18
rmṯ mr iw bwpw=f irt m[šꜥ ..]
A man is ill who has not made [a journey].

O. DeM 418, rt. 2–4
tw=ì spr.tw ḥwt iry n=ì imn-ms m mitt pȝ-ḥm-nṯr ḥrt nbt nfrt
I have reached Hut. Amenmose as well as Pahemnetjer have taken good care of me.

O. IFAO 562
nȝ ḫdi=ì mtw=ì šm n=ì mtw=ì mḥ bsy
Will I go north? Will I go away alone? Will I finish the introduction?

The last one is an oracle question and not a letter, but I have included it here to demonstrate that journeys and travelling are mentioned also in other text groups than private letters only.

Conclusion

Overall it thus would appear that the negative expressions towards being away occur in the introductory and terminal formula in the beginning and end of a letter, but not so much in the main body of the message. One could argue that these epistolary formulae were standardised. Certain elements were included because they established the norm of proper Ramesside letter-writing,. not because these elements actually reflected on the writer's subjective opinion. This argument is supported by the fact that both negative expressions in the introductory or terminal formula and neutral or even positive expressions in the main body can be found in the same letter, e.g. BM EA 10284 and Turin Cat. 1972.

It is interesting that another corpus of letters containing references to travelling, the letters from el-Hibe, do not in general include this kind of introductory formula with negative expressions. The el-Hibe letters date to the Twenty-first Dynasty and are thus slightly younger than the Ramesside letters from Deir el-Medina (Spiegelberg 1917). They were written by two scribes of the local god, Horus of the Camp, in Late Egyptian, substantially the same written language as that of the Late Ramesside Letters (Sweeney 2001, 12). In my dissertation I will use the el-Hibe letters as comparative material to the letters from Deir el-Medina and the New Kingdom. By doing this I hope to be able to give a broader insight into perspectives of and changes of phraseology referring to travelling in the textual material over time.

The main body of the letter is of greatest interest for my study, due to the wide range of expressions referring to actual travelling found in the aforementioned text section. It is here that the real attitudes of the Egyptians are, in my opinion, likely to be found. In view of these references one might suggest that the Egyptians indeed possessed a great spectrum of attitudes to mobility, some of which, if not positive, were at least neutral where going away and confronting 'the foreign', or coming back home was the issue.

Acknowledgements

I would like to thank the organisers of the Current Research in Egyptology IX for the opportunity to present my paper at the symposium. I should also like to express my gratitude to my supervisors Associate Professor Dr. Jaana Toivari-Viitala and Professor Dr. Antonio Loprieno for valuable comments on the topic of my dissertation at this early stage. I hope to be able to present full results of my research project in the near future.

Bibliography

Assman, J. (1974) 'Die literarische Text im alten Ägypten. Versuch eine Begriffsbestimmung', *Orientalische Literaturzeitung* 69, 117–26.

Assman, J. (1996) 'Kulturelle und Literarische Texte', in A. Loprieno (ed.) *Ancient Egyptian Literature. History and Forms.* (Probleme der Ägyptologie 100), 59-82. Leiden, Brill.

Assman J. (1999) 'Cultural and Literary Texts', in G. Moers (ed.) *Definitely: Egyptian Literature* (Lingua Aegyptia. Studia monographia 2), 1–15. Göttingen, Seminar für Ägyptologie und Koptologie.

Allam, S. (1973) *Hieratische Ostraka und Papyri aus der Ramessidenzeit. Urkunden zum Rechtsleben im alten Ägypten*. Tübingen, Im Selbsverlag des Herausgebers.

Baines, J. (2004) *Die Bedeutung des Reisens im alten Ägypten*. Leipzig, Ägyptisches Museum der Universität Leipzig.

Baines, J. and Eyre, C. (1989) 'Interactions between Orality and Literacy in Ancient Egypt', in K. Schousboe and M.T. Larsen (eds). *Literacy and Society*, 91–119. Copenhagen, Akademisk Forlag.

Bakir, A. M. (1970) *Egyptian Epistolography from the Eighteenth to the Twenty-first Dynasty* (Bibliothèque d'Étude 48). Cairo, Institut français d'archéologie orientale.

Černý, J. (1939) *Late Ramesside Letters* (Bibliotheca Aegyptiaca IX). Brussels, Fondation Égyptologique Reine Élisabeth.

Černý, J. (1973) *A Community of Workmen at Thebes in the Ramesside Period* (Bibliothèque d'Étude 50). Cairo, Institut français d'archéologie orientale.

Černý, J. and Groll, S. I. (1993) *A Late Egyptian Grammar* (Studia Pohl: Series Maior. Dissertationes Scientificae de Rebus Orientalis Antiqui 4). Rome, Pontificio Instituto Biblico.

Fech, G. (1990) *Metrik des Hebräischen und Phönischen* (Ägypten und Altes Testament 19). Wiesbaden, Harrassowitz Verlag.

Fischer-Elfert, H.–W. (2006) 'Literature as a Mirror of Private Affairs. The Case of *Mnn3*(i) and his Son *Mrỉ–šm.t* (iii)' in A. Dorn and T. Hofmann, (eds) *Living and Writing in Deir el-Medina. Socio-historical Embodiment of Deir el-Medina Texts* (Aegyptiaca Helvetica 19), 87–92. Basel, Schwabe Verlag.

Foster, J. L. (1980) 'Sinuhe. The Ancient Egyptian Genre of Narrative Verse', *Journal of Near Eastern Studies* 39, 89–117.

Galán, J. M. (2005) *Four Journeys in Ancient Egyptian Literature* (Lingua Aegyptia. Studia Monographica 5). Göttingen, Seminar für Ägyptologie und Koptologie.

Gardiner, A. H. (1932) *Late Egyptian Stories* (Bibliotheca Aegyptiaca 1). Brussels, Fondation Égyptologique Reine Élisabeth.

Gasse, A. (1990) *Catalogue des ostraca hiératiques littéraires de Deir el-Médineh, Tome IV, Fasc. 1 (Nos 1676–1774)* (Documents de fouilles de l'Institut français d'archéologie orientale du Caire 25). Cairo, Institut français d'archéologie orientale.

Gasse, A. (1992) 'Les Ostraca Hiératiques Littéraires de Deir el-Medina Nouvelles Orientations de la Publication', in R. J. Demarée and A. Egberts (eds) *Village Voices. Proceedings of the Symposium "Texts from Deir el-Medina and their Interpretation". Leiden, May 31–June 1, 1991*, 51–70. Leiden, Leiden University.

Gasse, A. (2005) *Catalogue des ostraca littéraires de Deir al-Medîna, Tome V (Nos 1775–1873 et 1156)* (Documents de fouilles de l'Institut français d'archéologie orientale du Caire 44). Cairo, Institut français d'archéologie orientale.

Gnirs, A. (1996) 'Die Ägyptische Autobiographie', in A. Loprieno (ed.) *Ancient Egyptian Literature. History and Forms* (Probleme der Ägyptologie 10), 191–241. Leiden, Brill.

Guglielmi, W. (1983) 'Eine "Lehre" für einen reiselustigen Sohn', *Die Welt des Orients* 14, 147–66.

Haring, B. (1992) 'Libyans in the Late Twentieth Dynasty', in R. J. Demarée and A. Egberts (eds) *Village Voices. Proceedings of the Symposium "Texts from Deir el-Me-*

dina and their interpretation". Leiden, May 31–June 1, 1991, 71–80. Leiden, Leiden University.

Janssen, J. J. (1991a) *Late Ramesside Letters and Communications. Hieratic Papyri in the British Museum VI*. London, British Museum Press.

Janssen, J. J. (1991b) 'Requisitions from Upper Egyptian Temples (P. BM 10401)', *Journal of Egyptian Archaeology* 77, 79–94.

Janssen, J. J. (1992) 'Literacy and Letters at Deir el-Medina', in R. J. Demarée and A. Egberts (eds), *Village Voices. Proceedings of the Symposium "Texts from Deir el-Medina and their Interpretation". Leiden, May 31–June 1, 1991*, 81–94. Leiden, Leiden University.

Koch, R. (1990) *Die Erzählung des Sinuhe*. Brussels, Fondation Égyptologique Reine Élisabeth.

Loprieno, A. (1988) *Topos und Mimesis. Zum Ausländer in der Ägyptischen Literatur* (Ägyptologische Abhandlungen 48). Wiesbaden, Harrassowitz.

Loprieno, A. (1996) 'Defining Egyptian Literature. Ancient Texts and Modern Theories', in A. Loprieno (ed.) *Ancient Egyptian Literature. History and Forms* (Probleme der Ägyptologie 10), 39–58. Leiden, Brill.

Loprieno, A. (2003) 'Travel and Fiction in Egyptian Literature', in D. O'Connor and S. Quirke (eds) *Mysterious Lands. Encounters with Ancient Egypt*, 31–51. London, UCL Press.

McDowell, A. (1999) *Village Life in Ancient Egypt. Laundry Lists and Love Songs*. Oxford, Oxford University Press.

Moers, G. (1999) 'Travel as Narrative in Egyptian Literature', in G. Moers (ed.) *Definitely: Egyptian Literature* (Lingua Aegyptica. Studia Monographica 2), 43–61. Göttingen, Seminar für Ägyptologie und Koptologie.

Moers, G. (2001) *Fingierte Welten in der ägyptischen Literatur des 2. Jahrtausends vor Christus. Grenzüberschreitung, Reisemotiv und Fiktionalität* (Probleme der Ägyptologie 19). Leiden, Brill.

Parkinson, R. B. (2002) *Poetry and Culture in Middle Kingdom Egypt. A Dark Side to Perfection*. London, Continuum.

Posener, G. (1938) *Catalogue des ostraca hiératiques littéraires de Deir el-Médineh, Tome I (Nos 1001 à 1108)* (Documents de fouilles de l'Institut français d'archéologie orientale du Caire 1). Cairo, Institut français d'archéologie orientale.

Posener, G. (1951) *Catalogue des ostraca hiératiques littéraires de Deir el-Médineh, Tome II (Nos 1109 à 1167)* (Documents de fouilles de l'Institut français d'archéologie orientale du Caire 18,1). Cairo, Institut français d'archéologie orientale.

Posener, G. (1952) *Catalogue des ostraca hiératiques littéraires de Deir el-Médineh, Tome II, Fasc. 2 (Nos 1168 á 1213)* (Documents de fouilles de l'Institut français d'archéologie orientale du Caire 18:2). Cairo, Institut français d'archéologie orientale.

Posener, G. (1956) *Littérature et politique dans l'Egypte de la XIIe Dynastie*. Paris, Honoré Champion.

Posener, G. (1972) *Catalogue des ostraca hiératiques littéraires de Deir el-Médineh, Tome II, Fasc. 3 (Nos 1214 à 1266)* (Documents de fouilles de l'Institut français d'archéologie orientale du Caire 18:3). Cairo, Institut français d'archéologie orientale.

Posener, G. (1977) *Catalogue des ostraca hiératiques littéraires de Deir el-Médineh, Tome III, Fasc. 1 (Nos 1267–1409)* (Documents de fouilles de l'Institut français d'archéologie orientale du Caire 20:1). Cairo, Institut français d'archéologie orientale.

Posener, G. (1978) *Catalogue des ostraca hiératiques littéraires de Deir el-Médineh, Tome III, Fasc. 2 (Nos 1410–1606)* (Documents de fouilles de l'Institut français d'archéologie orientale du Caire 20:2). Cairo, Institut français d'archéologie orientale.

Posener, G. (1980) *Catalogue des ostraca hiératiques littéraires de Deir el-Médineh, Tome III, Fasc. 3 (Nos 1607–675)* (Documents de fouilles de l'Institut français d'archéologie orientale du Caire 20:3). Cairo, Institut français d'archéologie orientale.

Shaw, I. (2000) 'Egypt and the Outside World', in I. Shaw (ed.) *The Oxford History of Ancient Egypt*, 314–29. Oxford, Oxford University Press.

Spiegelberg, W. (1917) 'Briefe der 21. Dynastie aus El-Hibe', *Zeitschrift für Ägyptische Sprache und Altertumskunde* 53, 1–30.

Sweeney, D. (1993) 'Women's Correspondance from Deir el-Medineh', in S. Curto, S. Donadoni, A. M. Donadoni Roveri and B. Alberton (eds) *Sesto Congresso Internazionale di Egittologia. Atti. Vol. II*, 523–9. Turin, Società Italiana per il Gas.

Sweeney, D. (2001) *Correspondence and Dialogue. Pragmatic Factors in Late Ramesside Letter-Writing* (Ägypten und Altes Testament 49). Wiesbaden, Harrassowitz.

Wente, E. F. (1967) *Late Ramesside Letters* (Studies in Ancient Oriental Civilization 33). Chicago, University of Chicago Press.

Wente, E. F. (1990) *Letters from Ancient Egypt*. Atlanta, Scholars Press.

The Realities of Battle in Ancient Egypt

Dan Boatright
University of Liverpool

Introduction

Evidence for military action is abundant within the archaeological record of ancient Egypt, whether depicted on temple walls, described in private tombs or etched into the bodies of fallen soldiers. Despite this wealth of information, there tends to be a dehumanisation of warfare in Egyptian military studies with the focus instead being on the role of the king or gods, legitimization of rule, the relationship between the king and the gods, or between the elite and their king (as seen in Nibbi 1976, Spalinger 1982, Eyre 1996 and Beylage 2002). This can be attributed to the way in which the Egyptians themselves depicted warfare, often employing a clinical narrative, where logistics, tactics and economy become the focal points. By default much of the modern scholarly focus has been directed towards these topics (including Breasted 1903, Shaw 1996 and Spalinger 2005). This, however, contrasts with the study of ancient Greek Hoplite warfare where Hanson (1991, 9) describes the battle experience of a soldier being the bloody pit of an ugly cock fight that could become a deliberate mini-holocaust.

The agenda of Egyptian sources, while drawing much scholarly attention towards their intended focus, is not believed to be the only cause of this more logistical and economy based analysis. Smith (2003, 81–2) suggests that our own assessment of ancient military events is hampered by a relic of a colonist mentality, prevalent throughout the twentieth century, that characterised many cultures, specifically Sub-Saharan cultures, in primitivist terms. This is especially witnessed by the use of such terms as 'Troglodite' and 'Negro' in Breasted's translations (1906, 30), which, although perhaps accurately portraying the Egyptian opinion of their foe, portrays more the social opinions of Breasted's time. This has then led to a suggestion that warfare was not particularly common, with the Egyptians deploying the army to intimidate the surrounding cultures with superior weaponry and organisation. However more recent studies have suggested that the Egyptians did not accurately depict their foe, with the Nubians being far from cave dwelling and possibly technological equals (O'Connor 1993, 31). In reality the invasion of Nubia or the Levant would have required a great amount of resources and, on occasion, the sacrifice of soldiers on the battlefield.

The agendas imprinted upon these Egyptian sources are also closely linked to their design, purpose and date. The Predynastic palettes, for instance, have a mythological connotation with mysterious long necked beasts, bulls and lions savaging the enemy soldiers, and the king smiting the fallen enemy leader (Stevenson Smith 1998; 11–14). In the Middle Kingdom tomb of Mesehti at Asyut the famous models of spearmen and bowmen marching in formation portray what the army aspired to be, with each spearman holding a large wood and cowhide shield in his left hand and a bronze tipped spear in his right (originally published in Grébaut 1890–1900, pls. 33–7 but better quality images reproduced in Arnold 1999, 108–9). This ideal conflicts with the reality, with the armoury at the contemporary fortress of Mirgissa containing hundreds of flint-tipped spears and arrows and no sign of bronze weaponry (Vila 1970, 175–6). While any bronze weaponry may have been removed, re-smelted or plundered, the fact that so many flint weapons were found suggests that metal may not always have been available in large enough quantities to keep the army fully equipped. The flint weapons would supplement this shortfall, if not replace metal spears and arrow heads altogether.

In the New Kingdom the role of the king in battle becomes the centrepiece of temple and royal tomb depictions. Tuthmosis III, Sety I, Ramesses II and Ramesses III all depicted their prowess on the battlefield within the temple of Karnak. While their often egocentric focus on the king singlehandedly destroying the enemy is a somewhat skewed interpretation, the actual role of a king in battle should not be underestimated. As seen in ancient Greece, King Leonidas of Sparta died at Thermopylae (Herodotus VII, 220–227), while Dark Age and Medieval European kings would often engage in battle, such as Richard I of England during the Crusades (Richard 1999, 228) and King Gustav II of Sweden who was killed during the Battle of Lützen in AD1632 (Kirby 1990, 176). It is certainly possible that Egyptian kings took an equally proactive role on the battlefield, while also using temple depictions and royal inscriptions as a tool of propaganda.

With these distinct agendas in mind it is important to consider to what degree there may be any truth in an Egyptian military text, scene or depiction. Spalinger (1982, 39) notes that the Egyptian mind was less preoccupied with presenting a historical account but instead focused on the inevitable victory of the Pharaoh over his worthless opponents. Bishop and Coulston (1993, 33), in the study of Roman military practices, take a different view noting that, while a scholar has to be aware of the strengths and weaknesses of their chosen evidence, the context should not be the only analysed feature. Such an approach will be used in this paper. Looking at tomb depictions, archaeological sites, texts and actual bodies of soldiers from the Middle and New Kingdom, the potential realities of Egyptian military activity will be considered, with a particular focus on the events a soldier could find himself in when on campaign. The types of battlefield injuries, potential treatments and the risk of death will all be discussed, with the contexts and agendas of sources noted, but not the primary focus. Where appropriate more modern parallels and theories will be considered, in a bid to reconstruct a fuller understanding of what warfare could have been like in ancient Egypt. This will by no means be an exhaustive analysis of Egyptian military encounters but will rather serve as an overview of one avenue of interpretation that can be pursued when analysing these sources

Siege warfare in ancient Egypt

It was during the Middle Kingdom that scenes of conflict and military activity became prominent, with siege warfare and the sacking of strongholds being central themes. This depictive focus is mirrored in the archaeology of the period, with the construction of many Nubian fortresses, defended by small regiments of soldiers and designed to support Egyptian interests in the region. This wealth of information makes siege warfare an ideal

Figure 1. The siege of a fortified town depicted in the tomb of Amenemhat at Beni Hasan (after Newberry 1893b, pl XIV).

Figure 2. A reconstruction of the west gate of the fortress of Buhen. The gate is believed to have been heavily defended, with the entrance surrounded by huge walls to enable defenders to engage the enemy from all angles. Bastions and towers are also a part of the defensive structure (Emery *et al* 1979, pl. 11. Picture provided courtesy of the EES).

case study to consider how the Egyptians fought and the importance of this military activity is most evident in the tombs of Beni Hasan (Fig. 1), with several scenes depicting groups of soldiers attacking fortresses, using both conventional weaponry and what is believed by McDermott (2002, 117) to be a battering ram. In defence the men within the fortress are shown firing arrows into the attacking force. Due to the frequency with which this scene appears, being found in the tombs of Baqt III, Khety and Amenemhat (Newberry 1893a, pls V and XV, and 1893b pl. XIV) it is usually suggested that these depictions are not historical but instead ideological in character (Spalinger 1982, 39; 1995, 275). Though the factual nature of these scenes can be disputed, the reality of what they depict is in fact feasible. The defence of fortresses using bowmen is believed to be the most likely strategy with parapets, loopholes and firing slots being found in the Middle Kingdom forts in Nubia (Emery *et al* 1979, 22).

The examination of the architecture of the Nubian fortresses has provided a wealth of information on how these structures were defended and how they could be successfully stormed. The Buhen fortress in particular has several defensive features worthy of note (Fig. 2). The West Barbican of the Outer Fortifications, a main entrance to the fortress, shows how any attack on an entrance would have been repelled, with towers either side of the causeway to allow an aggressive overhead assault (Emery *et al* 1979, 21–2). Along the walls bastions projected into the ditch to provide defenders with an additional angle to strike any attacker (Emery *et al* 1979, 27). Although these fortifications would have been very difficult to overcome there is some evidence that this was achieved. The inner fortifications show evidence of having been taken by storm in the late Middle Kingdom/early Second Intermediate Period with the Great West Gate in particular believed to have been breached and set alight (Emery *et al* 1979, 13). This evidence would suggest that while the Egyptians were more than prepared for a defensive battle they were not always successful.

The bodies of Middle Kingdom soldiers also provide evidence for siege warfare. The mass grave at Deir el-Bahri of sixty men demonstrates what types of deaths could occur on the battlefield, especially from a frontal assault of a fortified position. All of the bodies have suffered trauma conclusive to military activity with four men actually showing evidence of well-healed fractures, indicating they were veterans of earlier skirmishes (Filer 1997, 62). Additionally, a study of their teeth revealed that they were all between thirty and forty years old at death (Winlock 1945), an age when a man could still be called up for military service. Although these soldiers may have been seasoned veterans of previous campaigns it is worth considering how prepared these men were for such a battle. While four of the men show signs of being injured in previous skirmishes, the others may have suffered wounds that left no recognizable scars on their bodies (Winlock 1945, 9). Equally they may have never fought in battle before. Whether these soldiers had all been trained for battle, or had experienced similar events in previous wars is unknown but judging by their ages it would be expected that they would have experienced war previously, rather than being completely inexperienced.

All of these soldiers had been attacked from above, with injuries conclusive to attacking a fortified position. There is little evidence that can firmly establish any direct hand-to-hand combat, with only body 35 possibly being stabbed by a dagger, though this could also have been a wound from a since lost arrow (Winlock 1945, 11). Injuries included various cranial wounds caused by arrows or stones, one body in particular (Fig. 3) still having the ebony tip of the arrow in the left eye socket and penetrating 5.5 centimetres into the head (Winlock 1945, 12–13). The most disturbing fact about this situation is

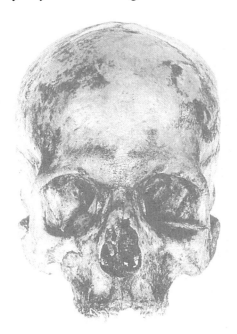

Figure 3. The skull of Body 21 with an arrow protruding from the left eye socket (Winlock 1945, pl. 8D).

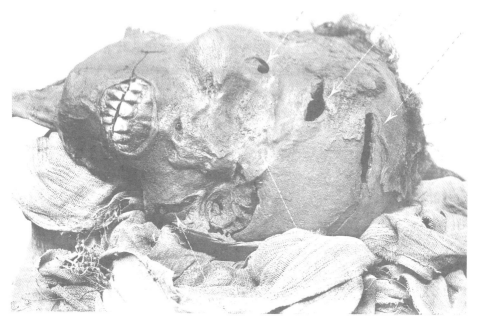

Figure 4. The skull of Seqenenre Tao II. The arrows point to wounds caused by various weapons. The condition of the body indicates a high level of decomposition prior to embalmment and burial (Smith 1912, pl II).

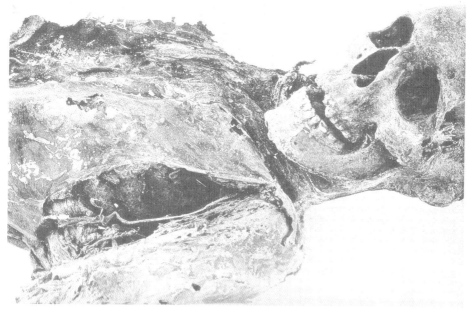

Figure 5. This body of a fallen soldier has damage symptomatic of bird attacks, likely a result of the body being left exposed after battle. This type of damage is to be expected if the body was left on the battlefield after withdrawal (Winlock 1945, pl. 12).

that, due to the relatively low energy impact of this type of arrow fire, and with the arrow not exiting the skull, the soldier would not have immediately lost consciousness (Sanchez 2000, 161). While the victim of such a wound would eventually succumb to the injury, he (and those around him) would face a harrowing experience before death.

Along with the penetrative wounds fifteen soldiers show evidence of being clubbed repeatedly about the head (Winlock 1945, 16–18). With many already receiving incapacitating wounds prior to the bludgeoning (Filer 1997, 62), it is possible that these soldiers were unable to escape after battle and were left for dead. Exactly why these men were left behind is unclear but it is possible that a hasty withdrawal from combat resulted in them being left in the hands of the enemy. Exactly who buried the bodies is unclear. Evidence of vulture attacks are witnessed on six of the bodies leading Winlock (1945, 19) to suggest that these soldiers were left exposed for a brief period before being preserved in sand and bandaged, probably while still in a state of rigor mortis. Whether the attacking forces were allowed to collect their dead is unclear but such events have been suggested in other ancient battle accounts, including the Battle of Kadesh (Spalinger 2005, pers. comm.).

The imperial battlefield

It was during the New Kingdom that Egypt developed more imperial tendencies, moving away from constructing a sphere of influence through routine and small scale skirmishes and instead extending the immediate boundaries of Egyptian rule (Redford 1992, 148). This more aggressive political stance clearly affected the artistic and textual record, showing a more militaristic attitude and the subjugation of the surrounding lands. The Tombos Stela clearly outlines this new foreign policy. Cut into the rock face opposite the island of Tombos, just north of the Third Cataract (Nibbi 1976, 91), this text describes an invasion of Tuthmosis I, one of the final battles that brought Nubia under the total control of Egypt. The poetic language and strong iconographic connotations have led scholars such as Beylage (2002, 676) to conclude that this was not an accurate portrayal of a battle but rather a deterrent for local Nubians against rebelling. The Tombos Stela has also been compared to the Middle Kingdom Semna Boundary Stela of Senwosret III which is believed to have been a marker of the geographical point at which Egyptian power and control began (Eyre 1990, 137). Whether such a text would have been a useful tool to prevent rebellion is unclear, as it is unlikely many local Nubians would be in a position to read and understand what it said. It is important to consider that this was an imposing structure, measuring over two metres high and, while it may not have been read, it certainly would have demonstrated the power of the invader.

Immaterial of the reasons for the stela's existence, the narrative describes an interesting battle that is arguably realistic. The text states that 'the '*Iwnw-sty* fell under the slaughter and were forced to the periphery of their land. Their decaying bodies inundate the valley. The blood (of) their mouths (flow) like a rainstorm' (Urk. IV, 84, 6–7). This suggests a large battle could have occurred with a significant loss of life on at least one side. O'Connor (1993, 31, 60), in his discussion of Nubia, notes that significant resources would have been required to bring down the Kushite Empire at the beginning of the New Kingdom and it is unlikely that a mere demonstration of military force would have been enough for the Egyptians to secure victory. A battle of some kind would therefore have been likely. Any physical evidence of this battle is currently unknown but the bodies of soldiers previously discussed above do support the description of the Tombos Stela. Though from a different type of battle, the Tombos Stela describing two forces striking one another on an open plain, several bodies from Deir el-Bahri show signs of decomposition symptomatic of the type of exposure described in the stela, while the body of Seqenenre Tao II is described as being severely decomposed prior to embalmment and burial (Elliot Smith 1912, 1–2; Harris and Weeks 1973, 122–3; Fig.4), and is one of the primary pieces of evidence used to support the belief that this king died on the battlefield. Under the African heat this decay could have been rapid, with the sun effectively cooking the flesh in hours (Vaughn 1993, 38). If describing a large scale battle, the Tombos Stela could be recounting what would have become of the bodies of the fallen soldiers.

The text continues, stating 'Birds of prey (swarm) over them (the dead). The mass of birds snatch and take them away to another place. The crocodile takes for himself the cowards' (Urk. IV, 84, 8–9). Birds of prey, such as the hawk, are common insignia of the king; however, there could also be an element of truth to this statement. Birds of prey are known to swarm battlefields, being described in accounts of World War I (Winter 1978, 207–8) but there is also evidence of bird attacks on the chest and cheek of body 26, from Deir el-Bahri (Winlock 1945, 18; see also Fig.5 for an example of this). Similarly crocodiles are used in Egyptian texts as personifications of the king (Eyre 1996, 419) but the description in the Tombos Stela of crocodiles killing soldiers may reflect reality. Crocodiles are also known to be opportunistic animals and would have taken advantage of the dead strewn across the valley or soldiers fleeing from the battle. It is also possible that the author is acknowledging a military tactic employed by the Egyptians. If the Nubians were forced towards the river it would cut off any escape route and leave them helpless against Egyptian and/or crocodile attack. While this can certainly be described as poetic language, a foundation in truth cannot be ruled out.

A large scale Nubian campaign in the reign of Tuthmosis I is also mentioned in the El-Kab tombs of Ahmose, son of Ebana (Urk. IV, 8) and Ahmose-Pen-Nehkbet (Urk. IV, 36, 5–8). Unlike the Middle Kingdom tombs at Beni Hasan, these tombs do not follow an identical structure, with form, style and content differing widely. Both soldiers describe contemporary campaigns they were actively involved in (as seen in Table 1) but they did not always serve at the same time. On one occasion where they did both serve, the Nubian campaign of Tuthmosis I, they describe the events in a different style to the others in their respective texts. Ahmose, son of Ebana, in contrast to his usual true-to-life description of campaigns, uses elaborate imagery, stating 'At this his majesty became like a leopard. His majesty shot and his first arrow pierced the chest of that foe. Then those enemies turned to flee, helpless before his uraeus. A slaughter was made among them' (Urk. IV, 8–9). Ahmose-Pen-Nekhbet, however, describes an unspecified but significant number of captives being brought from Kush (Urk. IV, 36, 5–8), unlike other campaigns where he describes specified, small numbers of captives. Exactly why there is such a different change in the description of these events is unclear but it is possible that something distinct occurred, possibly a huge battle in which heavy losses were incurred. Ramesses II uses similar images in the description of the Battle of Kadesh (Lichtheim 1974, 58–9) and this may indi

Ahmose, son of Ebana	Ahmose-Pen-Nekhbet
Avaris (Ahmose)	
Sharuhen, Palestine (Ahmose)	
	Djahy, Palestine ? (Ahmose)
Nubia (Amenhotep I)	Nubia (Amenhotep I)
	Northern Imukehek? (Amenhotep I)
Nubia (Tuthmosis I)	Nubia (Tuthmosis I)
Naharin (Tuthmosis I)	Naharin (Tuthmosis I)

Table 1. The battles described by Ahmose, son of Ebana, and Ahmose-Pen-Nekhbet, in relative chronological order

cate a literary tool employed by the Egyptians to describe large-scale battles whererlarge numbers of men fought and, potentially, died. Spalinger (2002, 361), in an in-depth analysis of the Kadesh narrative, notes that this extravagant phraseology should not detract from the historical reconstruction and the context may have significant relevance. While these descriptions may not be to the point and completely accurate, they are still based on the events witnessed by the Egyptians.

During these campaigns the soldiers would have been at significant risk. The Egyptians seem prepared for this and recorded the treatment of inflicted wounds. The Edwin Smith Surgical Papyrus describes a variety of treatments for injuries caused by trauma (either accidents or acts of violence). Case seven is a typical example of these injuries. It states '(If you treat a man for a gaping wound in his body, which has penetrated to the bone and violated the skull) you have to probe his wound... You should bandage him with an oil, honey and lint dressing' (Recto 3,3–3,6). The bandage with oil and honey dressing would have been very effective, honey being known to dry up a wound, heal it and have antibacterial properties to prevent infection (Mininberg 2005, 14). This treatment was not always effective, and the text continues, 'should you find his face damp from sweat, the vessels of his neck taut, his face ruddy, and his teeth and back, the smell of the box of his head like the urine of sheep and goats, his mouth clenched, his eyebrows knit and his face like something crying... an ailment for which nothing is done' (Recto 3,9–3,12). Despite the exposure of the brain the text does state that the victim could survive such an injury, however, a secondary infection posed a significant threat to survival. This text portrays a particularly grim, slow and painful death that, although not exclusively the result of battlefield activity, would have had a far higher prevalence there. Doctors are believed to have been depicted on the Kadesh battle scenes (McDermott 2004, 117) and are described in P.Anastasi IV (9,9–10,1), dealing with dysentery, lice and water pollution while on campaign. After large battles it is certainly possible these medics were faced with many injuries described in the Edwin Smith Surgical Papyrus and it may have been an invaluable resource for any Egyptian doctor.

The injuries and deaths depicted by the Egyptians on temple walls have also been analysed to determine authenticity. Sanchez, a neurosurgeon, studied the reliefs of Sety I (Sanchez 2000) and Ramesses II (Sanchez 2003) at Karnak, and found that the visible injuries to the abdomen, neck and head were very realistic. One Hittite soldier of the Ramesses II scenes was of particular significance as his posture was symptomatic of decerebrate rigidity, a body posturing reaction to a brain injury that disconnects the main part of the brain at the base from the upper brain stem (Sanchez 2003, 63). Though the Egyptian artist would not have understood what had happened, it is possible that it had been witnessed and later depicted at Karnak. With many deaths and injuries being depicted in an accurate manner it is possible that the author of these works had acquired a great deal of knowledge about battlefield injuries, either first hand or from those with battle experience.

Conclusion

The Egyptians produced a great quantity of material describing their military activity and utilised a variety of styles, some of which are common in other cultures. The descriptive style of Egyptian biographical texts and those found in royal contexts are quite similar to a modern genre of writing known as Landserhefte or 'Journals of the Ordinary Soldier.' These stories are usually set in periods of extensive combat, such as the world wars, with historic figures like SS soldier Otto Skorzeny playing a vital role in the narrative. These are designed to be uplifting stories, demonstrating heroism through graphic and brutal scenes, with enemies' bones being crushed, heads being blown off and soldiers impaled on bayonets (Mosse 1986, 498). Though not detailing exact historic events they do show the tactics that could be employed and the events that could happen to an individual soldier on the battlefield. With comparative descriptions in both texts of the elite, including the Ahmoses of El-Kab and Amenemheb, and in royal inscriptions, such as those of Tuthmosis I, Tuthmosis III and Sety I, it is certainly possible that much of the information given is based on the experiences of Egyptian soldiers who went into battle. As is the case with modern Landserhefte, where these fictional tales describe events that did occur on the battlefield during World War II, it is likely that the ancient texts could serve a similar purpose, describing the actions that may have occurred, if not the exact historic events.

To what degree these sources actually depict exact historical details can be argued but they do show the Egyptian attitudes to warfare and how they wished to be viewed on the battlefield. This information is further supplemented by the archaeology at such sites as Buhen, where the tactics depicted could have been used, and on the bodies of the soldiers, which show the numerous wounds shown in depictions and described in texts. While the first aim of Egyptian texts and inscriptions is to legitimise the rule of a king or portray the relationship between the king and gods, or an individual and his king, they also clearly demonstrate the warfare of the time which, as seen in the archaeology, could be particularly gruesome.

Acknowledgements

I would like to thank the organisers of the Manchester CRE IX conference for the opportunity to present and publish this paper. I am particularly grateful to Ian Shaw and Jennifer Cromwell for reading and commenting on the many forms this work has taken these past few years, and to Neil Smith for the French and German assistance.

Abbreviations

P.Anastasi: Gardiner, A. H. (1937) *Late-Egyptian Miscellanies*. Bruxelles, Fondation Egyptologique Reine Elisabeth.
Recto 3, 3–3, 6 etc: Allen, J. P. (2005) *The Art of Medicine in Ancient Egypt*. New Haven: Yale University Press.
Urk IV: Sethe, K. and Helck, W. (1906–21) *Urkunden der 18. Dynastie,* IV. Leipzig, Hinrichs.

Bibliography

Allen, J. P. (2005) *The Art of Medicine in Ancient Egypt*. New Haven, Yale University Press.
Arnold, D. (1999) 'The Middle Kingdom and Changing Notions of Kingship', in F. Tiradritti (ed.) *The Cairo Museum: Masterpieces of Art*, 90–135. London, Thames and Hudson.
Beylage, P. (2002) *Aufbau der königlichen Stelentexte vom begin der 18. Dynastie bi zur Amarnazeit. Teil I und II*. Weisbaden, Harrassowitz Verlag.
Bishop, M. C. and Coulston, J. C. N. (1993) *Roman Military Equipment; from the Punic Wars to the fall of Rome*. London, Batsford.
Breasted. J. H. (1903) *The Battle of Kadesh; a study in the earliest known military strategy*. Chicago, University of Chicago Press.
Breasted, J. H. (1906) *Ancient Records of Egypt. Volume II*. Chicago, University of Chicago Press.
Elliot Smith, G. (1912) *Catalogue Général des Antiquités Égyptiennes du Musée du Caire Nos 61051–61100; The Royal Mummies*. Cairo, L'Institut français d'archéologie orientale.
Emery, W. B., Smith, H. S., and Millard, A. (1979) *The Fortress of Buhen. The Archaeological Report*. London, Egyptian Exploration Society.
Eyre, C. J. (1990) 'The Semna Stelae; Quotation, Genre and Functions of Literature', in I. S. Groll (ed.) *Studies in Egyptology presented to Miriam Lichtheim*, 134–65. Jerusalem, Magnes P. Hebrew University.
Eyre, C. J. (1996) 'Is Egyptian Historical Literature "Historical" or "Literary"?', in A. Loprieno (ed.) *Ancient Egyptian Literature, History and Forms*, 415–33. Leiden, Brill.
Filer, J. M. (1997) 'Ancient Egypt and Nubia as a source of information for Cranial Injuries', in J. Carman (ed.) *Material Harm. Archaeological Studies of War and Violence*, 47–74. Glasgow, Cruithne Press.
Gardiner, A. H. (1937) *Late-Egyptian Miscellanies*. Bruxelles, Fondation Égyptologique Reine Élisabeth.
Grébaut, E. (1890–1900) *Le Musée Égyptien. Recueil de monuments et de notices sur les fouilles d'Égypt. Tome Premier*. Cairo, L'Institut français d'archéologie orientale.
Hanson, V. D. (1991) *Hoplites: The Classical Greek Battle Experience*. London, Routledge.
Harris, J. E. and Weeks, K. R. (1973) *X-Raying the Pharaohs*. London, MacDonald.
Herodotus (1972) *The Histories* (trans. A. de Sélincourt, revised by A. R. Burn). London, Penguin Books.
Kirby, D. (1990) *Northern Europe in the Early Modern Period*. London, Longman.

Lichtheim, M. (1974) *Ancient Egyptian Literature. A Book of Readings. Volume II*. Berkeley, University of California Press.

McDermott, S. (2002) *Ancient Egyptian Footsoliders and their Weapons. A Study Of Military Iconography and Weapon Remains*. Manchester University, unpublished PhD thesis.

McDermott, B. (2004) *Warfare in Ancient Egypt*. Stroud, Sutton Publishing.

Mininberg, D. T. (2005) 'The Legacy of Ancient Egyptian Medicine', in J. P. Allen (ed.) *The Art of Medicine in Ancient Egypt*, 13–14. New Haven, Yale University Press.

Mosse, G. L. (1986) 'Two World Wars and the Myth of the War Experience' *Journal of Contemporary History* 21(4), 491–513

Newberry, P. E. (1893a) *Beni Hasan, Part I*. London, Kegan Paul.

Newberry, P. E. (1893b) *Beni Hasan, Part II*. London, Kegan Paul.

Nibbi, A. (1976) 'The Great Tombos Inscription; Some Geographical Notes' *Journal of the American Research Center in Egypt* 13, 91–5

O'Connor, D. B. (1993) *Ancient Nubia; Egypt's Rival in Africa*. Philadelphia, University of Pennsylvania.

Redford, D. B. (1992) *Egypt and Canaan in the New Kingdom*. Beer-Sheva, Ben-Gurion University of the Negev Press.

Richard, J. (1999) *The Crusades, c.1071–c.1291* (trans. J. Birrell). Cambridge, Cambridge University Press.

Sanchez, G. M. (2000) 'A Neurosurgeon's View of the Battle of Reliefs of King Sety I; Aspects of Neurological Importance' *Journal of the American Research Center in Egypt* 37, 143–66.

Sanchez, G. M. (2003) 'Injuries in the Battle of Kadesh' *KMT* 14(1), 58–65.

Sethe, K. and Helck, W. (1906–21) *Urkunden der 18. Dynastie, Vol. 4*. Leipzig, Hinrichs.

Shaw, I. (1996) 'Battle in ancient Egypt; The Triumph of Horus or the cutting edge of the temple economy?', in A. B. Lloyd (ed.) *Battle in Antiquity*, 239–70 London, Duckworth.

Smith, S. T. (2003) *Wretched Kush, Ethnic Identities and Boundaries in Egypt's Nubian Empire*. London, Routledge.

Spalinger, A. J. (1982) *Aspects of Military Documents of the Ancient Egyptians*. New Haven, Yale University Press.

Spalinger, A. J. (1995) 'The Calendrical Importance of the Tombos Stela' *Studien zur Altägyptischen Kultur* 22, 271–81

Spalinger, A. J. (2002) *The Transformation of an Ancient Egyptian Narrative: P.Sallier III and the Battle of Kadesh*. Weisbaden, Harrasowitz.

Spalinger, A. J. (2005) *Warfare in Ancient Egypt*. Oxford, Blackwell.

Stevenson Smith, W. (1998) *The Art and Architecture of Ancient Egypt* (Rev. with adds by W. K. Simpson). New Haven, Yale University Press.

Vaughn, T. (1993) 'The Identification and Retrieval of the Hoplite-dead', in V. D. Hanson (ed.) *The Classical Greek Battle Experience*, 38–62 London, Routledge.

Vila, A. (1970) 'L'armament da la forteresse de Mirgissa-Iken' *Revue d'Egyptologie* 22, 171–99

Winlock, H. E. (1945) *The Slain Soldiers of Neb-hepet-rē' Mentu-hotpe*. New York, Metropolitan Museum of Art.

Winter, D. (1978) *Death's Men. Soldiers of the Great War*. London, Penguin Books.

Unpublished Coptic Limbo in the John Rylands Library, Manchester

Jennifer Cromwell
University College, Oxford

Introduction

The bulk of the John Rylands Coptic collection, housed in Manchester University's Special Collections library in Deansgate, was purchased by Mrs Rylands from the 26th Earl of Crawford (James Ludovic Lindsay, 1847–1913) in 1901. The collection, which consists exclusively of papyri texts, is in two parts. The first, older collection, was purchased by Alexander Lindsay, 25th Earl of Crawford (1812–1880) in the 1860s (for detail see Crum 1909, vii, updated by Emmel 1994). The second was bought by the 26th Earl during a visit to Egypt in 1898/9. Crum (1909, vii) notes 1898 as the year of acquisition, but on the basis of letters from February 1899 it appears that they were acquired at this later date (Choat 2007, 177). The manuscripts in the older collection contain items written in the two main Coptic dialects; Sahidic parchments, believed to be from the White Monastery, and Bohairic texts mostly from the Wadi Natrun. The provenance of the second collection is not as easy to fix but, while some are Fayumic and Achmimic, the large proportion is from Ashmunein, hence this group being known as the 'Ashmunein collection'. This material was supplemented by ad hoc acquisitions in the twentieth century, the most notable being the 1918 acquisition by Rvd. Harris who acquired a sizeable collection (no specific details are recorded, beyond the comment by Crum (1920, 497) that 'fifty odd pieces' seem worthy of study). The provenance of this material is less certain, as it was purchased from dealers throughout Egypt.

Of these Coptic items 478 (410 of which are Sahidic) were published by Crum in his 1909 catalogue: *Catalogue of the Coptic Manuscripts in the Collection of the John Rylands Library (P.Ryl.Copt.)*. This catalogued material constitutes less than half of the collection. Crum, in the introduction to his Catalogue, states that while all documents of the older collection are included, this is not the case with the "latter Ashmunein stock" (Crum 1909, ix). To quote Crum, 'I have been allowed to use discretion, and so have described but a selection of the great mass of fragments, abandoning a considerable quantity of impractical material to a limbo'. 'Limbo' is not merely the term employed by Crum, but is how the manuscripts are currently referred to by the Library itself. Seven boxes of textual material are uncatalogued. These are currently divided into 'Coptic Limbo', consisting of 506 fragments in boxes 1–4, and 'Coptic Limbo Additional', miscellaneous uncounted fragments in boxes 5–7. In total there are over a thousand unpublished fragments. This paper serves as a brief introduction to the preliminary work that has been undertaken on this 'limbo'-status corpus and a projection of the work to come.

Crum seemingly made no notes on the material which he omitted from his catalogue. Or, at least, no notes have survived, either in the Griffith Institute, Oxford, where his notes

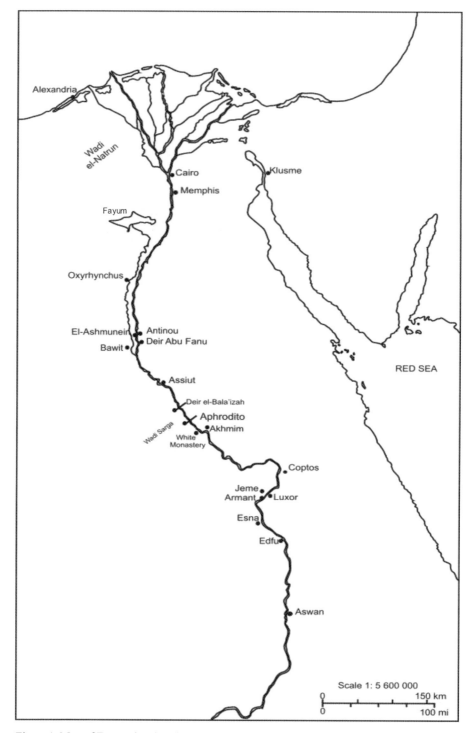

Figure 1. Map of Egypt, showing sites mentioned in the text.

are held, or in the John Rylands itself. The only record of work on these unpublished fragments are the notes compiled by Walter Till in 1950 and Monika Cramer in 1966–7. The notes are formed on an ad hoc basis, Till's notes are confined to the items in box 1, Cramer's to box 4. In total this accounts for 209 texts (some of which comprise multiple fragments): 104 by Till and 105 by Cramer; in total approximately twenty percent of the total material. Neither individual, however, was interested in compiling an entire catalogue; both were concerned instead with religious items, of which they published a small number of fragments (Cramer 1968; Till 1952).

That their remaining notes constitute only a preliminary study of the papyri is clear from their format and the inconsistency of the details provided for each item. This information includes: their material (predominantly vellum and papyrus), brief palaeographic notes (normally confined to 'bookhand' or 'letterhand'), possible provenance (only Cramer includes such information, and mentions only one site: Oxyrhynchus) and suggested date (again, such information is only found in the notes compiled by Cramer). Therefore, while these notes serve as a useful resource aid, especially in instances where the papyrus might have suffered damage in the intervening fifty years, they are not sufficient by themselves to constitute a catalogue of the unpublished collection.

At the moment the original designation numbers are being used. However, the problems inherent in this system are immediately apparent. While Cramer's box 4 fragments are predominantly numbered in the 400s, there are also a series numbered 1–22. These are not the same as the material in box 1, which is numbered 1–104. Beyond this conflict in the numbering system, it is also evident that fragments were simply grouped together and numbered consecutively, in no coherent manner. Their grouping follows neither geographic location, date, language nor genre. These latter two categories are how texts are normally grouped (see the Crum catalogue: texts are catalogued first by dialect, Sahidic, Middle Egyptian, Bohairic, and then further subdivided into genre). For example, only seven of the documents are identified by Cramer as being potentially letters (primarily on palaeographic grounds) and their current numbers are Limbo 1, 2, 484, 492, 497, 498 and 500. Furthermore, it appears that a number of fragments with different numbers actually belong together. Some of these are numbered consecutively, for example 479 and 480 (fragments of a late literary text?); some are more removed but in the same box, for example 486 and 490 (the latter of which comprises four separate fragments of a literary text); while others are divided between boxes, for example the five fragments of 488 in box 4 and box 6's 'limbo 2' (again, seemingly a late literary text, on vellum).

Project

The first aim of the project is to complete the catalogue. The preliminary activities already show that a variety of material is contained within the collection. Particularly significant is the potential that some fragments are from Oxyrhynchus. While the Greek material from this site is very well known and has been consistently published over the past century since their discovery, in what now totals 71 volumes and over 4800 items (for the most recent volume, see Gonis 2007), the Coptic material is considerably less well known. This is largely a result of the number and condition of the Coptic fragments, and the paucity of

Coptic papyrologists interested in this archive. Nevertheless, in Oxford there are approximately 400 such fragments, held in the Papyrology Rooms of the Sackler Library. This number far exceeds the original estimate of the size of the collection made by the excavators of the site, who hypothesized that no more than forty or fifty documents were likely to be of any value (Grenfell & Hunt 2007 [1896–7], 352). The Manchester collection could well provide an important supplement to this collection, especially as the collection is omitted from the most recent list of institutions known to hold Coptic Oxyrhynchite material (Clackson 2007, 333).

It is also hoped that amongst the unpublished material are more pieces belonging to the important fourth/fifth century archive of the letters of Apa Johannes. A number of these texts were published in the first catalogue (P.Ryl.Copt. 268–183) and a new edition of the entire dossier has recently been proposed by Malcolm Choat (2007). In this respect, box 1 might potentially bear fruit, as it contains more than twenty fragments of what may be letters. Until further study has taken place, especially concerning palaeographic similarities between the known letters and the remaining fragments, more definite statements cannot be made.

The larger majority of fragments in box 1 appear to be legal in nature, on the basis of surviving legal formulae, witness statements and dating formulae. An Ashmunein provenance is certain for some of these fragments: fragment 27 line 2 reads: [ⲡⲱⲙ]ⲉ ⲱⲙⲟⲩⲛ ⲧⲟ ⲙⲙⲛⲧⲣⲉ '[the man] of Shmoun (Ashmunein) acts as witness' and fragment 32 line 8 mentions ⲛ̣ϣⲙⲟⲩⲛ ⲧⲡⲟⲗⲓⲥ 'of Shmoun, the city'. A number of documents preserve dating formulae: fragment 39 is dated 4th Paoni, 11th Indiction, while 53 is dated 27th Paremhotep, 5th Indiction (the Indiction year being the standard dating method employed in documents, based on the 15 year tax cycle introduced by Diocletian). While these documents cannot be dated precisely using these formulae alone, the combination of features exhibited points to a post-Arabic invasion date.

On the literary front, fragments have already been identified bearing the names David and Goliath. Fragment 14, from box 4, written on vellum, preserves both names: ⲇⲁⲩⲉⲓⲇ on line 4 and ⲅⲟⲗⲓⲁⲑ at the beginning of line 5. These might, then, be part of a larger piece from the Old Testament, 1 Samuel 17. Further study of the other surviving traces might provide a more precise identification. The number of texts written in a 'bookhand' (that is, a type of majuscule hand normally used for writing literary texts, as opposed to the type of hand typically used for documentary and other non-literary purposes) indicates the existence of a large number of Biblical or other literary items.

The production of a comprehensive catalogue of the fragments is therefore required, which conforms to modern catalogue conventions. As Choat (2007, 175) has noted, the existing Ryland's catalogue is 'in places not easy to use even for a papyrologist, and most of the archive cannot be accessed without a sound knowledge of Coptic'. The new catalogue aims to avoid this pitfall. Included, therefore, will be a description of the physical properties and palaeography of each fragment, plus a transcription and commentary, primarily detailing its provenance, date and content. Translations will not be provided with the catalogue; full text editions are beyond the scope of the intended project, and would extend the time involved considerably (but this latter point is subject to change, depending on how the project advances).

The second goal is the conservation of the fragments. The storage methods for the fragments have not been updated since the start of the twentieth century, with the result that many of them have deteriorated and risk ongoing deterioration. Many fragments are still wrapped in newspaper dated January 1907, which are in turn placed in brown envelopes. An intermediary stage in the conservation process is currently being experimented with. This entails the fragments being placed in a plastic envelope, which is then stored within a cardboard folder. The type of plastic used for this is inert archive plastic, known by the trade name of either Mylar or Melinex. This has many of the benefits of glass mounting. Most importantly, if means both sides of the papyrus can be examined without having to physically handle the manuscript. The final stage in the conservation process, mounting between framed glass sheets, is the most labour intensive stage and also first requires the final sorting of the fragments before it can take place, so that all related fragments are mounted together.

Manchester's unpublished Egyptian material is not confined to Coptic texts. There also remain to be studied 7 hieroglyphic and 19 hieratic items, dated from the fourteenth century BC to the second century AD, all of which are funerary in nature, plus an additional 60 Demotic items, primarily legal texts (for more information see the website: http://rylibweb.man.ac.uk/specialcollections/collections/guide/atoz/egyptian/). This Demotic material is in much the same situation as the Coptic: it has partially been published (Griffith 1909) but awaits further attention.

Although the current project is still very much in its infancy, the indications so far are that the 'limbo' collection presents an important addition to the current body of published Coptic material.

Acknowledgements

This project could not be possible without the support and enthusiasm of the curator of the collection, John Hodgson, and Anne Young, the assistant curator.

Bibliography

Choat, M. (2007) 'The Archive of Apa Johannes: Notes on a proposed New Edition', in J. Froesen, T. Purola and E. Salmenkivi (eds) *Proceedings of the 24th International Congress of Papyrology, Helsinki 1–7 Aug. 2004* (Societas Scientiarum Fennica: The Finnish Society of Sciences and Letters. Volume 1), 175–183.

Clackson, S. (2007) 'Coptic Oxyrhynchus', in A. K. Bowman, R. A. Coles, N. Gonis, D. Obbink and P. J. Parsons (eds). *Oxyrhynchus: A City and Its Texts* (EES Graeco-Roman Memoirs 93), 332–41. London, Egypt Exploration Society.

Cramer, M. (1967–8) 'Some Unpublished Coptic Liturgical Manuscripts in the John Rylands Library', *Bulletin of the John Rylands Library* 50, 308–316.

Crum, W. E. (1909) *Catalogue of the Coptic Manuscripts in the Collection of the John Rylands Library*. Manchester, Manchester University Press.

Crum, W. E. (1920) 'New Coptic Manuscripts in the John Rylands Library', *Bulletin of the John Rylands Library* 5.5 (December 1919–July 1920), 497–503.

Emmel, S. (1994) 'The Coptic Manuscript Collection of Alexander Lindsay, 25th Earl of

Crawford', in S. Giversen, M. Krause and P. Nagel (eds) *Coptology: Past, Present, and Future*. Leuven, Peeters.

Gonis, N. (2007) *Oxyrhynchus Papyri 71* (Graeco-Roman Memoirs 91). London, Egypt Exploration Society.

Grenfell, B. P. and Hunt, A. S. (2007) 'Excavations at Oxyrhynchus', in A. K. Bowman, R. A. Coles, N. Gonis, D. Obbink and P. J. Parsons (eds) *Oxyrhynchus: A City and Its Texts* (EES Graeco-Roman Memoirs 93), 345–68. London, Egypt Exploration Society. [Originally published as 'Oxyrhynchus and Its Papyri', in *EEF Archaeology Report* 6 (1896–7), 1–12].

Griffith, F. Ll. (1909) *Catalogue of the Demotic Papyri in the John Rylands Library, Manchester*. Manchester, Manchester University Press.

Till, W. C. (1952) 'Coptic Biblical Fragments in the John Rylands Library', *Bulletin of the John Rylands Library* 34, 432–58.

Ḫnm.t, šd.t, ẖnw.t, and bꜥr: Ancient Egyptian *Emic* Terms for Wells and Cisterns

Henning Franzmeier
University of Göttingen

Introduction

As part of my MA thesis, written in 2006 at the University of Göttingen (Franzmeier 2006; Franzmeier 2007), which was concerned with ancient Egyptian well technology, I tried to gather additional information from textual sources from pharaonic Egypt. This short study presents the results and focuses also on some very important methodological considerations that deal with the differences between the recent, *etic* terminology used by archaeologists to describe and classify features and finds from excavations and the ancient *emic* terminology and classification.

Emic *and* etic

The basic terms employed in my study are *emic* and *etic*. This terminology had been developed by the linguist Kenneth Lee–Pike in his influential study 'Language in Relation to a Unified Theory of the Structure of Human Behaviour', published in 1967, out of the linguistic terms *phonetic* and *phonemic*.

Etic thus indicates a viewpoint of study from the outside of a particular system whereas *emic* refers to the study of a system from within (Lee–Pike 1967, 37). In this short inquiry *etic* denotes the modern terminology used to refer to wells and cisterns in general and the terminology used by archaeologists in particular. *Emic* thus basically denotes the ancient Egyptians' way of talking (or better writing) about such features.

Terminology, classification and typology

To deal with any archaeological material, features or finds, archaeologists first invent a terminology to classify the objects (the division between classification and typology is made according to Hayden 1984, 80). In most cases this first step is descriptive. The outer appearance of objects is translated into terms, thus into language. Egyptologists' way of referring to pottery is a good example. A term like 'funnel–necked jar' is used. If more accuracy is needed, the material might be included and a term like 'funnel–necked jar, Fabric I.E.01' is invented.

Primarily this is only a classification, used as a mode of communication, to enable archaeologists to talk about things. For an appropriate analysis a second step is needed: a typology. The typologies are made to provide clues to answer specific questions posed about the material and can be said to be a tool for the analyst. To stay with pottery analysis, terms like 'Canaanite jar' or 'Upper Egyptian marl clay vessel' are used for a type of pottery, found in New Kingdom contexts, to distinguish between local (or at least Egyptian) and imported pottery. Therefore this typology can be a part of the puzzle of the problem of trade relationships. Of course the term funnel–necked jar, mentioned above can thus gain new importance too and become a part of a typology.

The problem of 'loaned' terminologies and typologies

A further point has to be made about terminologies and typologies which the archaeologist imports from other sciences, no matter whether from the sphere of life sciences such as biology, technological sciences such as engineering or social sciences.

The archaeologist has to be aware that here a double translation or transfer is made. First a term is borrowed from another science, thus a system with an *emic* terminology of its own, and afterwards the term is applied to the archaeological material. This remark seems to be trivial but, as several examples show, it is not.

Wells and cisterns

Wells and cisterns – modern definitions and typologies

Wells and cisterns are modern basic terms for devices that 'produce' water. Wells are defined as features which enable human use of the groundwater, whereas cisterns are made to collect and store water, mainly surface water, such as rain or temporary runoff water. Therefore the 'mode of production' of the water makes the difference in this general classification. As specialists appear, lots of further terms are employed, as Hayden 1984, 85 already recognised:

> 'Another important aspect of emic categories is that they may vary within communities according to specific roles of individuals. For instance, full–time manufacturers may have elaborate categories for their products and their parts. On the other hand, traders and merchants may have very different concerns and may emphasize very different attributes in their terminology, such as size, weight, decoration and aspects related to selling and transport'.

For wells this means that engineers constructing wells do have terms such as 'shaft well' or 'open caisson well', depending on the building process and method used. People interested in different water qualities, whether the water is potable or just suitable for industrial purposes, will make distinctions on this level. Others might be interested in the legal status of wells or cisterns and classify them in a third way.

Therefore the situations of modern specialists, referring to recent wells, can be compared with the situation of an archaeologist who is interested in solving a specific problem concerning ancient wells.

Wells and cisterns – the etic typology used in my study

As my study was mainly focused on the relationship between environmental situations, consumers' demands and the actual whereabouts and constructions of the ancient Egyptian wells and cisterns I deduced a specific *a priori* typology (Tab. 1).

Anthropogenic situation	Consumer's demand	Environmental situation
spatial differentiation (anthropogenic)	quality of water	spatial differentiation (natural)
Settlement	Potable water	Desert (no other water available)
Temple	Water for other	Nile Valley
Workshop	purposes	
↘	↓	↙
	Lead to	
	↓	
	Built device	
	Well or cistern	
	Strengthened wall	
	Staircase	
	Decoration	
	Filtering device	

Table 1. The typological system used in my study of ancient Egyptian wells and cisterns and wells.

The first distinction I made was between different consumers' demands. This refers to the quality and the amount of water the device is able to produce. Wells might be suitable to deliver potable water or not. A possible case could have been a well near the coast where the groundwater might be brackish and therefore unfit for human consumption but adequate for an industrial use such as in pottery production or a ritual use in a temple.

Secondly a spatial differentiation between wells and cisterns in different natural environments seemed of eminent importance. The feature might be located in the Nile Valley close to the river or in the desert where no other water supply is available at all. This distinction is relevant for the purpose of the well. In the Nile Valley it might be about comfort or the improvement of the quality of the water. In the desert it is about survival. Without water no human life is possible. Furthermore the stability of the surrounding rock was taken into consideration. In the desert the wells were often sunk into solid bedrock whereas in the Nile Valley the ancient Egyptian engineers had to deal with soft alluvial material. Besides natural environments the anthropogenic spatial situation might be important too. Examples for this might be rural environs, settlements, workshops, military installations, or temples.

The third level of the typology was the actual construction of the wells and cisterns, thus the outer appearance of the archaeologically examined features. Most important in this respect was the treatment of the wells' walls. Some wells have walls of stone masonry but some do not. Furthermore some wells have access via a staircase, most do not. Last but not least I also tried to differentiate between wells and cisterns.

This framework was used for a typology of the archaeological remains and also provides the basis for the study of the textual sources as the aim was to add information to the archaeological investigation.

The ancient Egyptian terms and the sources

The ancient Egyptian terms and previous translations

The subjects of this study are four ancient Egyptian words that used to be translated as 'well' or 'cistern'. These words are *ḥnm.t*, *šd.t*, *ḫnw.t* and *bꜥr* (Tab. 2). The periods sur-

Hieroglyphs	Transliteration	Translation	Period of use	Number of examples
	ḫnm.t	well, cistern, desert well, well-station	OK, MK, NK, Late Period	39
	šd.t	well, cistern, waterhole	OK, NK, Late Period	10
	ḫnw.t	waters, desert well well-station	Late OK, 19th Dynasty	4
	bᶜr	well, bir	18th Dynasty, Late Period	1

Table 2. The ancient Egyptian terms for well and cistern, and their traditional translations (after Erman and Grapow 1957; Hannig 1997; Hannig 2003; Lesko 1982–90).

veyed are the Old Kingdom, Middle Kingdom, New Kingdom into the Third Intermediate Period. The most important terms are ḫnm.t and šd.t with the most records. ḫnw.t is quite rare while bᶜr is attested only once in the period examined.

A quick look already reveals that the translations are quite general and that some translations, especially the basic modern terms are applied to more than one ancient Egyptian term. This also holds true for the Coptic words ϣⲱⲧⲉ and ϩⲟⲛⲃⲉ, which stem from šd.t and ḫnm.t respectively (Westendorf 1965, 331 and 379; Crum 1939, 595 and 691).

The female term ḫnm.t studied here must not be confused with the male term ḫnmt which is used in the Papyrus Wilbour (Gardiner 1948, I, 16a, 36) and on a stela from Qantir (Habachi 2001, 225/226, Cat.–No. 133). This word is most often written with the sign Gardiner F 26 (𓄚) instead of the jar Gardiner W 9 (𓎼) the only exception is the stela from Qantir, mentioned above.

Also, the idea that ḫnw.t and ḫnm.t at least in the New Kingdom might be the same term (see Lesko 1982–90, II, 207 where both are subsumed under the lemma ḫnmt together with the male ḫnm.t) can be rejected by the fact that both words appear in the same text just a few lines apart and are written in a very distinct way (Kitchen 1975–89, I, 66,10 (ḫnm.t) and I, 66,8 (ḫnw.t)). The second argument for this is the fact that the oldest secure examples of these two terms show exactly the same orthography: the jar Gardiner W 9 for ḫnm.t and the sign Gardiner F 26 for ḫnw.t (for the example see below, ḫnm.t is securely attested from the Eleventh Dynasty onwards (Old Kingdom examples are not secure in their interpretation), ḫnw.t from the Sixth Dynasty). Few attempts have been made to get closer to the *emic* meaning of these terms. Gardiner (1947, 7–8) proposed a differentiation for ḫnm.t and šd.t, with šd.t being a term for wells in the cultivation and ḫnm.t being a well in the desert.

Eichler used the etymologies of šd.t and ḫnw.t in his trial to get a better understanding of some late Sixth Dynasty inscriptions in the Eastern Desert (1998, 263–5). He relates both terms to basic terms meaning 'skin' and especially 'waterskin'. As this etymology for ḫnw.t might hold true, for šd.t it probably does not as Schenkel (1983, 208, footnote 67) interpretes šd.t as a nominal form of šdj – 'to dig' and gives it the meaning '*das Gegrabene*' – '*the dug one*'. The word šd.t – 'skin, waterskin' is also only attested from the Middle Kingdom onwards (Erman and Grapow 1957, IV, 560). Furthermore Eichler did not reflect the modern terminology and seems to use well, cistern, and natural water accumulation synonymously. This is best reflected in his translation of the following phrase:

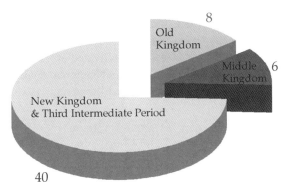

(after Rothe, Rapp and Miller 1996, 97, fig. 31)

jrj.n(=j) šd(.t) {r}ḫn<w>{t}.t (j)ptn

His translation was *'I dug (lit: made) a well–hole of these cisterns'* ('Ich grub (wtl: "machte") ein Brunnenloch dieser Zisternen') (Eichler 1998, 263). Therefore it can be concluded only that a *šd.t* can be made within a *ḫnw.t*, while his further assumptions must be seen critically.

The sources

The sources I used are texts from the Old Kingdom until the Third Intermediate Period and one Twenty-sixth Dynasty example. This choice is not random but was instead a result of the archaeological features I examined in my study. The Third Intermediate Period seems to be a good limit as afterwards foreign influences change the technological situation considerably and added new techniques. The most important amongst them are the adoption of qanat systems from Persia and the saqia probably under Greek influence. I also excluded most of the purely religious texts such as the Pyramid Texts, the Coffin Texts, and the Book of the Dead as these texts include no information in terms of the problems I wanted to examine.

Of course even this choice covers a huge interval of time but this is necessary due to the scarcity of texts surviving. I included 45 texts. By far the greatest amount of texts come from the New Kingdom while texts from the Old and Middle Kingdoms are very rare (Fig. 1).

Figure 1. The chronological distribution of all examined texts.

Besides the chronological dimension also the spatial and functional contexts of the texts have to be taken into account. The texts included in this study mostly come from two contextual situations. On the one hand there are royal inscriptions mentioning wells and their construction. These come from royal stelae or from inscriptions on the walls of temples. On the other hand many texts can be classified as inscriptions by the members of expeditions, therefore non–official texts but made by officials working in their function.

This situation has manifold implications for the interpretation of the texts. The function of the royal texts was in most cases just to say that the water supply in a given place (most often located in the desert) had been improved. It was not important which kind of device had been installed. Furthermore most of the texts come from the desert. This means that desert–wells and cisterns might be overrepresented in the material. Whether this had been caused by a real dominance of texts mentioning wells in the desert or by chance survival is hard to say.

Two texts might be considered to speak in favour of the hypothesis of selective preservation. These texts which might be classified as expert's texts by the actual 'engineers' survive from Deir el–Medina, mentioning as far as can be concluded the *grands puits* (Ventura 1987, 155). As they are written on an ostracon and a papyrus, the materials they are written onto are more likely to be destroyed, at least as seen against monumental inscriptions and rock inscriptions. A further influential factor in getting to the meaning of a term is the question of whether a specific installation is described, or rather just a category of installation. If a text refers to a specific installation the whole situation can be more informative – information might be added by the examination of the building itself. Therefore, one has to be aware of this situation concerning the source materials as a potential factor which might skew the results of this study.

The study

The main part of this study seeks to propose translations which are closer to the *emic* meanings of the ancient Egyptian terminologies. As this study was borne out of an archaeological study and the aim was to use the texts as an aid in the interpretation of excavated features, specific questions, oriented to the typological system, had been posed about the material.

As already mentioned above, the first to try to differentiate the terms *ḫnm.t* and *šd.t* was Gardiner (1947, 7–8). His proposal that *ḫnm.t* might be a term designating wells in the desert whereas *šd.t* might refer to wells in cultivated areas is a suitable starting point. His differentiation is located on the level of environmental spatial definitions. Unfortunately this assumption does not hold true. In the Eighteenth Dnasty a well in the desert is termed a *šd.t*:

(Helck 1980, 123).

gm.n=tw nꜣ n ḫr.w r gs jꜣbt(.j) n jtrw ḥr mḥt(.j)n šd(.t) bj<ꜣ>.t

'The enemies have been found on the eastern side of the river, north of the šd.t of the mining region' (after Helck 1980, 122).

Ḫnm.t seems to be fairly restricted to the deserts and areas without any other permanent water supply but not exclusively. In the Twenty-second Dynasty a well or probably even a spring in the Dakhla Oasis is termed *ḫnm.t* which is definitely located in a cultivation area with the specification *ḫnm.t–ww* making it an installation used for irrigation:

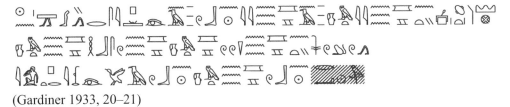

(Gardiner 1933, 20–21)

hrw n šm(.t) r sjp(.t) nꜣ wbn.y nꜣ ḥnm.yt ntì (m) Šꜣ-wꜣḥ.t
ḥnm.t-ḥbs.w ḥnm.t-ww ntj sw pḥ.w
{j} <r> ptr pꜣ wbn-ḥnm.t Wbn[-Rꜥ]

'The day he went for the inspection of the *wbn.y* and the *ḥnm.yt* which are in *Sꜣ-wꜣḥ.t*, *ḥnm.t-ḥbs.w* (closed wells) und *ḥnm.t-ww* (irrigation–well?), he arrived to see the *wbn–ḥnm.t Wbn[-Rꜥ]*' (after Gardiner 1933, 20–1)

A second level of classification to be examined is the anthropogenic spatial situation. Contexts such as temples, fortresses, domestic areas, or mines and quarries are referenced from the archaeological record. Unfortunately only for mines and fortresses is more than one meaningful example known. These show clearly that in both cases *šd.t* and *ḥnm.t* can be used to denote installations in those contexts.

For a *šd.t*, with regard to mines I quoted the example from the Eighteenth Dynasty above, examples for *ḥnm.wt* are more frequent. From the Nineteenth Dynasty comes the following example, talking about a failed attempt to sink a well under the reign of Seti I en route to the gold mines of Wadi Allaqi, written on the so–called Kuban stela:

(Tresson 1922; Kitchen 1975–89, II, 357)

jw ꜣby.n nsw nb n ḥr-ḥꜣ.t wbꜣ ḥnm.t ḥr=s bw ḫpr rwḏ=sn jw jr.n
nsw Mn-Mꜣꜥ.t-Rꜥ m mjt.t rdj.n=f šd.tw ḥnm.t n mḥ 120 m mḏ.wt m
h(ꜣ)w=f ḥꜣꜥ.n.tw =s ḥr wꜣt bw prj mw jm=s

'Every previous king desired to open a well in it, they had no success. King Men–Maat–Ra (Seti I) did the same. In his age he ordered a *ḥnm.t* to be dug 120 cubits in depth, but it was given up, no water coming out of it' (after Kitchen 1993–2003, II, 190/91).

Wells in fortresses do not have a single term referring to them either. The wells or cisterns located at the ways of Horus in North Sinai and depicted in the reliefs of Seti I in Karnak are all referred to as *ḥnm.wt:*

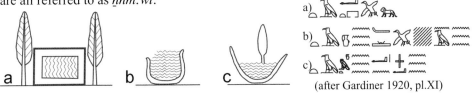

(after Gardiner 1920, pl.XI)

a) *tꜣ ꜥt pꜣ mꜣj*; 'The migdol of the lion'.
b) *tꜣ ḫnm.t Ḥpn;* 'The *ḫnm.t Ḥpn*'
c) *tꜣ ḫnm.t ꜥ n Jmj-ꜥ;* 'The *ḫnm.t* of *Jmj-ꜥ*'

(after The Epigraphic Survey 1986, 21).

Compared with these examples the excavated wells of Zawiyet Umm el–Rakham are
referred to as *šd.wt* in an inscription on one of the main gates of the fortress which dates
to the time of Ramesses II:

///[ḫꜣs.t] ṯmḥ šd.wt m–ḫnw=sn r s<qb>b

'...foreign land of Tjemhu (and) the *šd.t*–wells within them to refresh...'
(Morris 2005, 624).

These two examples lead to the next further distinction that could have been made by the
Egyptians: the modern basic differentiation between well and cistern. The *šd.wt* of Zawiyet Umm el–Rakham are archaeologically known to be wells (Snape 2003, 5), whereas
the *ḫnm.wt* at the Ways of Horus can be considered cisterns as can be concluded from the
depictions and from excavations at New Kingdom fortresses in North Sinai, such as Deir
el–Bala (Dothan 1987, 125). But this idea is clearly wrong too, as the *ḫnm.t*–installation
on the way to the goldmines of Wadi Allaqi, shown above, is definitely a well. For all the
other typological groups I used in the course of my study, except one, the same holds true:
no knowledge can be gained from within the texts.

But one point brings us one step closer to the Egyptian perspective. If one considers
the way a feature was built, it can be shown that *šd.t* refers exclusively to man–made
features whereas *ḫnm.t* can also be a natural water accumulation in the desert. As already
mentioned, on the one hand the etymology of *šd.t* points towards this direction. *šd.t* seems
to derive from a nominal form of the verb *šd(j)* – *'to dig'* (Schenkel 1983, 208, n.67: *'das
Gegrabene'*). This verb is also often used when the building of a well is described, for
example on the Kuban Stela, to be seen above.

The fact that *ḫnm.t* can, on the other hand, be used to describe a natural feature which
holds water, probably what is called *qalt* (plur. *qulût*) in modern Arabic, is shown by a text
from the Wadi Hammamat. *qulût* are depressions to be found mainly in the mountains of
the Eastern Desert which fill after the occasional rainfalls and keep the water for a considerable period of time (Attia 1953, 213):

(Couyat and Montet 1912, No. 191)

…whm bjȝ.(y)t jr.t ḥw(.t) mȝȝ ḫpr.w n.w nṯr pn dj.t bȝw=f n rḫ.yt
jr.t ḫȝs.t m nwy bs.t mw ḥr nhȝ n jnr gm.t ẖnm.t m ḥr (.j)–jb jn.t
mḥ 10 r mḥ 10 ḥr r=s nb mḥ.t m mw r npr.wt=s sqbb.t stwr.tj r mȝ.(w)–ḥḏ(?)
s.štȝ.tj r jwn.tjw…

'The wonder was repeated, it rained, the manifestations of this god were seen, his power was given to the people. The mountainous area was made water, water flowed out of the uneven stone. A *ẖnm.t* was found amidst the valley, 10 by 10 cubits on each side filled with water to the edge, cool and kept clean from the Oryx–antelopes, kept secret from the dwellers of the Eastern Desert.' (after Breasted 1906–7, 1, 216)

This text, known as the 'Brunnenwunder' is a clear indication for this facet of meaning of *ẖnm.t*. As *ẖnm.t* does definitely also refer to man–made features it seems quite clear that *ẖnm.t* is the most general term. A further hint towards this generality of meaning can be gained from the metaphorical use of *ẖnm.t* as in the Twenty–sixth Dynasty text below:

(Quack 1993,152)

n tr ḫpr.n js p.t n Jwn.w pn m ẖnm(.t) n.t nṯr nb

'Didn't this heaven and this Heliopolis come into existence as the *ẖnm.t* of every god?' (Goyon 1972, 75; Goyon 1974, pls XII, XIIA; Quack 1993, 152)

Here a meaning such as 'wellspring' or 'well' can be proposed for *ẖnm.t*.

The two other ancient Egyptian terms for well and cistern are even harder to give a more closely defined meaning because of their rare occurrence. Both might be related to water supply in extremely arid regions such as the deserts. *Ḥnw.t* and *bꜥr* are only attested in desert related contexts. *Ḥnw.t* is restricted to rock inscriptions of the members of expeditions to the Eastern Desert in the late Old Kingdom, except one example from the Nineteenth Dynasty temple at Kanais, also located in the Eastern Desert close to Edfu. As *ẖnw. wt* are said to be made this term refers to man–made installations:

(Rothe and Miller 1999,100)

šps(w)–nsw jmj–rȝ ꜥw Nḏw ḏd=f
jnk šdj ẖn(w).t tn ẖnꜥ kȝ.wt n.t wts.t–¡r mḥ 10 wȝ=s r sš pn

'The noble of the king, the overseer of the foreign mercenaries, Nedju, he says: I dug this *ẖnw.t* with the workers of the nome of Edfu. It is at a distance of 10 cubits from this inscription.' (after Rothe and Miller 1999,100)

But unfortunately the assumption that *ḥnw.t* refers to man-made features might not be exclusive since in the other text shown above as the first example, *ḥnw.t* might designate a natural feature where a *šd.t* has been dug to improve its capacity. As Eichler (1998, 264) mentions, there is a natural basin located close to that inscription.

Bʿr is only attested once in a text referring to a raid into the Nubian desert as a place which seems to be used by the inhabitants. Therefore a connection with the desert might be plausible but is not more than guesswork.

Conclusion

Ḥnm.t is by far the most common term, designating installations of water supply (Tab. 3). It was used to designate a lot of different kinds of features, even naturally occurring pools in the Eastern Desert, probably what is today called *qalt* in Arabic. A close relationship to water supply in highly arid areas, where no other water supply exists, can be proposed. At least in the Third Intermediate Period this area was left, as is shown by the text mentioning *ḥnm.t*–features in agricultural areas in the Dakhla Oasis. Also both cisterns and wells can be termed *ḥnm.t*. Its metaphorical use makes the range of application for *ḥnm.t* more general.

Šd.t in contrast was used for man–made features only, which fits its etymology. Furthermore all different kinds of installations, located in different environmental and anthropogenic contexts, can be termed *šd.t*.

Both other terms might be related to desert–environments but as the evidence is scarce, not too much weight should be put upon these arguments. *Ḥnw.t* definitely refers to man–made features, but may also relate to natural features.

Finally it can be said that the information gained by a semantic analysis, in addition to the archaeological questions was limited. In several cases an archaeological excavation of the features mentioned, as far as they can be identified and their present state reflects the conditions, the text referred to, would add to our understanding of the text.

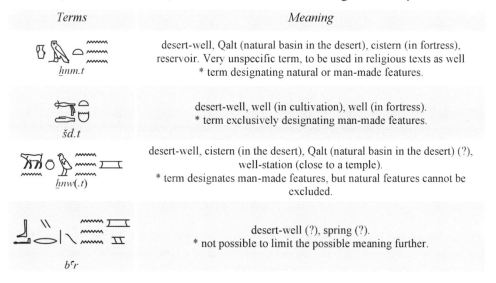

Terms	Meaning
ḥnm.t	desert-well, Qalt (natural basin in the desert), cistern (in fortress), reservoir. Very unspecific term, to be used in religious texts as well * term designating natural or man-made features.
šd.t	desert-well, well (in cultivation), well (in fortress). * term exclusively designating man-made features.
ḥnw(.t)	desert-well, cistern (in the desert), Qalt (natural basin in the desert) (?), well-station (close to a temple). * term designates man-made features, but natural features cannot be excluded.
bʿr	desert-well (?), spring (?). * not possible to limit the possible meaning further.

Table 3. The meanings of the four ancient Egyptian terms according to the reconstructions of this study.

This result leads towards two conclusions. On the one hand, one basic assumption by Lee–Pike is definitely confirmed to some extent: *emic* terminologies cannot be deduced from an *etic* perspective, they have to be discovered independently. (Lee–Pike 1967, 38). Therefore texts will not answer automatically to questions posed to them by archaeologists, as the *emic* classifications and the *emic* terminologies might have been completely different from our modern ones.

On the other hand a combination of archaeological examination and philological analysis seems to be a way in which to propose further results but probably more in favour of a gain of further philological knowledge.

Acknowledgements

I would like to express my gratitude to the organisers of CRE IX at Manchester for giving me the opportunity to present my paper at this symposium. I would like to thank Dr. Matthias Müller (Basel) for his help with the translations of the Egyptian texts and Campbell Price for adjusting my English. Last, but not least I thank Professor Friedrich Junge from the University of Göttingen for supervising my Masters thesis on this subject.

Bibliography

Attia, M. I. (1953) 'Ground Water in Egypt', *Bulletin de la Société de Géographie d'Égypte* 26, 207–25.

Breasted, H. (1906–7) *Ancient Records of Egypt* (5 vols). Chicago, Chicago University Press.

Couyat, J. and Montet, P. (1912) *Les inscriptions hiéroglyphiques et hiératiques du Ouâdi Hammâmât*. Cairo, Institut français d'archéologie orientale.

Crum, W. E. (1939) *A Coptic Dictionary*. Oxford, Clarendon Press.

Dothan, T. (1987) 'The Impact of Egypt on Canaan during the 18th and 19th Dynasties in the Light of the Excavations at Deir el–Balah', in A. F. Rainey (ed.) *Egypt, Israel, Sinai. Archaeological and Historical Relationships in the Biblical Period*, 121–36. Tel Aviv, Tel Aviv University.

Eichler, E. (1998) 'Neue Expeditionsinschriften aus der Ostwüste Oberägyptens, Teil II: Die Inschriften', *Mitteilungen des Deutschen Archäologischen Instituts Kairo* 54, 250–66.

The Epigraphic Survey (1986) *Reliefs and Inscriptions at Karnak. 4. The Battle Reliefs of King Sety I* (Oriental Institute Publications 107). Chicago, The Oriental Institute.

Erman, A. and Grapow, H. (1957) *Wörterbuch der ägyptischen Sprache* (2nd Edition) 6 vols. Berlin, Akademie–Verlag.

Franzmeier, H. (2006) *Ein Brunnen Ramses' II. in Samana – Untersuchungen zu Typologie und Funktion von Brunnenbauwerken im ramessidischen Ägypten*. Unpublished M.A. thesis, University of Göttingen.

Franzmeier, H. (2007) 'A Ramesside Well at Samana near Qantir – A New Insight into the Hydrological Technology of Pharaonic Egypt'. in K. Endreffy and A. Gulyás (eds) *Proceedings of the Fouth Central European Conference of Young Egyptologists. Studia Aegyptiaca XVIII*, 121–32. Budapest, Chaire d'Egyptologie de l'Université Eötvös Loránd de Budapest.

Gardiner, A. H. (1920) 'The Ancient Military Road between Egypt and Palestine', *Journal of Egyptian Archaeology* 6, 99–116.

Gardiner, A. H. (1933) 'The Dakhleh Stela', *Journal of Egyptian Archaeology* 19, 19–30.

Gardiner, A. H. (1947) *Ancient Egyptian Onomastica* (3 vols.). Oxford, Oxford University Press.

Gardiner, A. H. (1948) *The Wilbour Papyrus* (3 vols.). Oxford, Oxford University Press.

Goyon, G. (1972) *Confirmation du Pouvoir Royal au Nouvel An [Brooklyn Museum 47.218.50]*. Cairo, L'Institut français d'archéologie orientale.

Goyon, G. (1974) *Confirmation du Pouvoir Royal au Nouvel An [Brooklyn Museum 47.218.50]. Planches*. Oxford, Oxford University Press.

Habachi, L. (2001) *Tell el–Dabʿa I. Tell el–Dabʿa and Qantir. The Site and its Connection with Avaris and Piramesse*. Vienna, Verlag der Österreichischen Akademie der Wissenschaften.

Hannig, R. (1997) *Großes Handwörterbuch Ägyptisch–Deutsch*. Mainz, Phillip von Zabern.

Hannig, R. (2003) *Ägyptisches Wörterbuch I: Altes Reich und Erste Zwischenzeit*. Mainz, Phillip von Zabern.

Hayden, B. (1984) 'Are Emic Types Relevant to Archaeology?' *Ethnohistory* 31(2), 79–92.

Helck, W. (1980). 'Ein „Feldzug" unter Amenophis IV. gegen Nubien', *Studien zur Altägyptischen Kultur* 8, 117–26.

Kitchen, K. (1975–89) *Ramesside Inscriptions* (8 vols.). Oxford, Blackwell.

Kitchen, K. (1993–2003) *Ramesside Inscriptions. Translated and Annotated* (4 vols.). Oxford, Blackwell.

Lesko, L. H. (1982–90) *A Dictionary of Late–Egyptian* (5 vols.). Berkeley, B.C. Scribe Publications.

Morris, E. F. (2005) *The Architecture of Imperialism. Military Bases and the Evolution of Foreign Policy in Egypt's New Kingdom*. Leiden, Brill.

Lee–Pike, K. (1967) *Language in Relation to a Unified Theory of the Structure of Human Behaviour*. The Hague, Mouton & Co.

Quack, J. F. (1993) 'Philologische Miszellen 2', *Lingua Aegyptia* 3, 151–2.

Rothe, R. D., Rapp, G. and Miller, W. K. (1996) 'New Hieroglyphic Evidence for Pharaonic Activity in the Eastern Desert of Egypt' *Journal of the American Research Center in Egypt* 33, 77–104.

Rothe, R. D. and Miller, W. K. (1999) 'More Inscriptions from the South Eastern Desert', *Journal of the American Research Center in Egypt* 36, 87–101.

Schenkel, W. (1983) *Aus der Arbeit an einer Konkordanz zu den altägyptischen Sargtexten*. Wiesbaden, Otto Harassowitz.

Snape, S. (2003) 'New perspectives on distant horizons: aspects of Egyptian imperial administration in Marmarica in the Late Bronze Age', *Libyan Studies* 34, 1–8.

Tresson, P. (1922) *La Stèle de Koubân*. Cairo, L'Institut français d'archéologie orientale.

Ventura, R. (1987) 'On the Location of the Administrative Outpost of the Community of Workmen in Western Thebes', *Journal of Egyptian Archaeology* 73, 149–60.

Westendorf, W. (1965) *Koptisches Handwörterbuch*. Heidelberg, Carl Winter.

Aegyptus, or the Western Conception of Egypt from the Fifteenth to the Eighteenth Century

Lucile Haguet
Université Paris IV Sorbonne

This paper is a discussion of the concept I have termed the 'Egypt of the West', an idea developed in my thesis which was entitled '*Aegyptus*, the Egypt of the West. Concept and Representation of Egypt in Western Cartography from the Fifteenth to the Eighteenth Century'. Many studies have been published on the concepts of Egyptomania or Egyptophily. However, these notions are not as inclusive as that summarised by the expression 'Egypt of the West'. Indeed, Egyptomania is an art movement, while Egyptophily designates only the positive expression of an interest towards Egypt. To this day, no real attempt to define that concept of Egypt elaborated in the West has ever been made. To distinguish it from true Egypt, I have decided to call it '*Aegyptus*', a word which is largely used in modern times.

Aegyptus is well documented by maps and my analysis uses these maps as source data. This is why I have chosen to limit my study to the period between the fifteenth to the eighteenth century. The first Latin translation of Ptolemy's *Geography* dates back to the fifteenth century and the period closes at the very beginning of the nineteenth century, when the *Atlas* of the *Description de l'Égypte* was published. Indeed, thanks to its encyclopedic aims, cartography is a particularly relevant source for the definition of *Aegyptus* and for the study of its various aspects. The complex nature of this multi-faceted concept makes it a difficult one to define, for it refuses to limit itself to a word, a period or even a definite place. This study aims at shedding new light on our understanding of the Western perception of Egypt by showing how *Aegyptus* goes far beyond the limited clichés such as the pyramids and the episode of the Exodus and is, instead, a multi-faceted concept.

The state of studies concerning the 'Egypt of the West'

Why should we study the Egypt of the West? Many researchers have already studied topics as varied as decipherment, hieroglyphs and travelogues, with the relevant data listed, published and analyzed (e.g. Munier 1828; Jolowicz 1857; Gay 1875; Paulitschke 1882; Atkinson 1927; Carré 1933, 1956; Sauneron 1970–90), Egyptomania, including subjects as diverse as paintings, operas, wallpaper and tea sets (Bissing 1912; Humbert 1989, 1994; Syndram 1989; Curl 2005), the history of esoterism (Cumont 1937; Hornung 2001), the conception of Egypt in the Bible and the Scriptures (Halbwachs 1971; Assmann 1998), and orientalism in general (Dufrenoy 1946; Tinguely 2000; Balard 1987).

The concept of the 'Egypt of the West' is dispersed amongst numerous subjects of study, so disciplinary approaches are quite heterogeneous too. The history of Egyptology, literary studies, social history of sciences and art history have all dealt with this topic.

Among these studies, the epistemological analysis is often given great importance. Seen through that lens, the 'Egypt of the West' becomes a history of Egyptology. However, since the dawn of Egyptology as a discipline is considered to be the decipherment of hieroglyphs, every earlier fact is generally analysed with this in mind, hence the considerable weight given to the scholars who tried to decipher the hieroglyphs. Travelogues recording the rediscovery of a site, thanks to a description or an engraving, are also favoured. We shall for instance recall those compiled in Porter and Moss' *Topographical Bibliography* (1960–75). Finally, studies on 'cabinets of wonder' containing Egyptian objects may document the custodial history of museum objects and, sometimes, reconnect the scattered parts of some of them. This method is thus not without interest.

These approaches can nevertheless be criticised. On the one hand, a chronological and descriptive approach is more often used than an analytical one. On the other hand, one could object that this approach considers historical facts *a posteriori* in the sense that pioneers and key events are chosen according to current Egyptological criteria. This narrows quite artificially the concept of 'Egypt of the West' to pharaonic Egypt alone.

In spite of the bulk of documentation and approaches available, cultural studies on *Aegyptus* remain rare. This is all the more surprising considering the notorious role played by *Aegyptus* in Western culture (a role it already played long before the nineteenth century and its sudden interest for Egypt). Consequently, when the French specialist Chantal Grell (2001), who specialises in the eighteenth century, suggested the idea of an assembly about Egypt in Western culture, she realised that there were only three books devoted to that topic: *The Myth of Egypt and its Hieroglyphs* by Erik Iversen (1961), *La Quête d'Isis* by Jurgis Baltrusaïtis (1967), and *Moïse* by Jan Assmann (1998). However, none of these offers a panoramic study, each one dealing instead with specific problems.

Suggestions for a new terminology

Therefore, a new study dedicated to the Western cultural representation of Egypt in the modern era does not seem to be a pointless endeavour. However, as I mentioned in the introduction, such a study is met with an incomplete terminology, words like 'Egyptophily', 'Egyptomania', and 'Egyptology' being unable to describe such a complex reality.

Chantal Grell (2001) proposed to refer to this concept through the expression 'imaginary Egypt'. However, the adjective 'imaginary' seems too ambivalent. Indeed, it could suggest that the Western representation of Egypt doesn't contain any objective facts, an assertion which is incorrect. 'Imaginary' could also imply that people living in modern times made a distinction between scholarly Egypt, known through objective facts, and an imaginary Egypt, known through legends, while for them, positive and wonderful facts belonged equally to the realm of knowledge. This is why I have selected the more neutral expressions: 'Egypt of the West' and '*Aegyptus*'. I tend to favour the latter because the Latin ending underlines the foreign origin of the word.

Suggested documentation, or how to study Aegyptus

A single document summarizing Egypt in Western culture has still to be found. Until now, studies about how Egypt was perceived in the West relied on texts, especially on travelogues. Yet in modern times few travellers went to Egypt and their representation of the country was directly influenced by their contact with it. Even though they were filled with knowledge and a textual culture, their points of view remained specific and personal, different from the experience of the 'arm-chair' reader. Moreover, texts about hieroglyphs or esoterism in general were often very scholarly, and consequently meant for a limited public.

On the other hand, paintings, sculptures and above all engraved plates are probably more widely known. But unfortunately, they often represent very specific themes, such as Moses saved from the waters, an episode of the Exodus or pictures of ruins. That is why I finally favoured a kind of documentation that remains very original: maps.

Why mapmaking?

In modern times, maps were not solely morphological plans. They constituted encyclopedic abstracts of historical, geographical, natural, religious, or commercial topics emblematic of how the West saw Egypt. As overviews of textual, iconographical and cartographical influences, they summarised all the knowledge of that time, that is not only of the sixteenth century, but also of the period up to the eighteenth century (Dainville 1940, 74).

In addition, even then, maps were not documents meant for few experts only. The reception of Egypt's maps is largely attested in geographical education, textbooks, and even literature. Such an interest for Egyptian geography is no surprise for, at that time, Egypt and cartography worked together. Through different founding myths of mapmaking and geography, the disciplines were tightly linked to pharaonic civilization. Here, Isis is teaching geography to her son Horus, according to the *Corpus Hermeticum* (Rivière 1980, 86). There, Ptolemy's *Geography* is attributed to the pharaoh of the Hellenistic age who bore the same name as the Egyptian geographer (Broc 1975, 9). In the eighteenth century, the entry 'geography' in Denis Diderot and Jean d'Alembert's *Encyclopédie* designated the pharaoh Sesostris as the first mapmaker (Robert de Vaugondy 1751–80, 612).

Besides, according to Greek and Latin geographers, whose points of view have been largely taken up by modern Western geographers, the Egyptian territory generated the very idea of mapmaking, not only because the Nile and its canals seem to foreshadow the artificial layout of meridian lines and parallels, but also because it constitutes a clean surface each year, when the annual flood of the Nile made a clean sweep of all signs. Because of the lack of permanent landmarks resulting from the flood, the required dividing of the Valley into equal and square pieces of land with the help of measuring tools was believed to have given birth to mapmaking. For this reason, and even though some of the ancients claimed that cartography was invented by Thales in Greece, Herodotus and Isidore of Seville believed that it was born in Egypt (Froidefond 1971, 124–5).

Therefore, maps have an Egyptian origin. And reciprocally, *Aegyptus* developed itself largely from geography. Information concerning territory and toponymy made up an essential part of Graeco-Latin authors' discourses. Thanks to Herodotus, Strabo, and Ptolemy, very detailed maps of Egypt have been produced. They contrast with the fragmentary knowledge regarding the rest of Africa during the same period. With regard to biblical episodes, they often centre on journeys such as the Exodus or the Flight into Egypt. So they too lead to a representation of *Aegyptus* related to an itinerary. For this reason, I postulate that mapmaking is the most legitimate documentation with which to study *Aegyptus*: maps derive from *Aegyptus* and, reciprocally, knowledge about Egypt is shaped by the Egyptian territory and summarised through canals and mountains, vignettes, icons and texts, as an *ars memoriae*.

The art of memory has been studied by Frances Yates in the 1960s (Yates 1966). She has demonstrated that ancient Greece and Rome bequeathed a mnemonic method to modern times. This method consists of organizing memory in space. First, words, facts or ideas meant to be memorised have to be converted into metaphors (for instance criss-cross sabers to symbolise a victory). Then, the metaphoric images have to be placed somewhere (for instance in a house, a garden, or, in the present case, on a map). By visiting mentally the places where metaphors were put, one should be able to recollect a whole speech. The art of memory was still very popular in modern times, and people believed in its efficiency. The word 'commonplace', to mention a cliché, originated from this art which links space and memory.

Finally I have decided to dedicate my research to the production of an inventory of more than six hundred maps. These maps come from Paris and Cairo. Some facsimiles have also been studied (Jomard n. d.; Santarem 1841; Kamal 1926–51; Kammerer 1929; Tooley 1969; Al-Ankary 2001). In order for these sources to be properly analyzed, I have developed a grid, for no consensual model of chart description existed so far. While doing this, I had two aims in mind: to set up preliminary work, and to create a catalogue which could be easily consulted by readers.

Let us see if this grid enables us to answer the question 'what is *Aegyptus*?'

Definition attempts

I have managed to answer this question by studying the various names given to Egypt in charts, and by defining its space.

Egypt's name

The study of a concept begins quite obviously with an analysis of the word used to designate it. Denomination is the founding act by which men view the world, as exemplified by Adam in the Book of Genesis. The geographers of the modern age understood this very well. This is why, from the sixteenth to the eighteenth century, the entries of an atlas very often started with a list of names. Following this habit, the geographer Giovanni Antonio Magini (1555–1617), professor of astronomy at the university of Bologna, quoted all the names of Egypt he knew: 'Aeria, Aetia, Potamia, Ogygia, Melambolos, Hephaestia, Myara, Aethiopia'(1617, 195).

In maps, the name given to Egypt appears to be more constant. The use of '*Aegyptus*' has generally been used under various written forms since the sixteenth century. However, '*Aegyptus*' may refer to a chart of ancient Egypt similar to a chart of modern Egypt. In addition, other names were sometimes preferred, as in this *Carte de l'ancienne Thébaïde* (1696), '*Thébaïde*' being here a synonym for Egypt, deserts included.

Sometimes, the local name of Egypt was restored. For instance, we may think of 'Chibet', used during the 17th century following Leo Africanus' *Description of Africa*. Under the influence of travelogues, it became 'Missir' in the course of the eighteenth century. Consequently, the proliferation of names became for cartographers the only way to encompass the various aspects of Egypt. Thus, in 1799, a map was entitled: *Aegyptus, Mesraim, Egypt*.

Space

Though it cannot be restricted to one name or one period, Egypt can be defined by its indisputable morphologic reality. But here again, modern cartographers were confronted with several difficulties. First, they hesitated between locating Egypt in Asia or in Africa. The question of the African or Asian origin of Egypt is a controversy of Ionian origin, briefly evoked in the second Book of Herodotus' *Histories*. According to the summary of the Greek traveller, Upper Egypt is attached to Arabia, the Nile being the boundary between Africa and Asia (*Histories*, 1982, II, 15–16, p. 76–77).

Until the eighteenth century, this Ionian heritage was depicted on charts which located Egypt on both continents. According to the map *L'Egipte dressée sur le second livre d'Hérodote* (1669) created by the French geographer Pierre Duval, 'the Nile delimits Africa and Arabia'. In the chart Asia by Jodocus Hondius (1607), the pink wash drawing on the Western bank of Nile as well as the yellow one on the Eastern bank suggest that Egypt was seen as mid African, mid Asian. This central question was still relevant at the beginning of the nineteenth century, according to the *Préface historique* of the *Description de l'Égypte* (Fourier, 1821, 1): 'Egypt [is] placed between Africa and Asia'. That sentence appears at the very beginning of the *Description*, published following Bonaparte's Expedition.

The difficult mapping of Egypt

Egypt, which could not be defined by its borders, could then be described by its layout. And yet, according to Jean-Baptiste d'Anville, one of the most important French geographers of the eighteenth century, nothing is 'more simple & more easy' (d'Anville 1766, 1), since it can be typified by the rectilinear feature of the river.

This simplicity is however illusory. If Egypt is a territory easy to schematise, it is nevertheless difficult to mark out because the mapmaking of Egypt works out in opposition to other charts. The river, which commonly materialises a political border in Western geography, constitutes here the heart of the country. Against all expectations, the border is found in the unspecified vastness of the desert, instead of drawing a quite clear limit, materialised by a mountainous or marine/riverine barrier.

Some geographers get around the problem by schematizing the mountainous chains on both sides of the Nile (Dainville, [1964] 2002, p.166). As for regional borders, they were represented by soft shapes, as is the case in Nicolas Sanson's map *Royaume et désert de Barca, et l'Aegypte*, by braces as in Melchior Tavernier's *Patriarchatus alexandrini* (1640), or by dashes cutting out the Nile as in the map *Sixième partie de la carte du cours du Nil* by Frederick-Ludwig Norden. These strategies exempted from evoking the borders' extent in the East and in the West. This is clearly visible in Adrien-Hubert Brué's map *Carte générale de l'Égypte ancienne* (1822).

After all, not time, nor space, nor culture, nor any specific criterion really defines Egypt. One could almost see in these maps many 'Egypts' rather than a discrete one. However, the present study claims that in the Western culture, *Aegyptus* cannot either be reduced to an accumulation of discontinuous aspects, for maps show that it constituted a coherent concept to their contemporaries. On maps, *Aegyptus* is thus successively related to the cabinet of curiosities, the emblem, or the mosaic, all these objects being characterised by heterogeneous, often marvellous details coherent only at global glance.

This paper is of course quite limited. Its purpose was to arouse some interest for 'Egypt as seen by the Western world', an Egypt which, I hope, will not be reduced to the pharaonic period, for that is only one element among all those which define *Aegyptus*. Indeed, once we refuse to restrict our analysis to this sole filter, it is striking to see the important role played by geographical curiosities such as islands, deserts, and channels in the building of Western cultural representations of Egypt. Such analyses also make it possible for us to highlight some modern questions. Thus, the debate on whether Egypt belongs to Africa or Asia here finds its Greek origin.

Acknowledgements

My thesis and this paper would not have been possible without the support and comments of my Ph.D supervisor, Michel Dewachter, the help of many professors, Frank Lestringant, Jean-Marc Besse, Isabelle Surun, Gilles Palsky, Marie-Noëlle Bourguet, and the kindness of the curators of the Bibliothèque nationale de France who allowed me to work on rare documents.

Bibliography

Anville, J.-B. d' (1766) *Mémoires sur l'Égypte ancienne et moderne*. Paris, Imprimerie royale.

Al-Ankary, K. (2001) *La Péninsule arabique dans les cartes européennes anciennes*. Paris, Institut du monde arabe.

Assman, J. (1998) *Mose der Ägypter, Entzifferung einer Gedachtnisspur*. Munich, Hanser.

Atkinson, G. (1927) *La Littérature géographique française de la Renaissance*. Paris, Picard.

Balard, M. (1987) 'L'Orient: concept et images dans l'occident médiéval', in J.-P. Charnay (ed.) *L'Orient: concept et images, XVe colloque de l'Institut de recherche sur les civilisations de l'Occident moderne*, 17–26. Paris, Presses de l'université de Paris-Sorbonne.

Baltrusaitis, J. (1967) *Essai sur la légende d'un mythe, la quête d'Isis, introduction à l'égyptomanie*. Paris, Perrin.

Bissing, F. W. von (1912) *Der Anteil der aegyptischen Kunst am Kunstleben der Völker*. Munich, Roth.

Broc, Numa. (1975) *La Géographie de la Renaissance*. Paris, Ophrys.

Brué, A. H. (1822) 'Carte générale de l'Égypte ancienne, de la Palestine et de l'Arabie Pétrée', in Kamal, Y. (1926–51) *Monumenta cartographica Africae et Aegypti t. II, fasc. 4, n°AA 58*. Cairo, n. p.

Carré, J.-M. (1933) 'La connaissance de l'Égypte en France au XVIIIe siècle en France',

Chronique d'Égypte. 15, 124–5.

Carré, J.-M. (1956) *Voyageurs et écrivains français en Égypte*. Cairo, Institut français d'archéologie orientale.

Cumont, F. (1937) *L'Égypte des astrologues*. Brussels, Fondation Égyptologique Reine Élisabeth.

Curl, J. S. (2005) *The Egyptian revival, ancient Egypt as the inspiration for design motifs in the West*. London, Routledge.

Dainville, F. de (1940) *La Géographie des humanistes*. Paris, Beauchesne.

Dainville, F. de (2002) *Le Langage des géographes*. Paris, Picard.

Dufrenoy, M.-L. (1946) *L'Orient romanesque en France, 2, Bibliographie générale*, Montréal, Éditions Beauchemin.

Duval, P. (1669) *L'Egipte dressée sur le second livre d'Hérodote*. Paris, Bibliothèque nationale de France, Collection d'Anville Ge DD 2987 (10187).

Fourier, J.-B. (1821) 'Préface historique', *Description de l'Égypte*. Paris, Panckoucke.

Froidefond, C. (1971) *Le Mirage égyptien dans la littérature grecque, d'Homère à Aristote*. Gap, Ophrys.

Gay, J. (1875) *Bibliographie des ouvrages relatifs à l'Afrique et à l'Arabie, Catalogue méthodique de tous les ouvrages français et des principaux en langues étrangères traitant de la géographie, de l'histoire, du commerce, des lettres & des arts de l'Afrique et de l'Arabie*, Paris, Maisonneuve.

Grell, C. *et al* (eds) (2001) *L'Égypte imaginaire de la Renaissance à Champollion, Colloque en Sorbonne, 21 et 22 mai 1991*. Paris, Presses de l'Université de Paris-Sorbonne.

Halbwachs, M. (1971) *La Topographie légendaire des évangiles en terre sainte*. Paris, Presses universitaires de France.

Herodotus (1982) *Histoires II, Euterpe* (trans. Ph. E. Legrand). Paris, Les Belles lettres.

Hondius, J. (1607) 'Asia', in K. Al-Ankary. (2001) *La Péninsule arabique dans les cartes européennes anciennes*, 160–1. Paris, Institut du monde arabe.

Hornung, E. (2001) *L'Égypte ésotérique*. (trans. N. Baum). Paris, Éditions du Rocher.

Humbert, J.-M. (1988) 'Égyptologie et égyptomanie: imprégnation dans l'art occidental de quatre siècle d'une cohabitation harmonieuse', in *Les Collections égyptiennes dans les musées de Saône-et-Loire*, 51–71. Autun, la Ville.

Humbert, J.-M. (1989) *L'Égyptomanie dans l'art occidental*. Courbevoie, ACR.

Humbert, J.-M. (1994) *Egyptomania. l'Égypte dans l'art occidental 1730–1930*. Paris, Réunion des musées nationaux.

Iversen, E. (1961) *The Myth of Egypt and its Hieroglyphs in European Tradition*. Copenhagen, Gad.

Jolowicz, H.(1857) *Bibliotheca Aegyptiaca*. Leipzig, Engelmann.

Jomard, E.-F. (n. d.) *Les Monuments de la géographie, recueil d'anciennes cartes européennes et orientales*. Paris, Lainé et Havard.

Jondet, G. (1921) *Atlas historique de la ville et des ports d'Alexandrie. Mémoires présentés à la société sultanieh de géographie*. Cairo, Institut français d'archéologie orientale.

Halbwachs, M. (1971) *La Topographie légendaire des évangiles en terre sainte*. Paris, Presses universitaires de France, [1941].

Kamal, Y. (1926–1951) *Monumenta cartographica Africae et Aegypti*. Cairo, n. p., 14 v.

Kammerer, A. (1929) *La Mer rouge, l'Abyssinie et l'Arabie*. Cairo, Société royale de géographie d'Égypte, 11 v.

Magini, G. A. (1617) *Geographiae, tum veteris, tum novae*. Arnheim, J. Janssonius.

Munier, H. (1828–1929) *Bibliographie géographique de l'Égypte*. Cairo, Institut d'archéologie orientale pour la société royale de géographie d'Égypte.

Paulitschke, P. (1882) *Die Africa-Literatur in der Zeit von 1500 bis 1750*. Vienna, Brockhausen und Brauer.

Porter, B. and Moss, R. (1960–75) *Topographical Bibliography of ancient Egyptian hieroglyphic texts, reliefs, and paintings*. Oxford, Clarendon Press [2nd edition].

Rivière, J.-L. .(1980) 'La carte, le corps, la mémoire, in J. Bertin *et al* (eds) *Cartes et figures de la Terre*, 83–91. Paris, Centre Georges Pompidou.

Robert de Vaugondy, D. (1751–80) 'Géographie', in D. Diderot and J. d'Alembert (eds) *Encyclopédie, ou Dictionnaire Raisonné des Sciences, des Arts et des Métiers*. Paris, Briasson.

Santarem, M. F. (1841) *Atlas de Santarem, Fac-similé*. Paris, n. p.

Sauneron S. (ed) (1970–90) *Collection des voyageurs occidentaux en Égypte*. Cairo, Institut français d'archéologie orientale.

Syndram, D. (1989) *Ägypten-Faszinationen. Untersuchungen zum Ägyptenbild in europäischen Klassizismus bis 1800*. Frankfort, Peter Lang.

Tinguely, F. (2000) *L'Écriture du Levant à la Renaissance. Enquête sur les voyageurs français dans l'empire de Soliman le magnifique*. Geneva, Droz.

Tooley, R. V. (1969) *Collector's guide to maps of the african continent*. London, Carta Press.

Yates, F. (1966) *The Art of Memory*. London, Routledge and Kegan Paul.

Water Basins in Middle Kingdom Planned Settlements

Kate Liszka
University of Pennsylvania

Introduction

Water basins are architectural features frequently found in Middle Kingdom settlements. Yet, publications which mention these features rarely discuss them in detail because their purpose seems enigmatic. When they are examined as a group, however, many differences appear that pertain to their functions. This study will demonstrate that most water basins in Middle Kingdom settlements function as hospitable and bureaucratic features, some are associated with production, industry, and storage, and a few exhibit a possible 'ritualistic' function.

In First Intermediate Period autobiographies, provincial rulers frequently boasted of their ability to provide water to their hometowns. For example, pharaoh Khety II noted that he created a canal for Herakleopolis. This task was an exceptional gift for his town because he did not use corveé labour (Badawy 1967, 106). The Eleventh Dynasty steward Samentuser also states 'I organised a water supply for my city and let my fellow citizens cross [the Nile] in my boat' (Badawy 1966, 11). Governor Sarenput I provided a 'drinking place of Elephantine' located in the courtyard of the Satet Temple (von Pilgrim 1997, 17–18). In addition to the large-scale provisioning of water for a city, water provision was incorporated into simpler forms of generosity.

In the Middle Kingdom, water storage facilities took a prominent place in the main areas of many homes, workshops, and administrative centres. These facilities assume various forms. There are large water jars, or *zirs*, resting on ground level (Arnold 1996, fig. 3, House 1 and 1.2; von Pilgrim 1996, 134–9, 214, Abb. 48), and large water storage jars fully sunken into the ground (Czerny 1999, 17–23, Abb. 2–3; Adams 1992, 6; von Pilgrim 1996, 165–72, 214, Abb. 68). There are also water basins resting on ground level (Dunham 1967, 116), as well as water basins sunken into the ground. Organic settlements only contained the first three types of water facilities, whereas planned settlements contained all four. As such, inset water basins only occur in planned settlements during the Middle Kingdom. Moreover, the majority of water basins have been discovered in the Nubian forts and at Kahun. A correlation between water basins and house types (as defined by Arnold 2001, 123–4 or Bietak 1996, 22–3) does not exist. However, water basins frequently occur in administrative buildings, governmentally-organised production areas, elite housing, and structures associated with temple administration. They never seem to occur in non-elite houses, which instead may rely on ceramic vessels to fulfil the same functions.

Water basins occur in three distinct shapes: square, rectangular, and cruciform. Square basins (Fig. 1) and rectangular basins (van Siclen 1996, fig. 5) typically measure between half a meter and one meter wide. The tops of most basins are flush with the ground. How-

Figure 1. Example of a square water basin from the mortuary temple of Senusret III at Abydos (photograph courtesy of Josef Wegner, see also Wegner 2007, pl.17a).

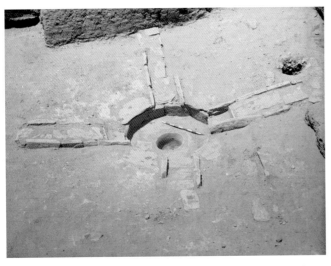

Figure 2. Example of a cruciform water basin from Semna. Photograph © 2008 Museum of Fine Arts, Boston (see also Dunham and Janssen 1960, pl. 8d).

ever, the top third of some basins rise above ground level (Wegner 2007, 93, 108; see Fig. 1). Cruciform basins (Fig. 2) typically measure 1.5 to 2.5 metres in width. The cruciform shape is created from stone slabs which radiate at 90 degree angles from a central basin. These slabs slope downward permitting liquid to flow along them into the central basin. Sometimes upturned ridges on the sloping slabs exist that would have controlled the flow. The central basin is round and up to 50 cm deep. Moreover, at Mirgissa (Dunham 1967, 144) and Semna (Dunham and Janssen 1960, 115), large pottery jars were found inside the central basin, allowing the liquid to be caught and removed. As will be seen below, the shape of cruciform basins may be associated with a specific activity or industry.

Water basins are primarily made out of limestone. However, fired ceramic basins are known from the so-called 'Campaign Palace' at Uronarti (Dunham 1967, 24–7). Water basins inset into the ground kept their contents cooler than those that remained above ground (Endruweit 1994, 82). On the ground surrounding the water basins, there are typically water-resistant limestone or fired-brick pavement (Figs. 5, 6, 9, 10, 11). Occasionally, basins can include an inflow drain (Figs. 3, 4), or an overflow drain (Figs. 3, 5, 6, 9). Water basins also frequently occur in the middle of open courts, or in the main halls of various types of structures. These locations are often the most public spaces within buildings.

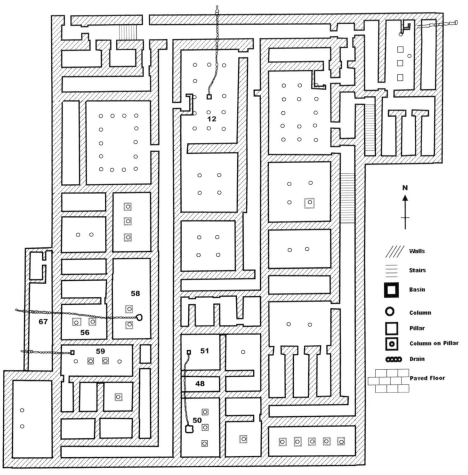

Figure 3. Plan of the 'Campaign Palace' of Uronarti depicting water basins and drains in rooms 12, 50, 51, 58, 59 (after Dunham 1967, Map VI).

To better understand the various functions of these water basins, we must first survey the types of locations in which they occur.

'Campaign Palace' of Uronarti

Several water basins were found at a large palatial structure located on the east side of Uronarti island opposite the Middle Kingdom fort (Fig. 3). Kemp has suggested that this structure was a ritualised campaign palace for Senusret III, because it aligns with true north, ignoring changes in topography. Furthermore the paucity of its archaeological remains suggests that it was only occupied for a short time (Kemp 1986, 134–6; Kemp 2006, 241). This structure contains five square water basins, all of which are made out of fired ceramic. The use of fired ceramic instead of more expensive limestone for the basins further supports Kemp's theory about the transitory nature of this structure. Three of these five water basins—present in rooms 12, 58, and 59—connect to drains that flow underneath other rooms and continue out of the structure. However, the water basin inside room 51 travels under room 48 and surfaces in room 50, connecting to that room's water basin (Dunham 1967, 24–7). The function of these rooms is unclear. These five water basins may have served in some ritualised purification ceremony for which—as Kemp argued—this building was specially constructed.

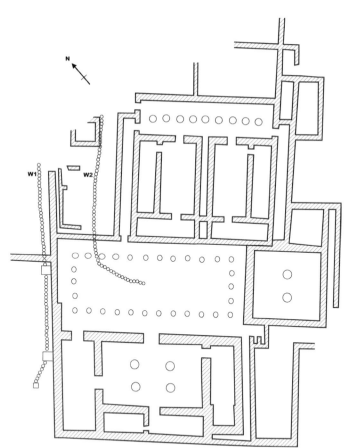

Figure 4. Plan of the Thirteenth Dynasty 'palace' at Tell el-Daba depicting an inflow drain (W2) emptying into the central court, where a water basin once was located (after Eigner 1997, 76-77).

Tell Basta 'Palace' and Tell el-Daba 'Palace'

Two so-called 'palaces' —residences of governors or mayors—contain water basins prominently located in the middle of large courts lined with columns. A Twelfth Dynasty palace found at Tell Basta contains a courtyard with shallow, rectangular basin (Fig. 5). This basin includes an overflow drain that

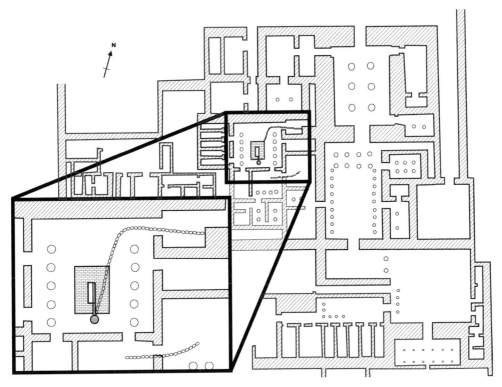

Figure 5. Plan of the Twelfth Dynasty 'palace' at Tell Basta depicting a water basin in the central court between two rows of columns (after van Siclen 1996, 239).

flows into a sunken pottery jar which also has an overflow drain. It is unclear where this drain leads (Farid 1964, 95; van Siclen 1996. 242–3). Similarly, at Tell el-Daba, there is a ceramic drain that begins in service areas of the palace, and empties into the middle of the large court, where a water basin was once located (Fig. 4). Moreover, around this basin were found drinking cups, bowls, pot-stands, and larger ceramic vessels (Eigner 1996, 76). These finds may indicate that the basin served as a focus for feasting. Judging from the central location of these basins amidst a columned courtyard in both 'palaces' and from the artefacts found at Tell el-Daba, it appears that these courts were foci for socializing, perhaps between officials, scribes or guests. Here the water basins act as a feature of hospitality, around which bureaucratic meetings or parties would take place. I believe that it may have provided visiting officials with water for drinking, personal cooling, or use in their administrative activities. The model garden courtyard from the tomb of Meketre (Winlock 1955, pls 9–12) may represent a schematic version of what is found in the palaces at Tell Basta or Tell el-Daba.

Military headquarters at Buhen and Uronarti

Basins were also found at the military headquarters of the Buhen and Uronarti forts. These buildings probably acted as administrative centres in which officials and members of the

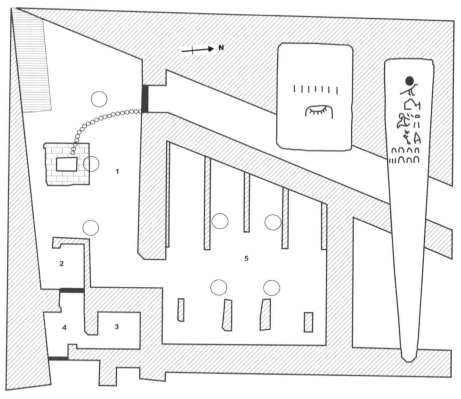

Figure 6. Plan of the military headquarters at Uronarti depicting a water basin with an overflow drain in room 1. In room 5 were found inscribed stone weights and wooden models of bread loaves that may have been used as tokens for rations (after: Dunham 1967, Map III, pl. 28, and pl. 35b. See also Kemp 2006, 175-6).

forts' staffs worked on a daily basis. At Uronarti, room 1 is the first court or hall between the dog-leg entrance and the only staircase leading to the top of the fort's walls (Fig. 6). Between the entrance and the staircase, a water basin with an overflow drain is prominently displayed in the middle of the room (Dunham 1967, 8–9). This basin was located in an area where many people would pass by and spend time. It may have provided water for those soldiers working in the hot sun at the top of the wall. No artefacts were found in the room with the basin. However, in rooms 3 and 4 administrative seal impressions, scraps of administrative documents and letters written on papyri were found (Dunham 1967, 17, 38). Moreover, in room 5, the excavators found stone weights inscribed with a number above a *nbw* sign (= Gardiner S12), indicating the amount of deben of gold to which each weight is equivalent (Fig. 6; Dunham 1967 17, pl. 35b). Also in room 5, they found wooden models of bread loaves with inscriptions (Fig. 6; Dunham 1967, 17, pls 27–8) that indicate that they were used as tokens for bread rations (Kemp 2006, 175–6). It appears that workers or soldiers came to room 5 to receive their pay. They probably queued around the water basin in room 1. The artefact contents and structure of these rooms clearly demonstrate the administrative function of this building. Certainly, the water basin in room 1 was a focal point for various administrative gatherings and work-related activities.

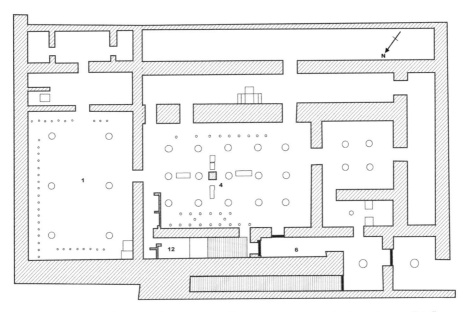

Figure 7. Plan of the military headquarters at Buhen. A square water basin with four flat flagstones around it is found in room 4 amongst 15 columns. (The basin is located immediately east of the number '4'). The small circles indicate small circular holes bored into the mud-brick flooring. The flagstones and the basins create a decorative cross form (after Emery et al 1979, pl. 16).

Similarly, at Buhen's military headquarters, an entrance provided access to the top of the defensive wall via a stairway (Fig. 7). However, the room to the east side of the stairs opens into room 4, the 'Painted Hall'. Smith, this building's excavator, describes the hall thus:

> *'The 'Painted Hall' was the largest, most stately, and best decorated chamber any-where in the Inner Fortress at Buhen; Block A as a whole was the most spacious, best appointed, and best-guarded building there, and it occupied the corner of the fort best sheltered from wind and the elements. There can be little doubt that at all times it was the audience chamber of the chief official at Buhen'* (Emery *et al* 1979, 48).

In the centre of the 'Painted Hall' lay a decorative water basin prominently displayed among 15 columns. Technically, this basin is cruciform in shape, but its four slabs lay flat on the floor and did not directly connect to the central basin. The cruciform shape in this case is decorative and not related to the basin's function. Furthermore, the artefacts found in the room suggest that eating, perhaps in large banquets, and administration took place in this hall. Inside the basin, were found animal bones, dom-palm nuts, a hemispherical cup, a small open bowl, and a small closed vessel (Emery *et al* 1979, 48). These items indicate that food was probably consumed in this room on a regular basis, and as the room was swept clean, remnants of the meals fell into the basin. Furthermore, in the floor around the edges of the room, a number of small holes were cut into the mud-brick floor-ing. Emery suggests that they may have been used to hold upright small food stands or

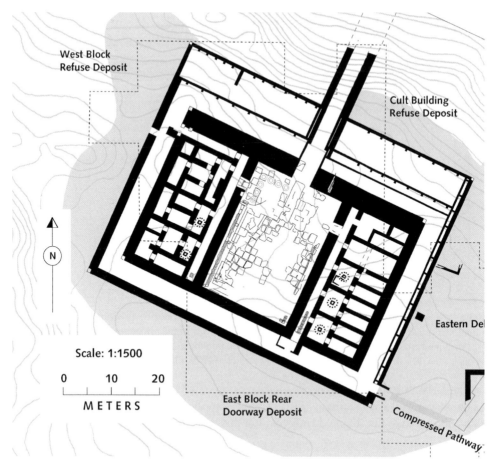

West Block
Refuse Deposit

Cult Building
Refuse Deposit

N

Eastern De

Scale: 1:1500

0   10   20

M E T E R S

East Block Rear
Doorway Deposit

Compressed Pathway

Figure 8. Plan of the Mortuary Temple of Senusret III at Abydos. Square water basins were found in the west administrative block and the east storage block. They are highlighted in the image above with dashed circles (courtesy of Josef Wegner, see also Wegner 2007, 50).

wine cups (Emery *et al* 1979, 9). Administrative seals and parts of administrative papyri were also found nearby in room 12 (Emery *et al* 1979, 9, 51). These objects and features indicate the administrative function of the painted hall. Therefore, room 4 would have been filled with various people either performing daily military duties and administrative functions, or attending occasional audiences with the chief official of Buhen. Food and refreshment were possibly provided during these activities. Therefore the water basin in the 'Painted Hall' was one of many marks of hospitality towards employees and guests and may also have been used for administrative activities.

Mortuary Temples at Dahshur, Kahun, and Abydos

Water basins of the Middle Kingdom are also associated with mortuary temple administration. The priests' house in front of the Mortuary Temple of Amenemhet III at Dahshur (Arnold 1987, pl. 36), the so-called 'Porter's Lodge' in front of the Temple of Senusret II at Kahun (Petrie, 1890, pl. 15), and the West Block of the Mortuary Temple of Senusret III at Abydos (Fig. 8) all have water basins located in the most public room of each structure. This location is probably where temple administration took place (certainly at Abydos: Wegner, 2007, 111–8). Water basins here provided water for short term storage or water for personal cooling, or water to aid administrative activities that took place around them.

It is noteworthy that the Mortuary Temple of Senusret III at Abydos also has three other water basins found in the temple's east block (Figs. 1, 8). The temple's excavator, Wegner, has definitively shown that these rooms were used as magazines for the storage of temple offerings and equipment (Wegner, 2007, 102–4). The three main rooms in front of the magazines each contained a water basin in the centre (Wegner, 2007, 93–6). Clearly, water in these basins must have been used for some type of administrative activity pertaining to the storage of food or supplies for the temple cult. Perhaps the basins held water to be used for sealing. Or perhaps water was left in these basins for the use of scribes and priests who worked in these magazines daily.

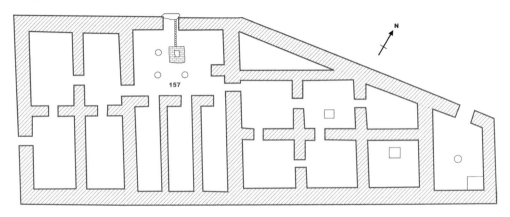

Figure 9. Plan of the granary block at Uronarti. According to Kemp (1986, 123) the left block was the treasury, the central block containing a basin with an overflow drain was used for granary administration, and the right block was the granary (after Dunham 1967, Map III).

Water basins and granaries

Water basins have been periodically discussed in conjunction with granaries (Arnold 2005, 55–60). This discussion began when Kemp utilised the granary block at Uronarti (Fig. 9) as his case study in an examination of the state-run granaries of the Middle Kingdom (Kemp 1986, 124–5). A water basin with an overflow drain leading out of the fort existed in the middle of room 157, which Kemp demonstrated was the administration centre of this granary. However, no other definite granary administrative centre from the Middle Kingdom contains a water basin. Askut, which had the largest granary of the Middle Kingdom forts, had no such basin (Smith 1995, 69–75). At Mirgissa (Fig. 10), Room 47 is most comparable to the granary administration centre at Uronarti (Dunham 1967, 7–8, 145). Yet there is no water basin. Room 32 at Mirgissa does have a stone pavement and an overflow drain leading out of the fort. This feature may have provided the same

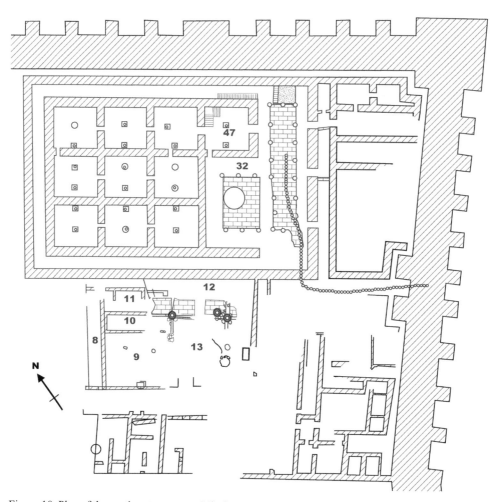

Figure 10. Plan of the northeast quarter at Mirgissa. A granary and buildings belonging to the granary administration form the northern half. Room 47 is the most comparable to Uronarti room 157, but room 32 has a podium for an official at the north end and an outflow drain laid into the floor. No water basin appears in these rooms. Three cruciform basins can be found in the structures south of the granary in rooms 10-13. These areas clearly are physically separated from the granaries (after Dunham 1967, Map 17).

function as the basin and drain at Uronarti. The basin at Uronarti provided water for the administrative activities that took place in the magazines and treasury of this same block, rather than provided water for the granary's administration.

Water basins and drains

The majority of water basins are not connected to an inflow or overflow drain. Most of the examples of basins with drains have been discussed above. The Thirteenth Dynasty 'palace' at Tell el-Daba (Fig. 4) contains the only known example of a drain flowing into a water basin. Overflow drains are accessed from the top of the basin, allowing the contents in the bottom of the basin to remain, as at Uronarti (Dunham 1967, 7–8). Overflow drains connected to basins are present at the Twelfth Dynasty 'palace' at Tell Basta (Fig. 5), the military headquarters at Uronarti (Fig. 6), and the granary administration centre of Uronarti (Fig. 9). Furthermore, an outflow drain that is not connected to a basin is also featured in the floor of the granary administration centre, room 32, at Mirgissa (Fig. 10). The locations, which include drains, are in administration centres. Drains therefore indicate the need to remove used liquid from these areas as part of the activities that took place here. This link between drains and administration centres does not pertain to the features in the 'Campaign Palace' of Uronarti.

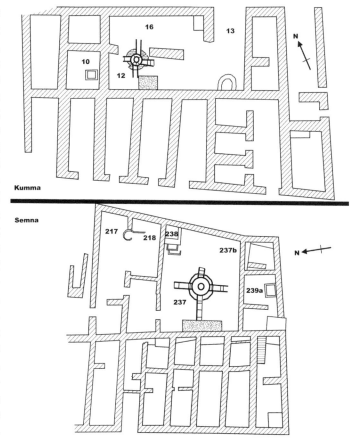

Figure 11. Top: Plan of the northeast corner of Kumma depicting a workshop with a cruciform basin in the centre (after Dunham and Janssen 1960, Map XVI). Bottom: Plan of the southeast corner of Semna depicting a workshop with a cruciform basin in the centre (after Dunham and Janssen 1960, Map IV).

The presence of a basin with a drain suggests that officials and scribes would spend time working in these areas. Water was necessary for the diverse activities taking place in these areas such as erasing clerical mistakes, sealing, or refreshment. This water was provided for employees in the portable water jars, or in the water basin itself. The water was then disposed of through the drains as part of the daily activities.

Cruciform water basins

Water basins also exist at Mirgissa (Fig. 10), Semna (Fig. 11), Kumma (Fig. 11), and Serra East (Hughes 1963, pl. 2) that are not associated with granaries or military headquarters. Each of these forts has a large workshop. In the middle of the central room of these workshops lay large cruciform basins. Each basin has four arms with upturned edges that slope into a central basin (Fig. 2). Their design suggests that a liquid flowed down the arms into the central basin. Large pottery jars were found inside the central portion of the cruciform basins at Mirgissa (Dunham 1967, 144) and Semna (Dunham and Janssen 1960, 115). Presumably, the jars caught the liquid and could be easily removed to be emptied elsewhere. The cruciform basins at Semna and Kumma (Fig. 11) are surrounded by five or six rooms almost certainly associated with the activity that took place at the cruciform basins. In both forts, a rectangular platform overlooks the basin, possibly for the use of the workshop's overseer. These workshops both have a small square or circular quern-like structure in the corner of the room and in an adjacent room. Moreover, large storage or production facilities are located behind the wall of the room that the basin is in. Both Mirgissa (Fig. 10) and Serra East (Hughes 1963, pl. 2) have a series of holes carved directly into the limestone bedrock around the basin. Hughes suggested that the activity that took place in these rooms at Serra East may have used wooden poles that needed to be temporarily affixed to the ground (Hughes 1963, 126–7). Unfortunately, the structures in which they were found were denuded.

It is important to note that the cruciform basins only occur in the Nubian forts (with one exception, see below). Because their location is limited to Lower Nubia, the cruciform basins may relate to localised activities. Additionally, they may relate to activities that needed to be conducted within the security of the forts' enclosure walls. From their design, it is almost certain that the cruciform basins were used in some type of production or industry in which a liquid, perhaps water or blood, spilled downhill in a controlled manner and needed to be removed easily. Four workers could have worked around the basin, each at one of the arms. Perhaps animals were slaughtered here, and the blood was collected below; a theory about the use of similar production spaces was suggested by Arnold (2005, 55–60). A number of net weights and some flints found at Mirgissa (Dunham 1967, 161) suggest that fish may have been cleaned here. It has also been suggested that laundry was washed here during a siege (Petrie 1890, 23; Wheeler and Dunham 1961, 115, 124).

The structure of the cruciform basins, with their sloping arms and their deep basins relate them closely to gold-washing tables and settling basins, found elsewhere in Lower Nubia (Smith 1991, 114; Vercoutter 1959, 120–8; Adams 1966, 269). Gold sluices found at Askut, Faras East, and elsewhere are always located next to the river banks, because a high volume of water is needed for sluicing gold. These cruciform basins, however, are on top of high hills inside of forts. Nevertheless, it is possible that the further separating of gold ore from intermingled minerals could have taken place here under the watchful eyes of an overseer and within the security of a structure in the fort. Representations of gold-washing from the Middle and New Kingdoms depict this process occurring inside of workshops on shallow tables, one of which is sloping (Newberry 1894, pl. IV; Martin 1991, 131; Ogden 2000, 161–2). In the tomb of Khay, the 'Goldwasher of the Lord of the Two Lands', he is depicted overseeing this activity in a workshop (Martin 1991, 131). Furthermore, the forts of Semna, Kumma, Mirgissa, and Serra East are all located at strategic points around the Second Cataract. The nearby mines produced gold which the Egyptians called the 'Gold of Kush' (Vercoutter 1959, 129). These mines were located relatively close to the Nile, rather than deep in the Eastern Desert like the mines called the

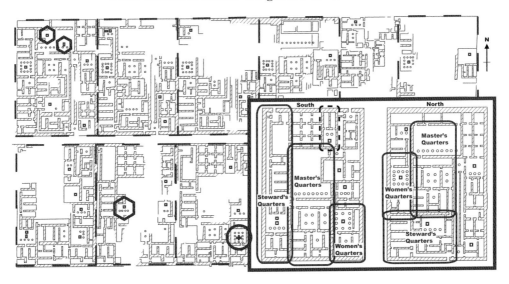

Figure 12. Plan of the northern and southern Kahun mansions containing square water basins in the middle of various courtyards (after Arnold 2005, 79 and after Bietak 1996, 32–3). The hexagons indicate water basins found in the 'Masters' Quarters'. The circle indicates the cruciform water basin at Kahun. The inset depicts a reconstruction of the 'typical' northern and southern mansions at Kahun, based on Bietak's reconstruction (1996, 32–3). The 'Master's Quarters', 'Women's Quarters' and 'Steward's Quarters' are sections that may have belonged to distinct members of the household (Arnold 1989, 84–8; Bietak 1996, 31–5; Quirke 2005, 55–68). The dashed oval on the southern mansion is another unit which contains a water basin that is discussed in the text. This plan does not include all of the basins at Kahun.

'Gold of Wawat' (Vercoutter 1959, 129). Thus, it would not have been a difficult task to move crushed gold ore from the mines to the forts for further refining.

The structure of the cruciform basins is similar to known gold-washing tables. The cruciform basins have coarse, sloping limestone arms and grooves between the slabs (Fig. 2) that could catch heavier gold pieces. Similar corrugated surfaces are found on gold-washing tables (Adams 1966, 269). At the bottom of the basins' sloping arms are shallow ledges onto which gold pieces could fall. A similar small holding area at the end of a sloping surface is part of the Faras East gold-washing table (Vercoutter 1959, 121). Lastly, the water of the cruciform basins falls into a deep basin which has a pottery jar in it. The water and the tailings in the cruciform basins could then be caught and reused or disposed. Similar deep basins are at the end of gold-washing tables (Smith 1991, 114; Vercoutter 1959, 121–2).

In addition to the cruciform basins in the Nubian forts, one was discovered at Kahun (Fig 12). Petrie referred to the same basin three times in his publications (Petrie 1890, 23, 24; Petrie 1891, 6–7; Gallorini 1998, 47–8) and sketched it twice in his notebooks (Petrie 2001, Notebook 39b, 72 and Notebook 48, 49). Yet, upon close scrutiny one can see that each reference refers to the same basin. This cruciform basin was located in the easternmost of the three southern mansions at Kahun in the 'Women's Quarters'. It also contained sloping sides that emptied into the central basin (Petrie 1890, 23, 24; Petrie 1891, 6–7; Gallorini, 1998, 47–8). Because this basin is a different shape than the basins in the centre of the other 'Women's Quarters', this cruciform shape may be a renovation to the original house that Petrie did not recognise. The appearance of this basin probably was not intended by the original architect who designed Kahun. Cruciform basins should still be considered primarily a feature of Nubian forts.

Elite mansions at Kahun

The majority of water basins of the Middle Kingdom come from the elite mansions of Kahun, accounting for about half of the excavated examples (Fig. 12). There are 36 potential basins from Kahun, although many of these identifications are questionable given the available evidence. Five water basins appear in the various reconstructions that scholars have made of the 'typical' northern and southern Kahun mansions as part of their discussion of spatial organization of domestic and administrative areas of these mansions (Badawy 1966, 24–35; Arnold 1989, 84–8; Bietak 1996, 31–5; O'Connor 1997, 398–400; Quirke 2005, 55–68). According to these reconstructions, certain quarters can be identified with either domestic or administrative activities based on the structure of the rooms. The function of the large courtyards belonging to the 'Master's Quarters' remain vague, due to the lack of features in them. Many of these reconstructions have overlooked the basins found in these courtyards. Two of the nine excavated mansions exhibit water basins in their large courtyards (Fig. 12). Unlike many other courtyard basins, these examples are not found in the very middle of the courtyard, but are off-centre. I believe that the addition of a water basin in these courtyards and the fact that many of these courtyards were renovated in the later Middle Kingdom to include granary silos (Kemp and Merrillees 1980, 79–101, esp. 86) indicate that the space had many functions. They probably accommodated administrative activities like the 'palaces' at Tell Basta and Tell el-Daba.

Water basins are sometimes connected to areas of granary administration in the Kahun mansions too. Although there is very little consensus as to which rooms in the Kahun mansions were used for administration of granaries (Kemp 1986, 122; Arnold 1989, 84–8; Bietak 1996, 31–4; O'Connor 1997, 397; Quirke 2005, 63), this study demonstrates that the presence of basins does not in fact correlate with granaries. When water basins are present near granaries, as at Uronarti fort (see above), they are almost certainly there for another reason such as production or storage, or even for aesthetic value.

Basins are also connected to other administrative activities in the Kahun mansions. They frequently appear in the courtyard of the housing unit identified with the steward (Fig. 12). This unit was identified with the steward because of its access to magazines and because it frequently has a separate entrance (Arnold 1989, 85; Bietak 1996, 34; Quirke 2005, 62–3). Much of the steward's business may have been conducted in the courtyard of this unit. Thus, the water basin commonly found in the centre of this housing unit would have served as a point of congregation for people, as also seen in the military headquarters of Nubian forts.

Water basins are also found in the housing unit known as the 'Women's Quarters' (Fig. 12). This unit is only accessible through the 'Master's Quarters'. This area consisted of a smaller housing unit, a courtyard and a basin surrounded by columns. This courtyard seems to be a central living and working area for the women and children in their daily activities (Arnold 1989, 84–8; Bietak 1996, 31–4; Quirke 2005, 61–2). The structure of these courtyards can best be compared with those in the 'palaces' at Tell el-Daba (Fig. 4) and Tell Basta (Fig. 5), each of which includes a basin surrounded by columns.

Basins are found in other areas in the Kahun mansions, the functions of which are unclear and consequently highly debated. Servant's quarters (Arnold 1989, 85; Bietak 1996, 31; Quirke 2005, 64, 67), guest rooms (Quirke 2005, 64–6), administrative areas (O'Connor 1997, 395), workshops (Bietak 1996, 31–2, 37; Lehner 2000, 293–4; Arnold 2001, 123; Kemp 2006, 216), food production areas (Arnold 2005, 57–60; Kemp 2006, 216), and animal pens (Quirke 2005, 68; Kemp 2006, 216) have all been suggested. Note that the unit enclosed with a dashed oval in Figure 12 takes the same shape as the store-rooms in the east block of the Mortuary Temple of Senusret III at Abydos (Fig. 8), which also contained water basins in the centre of those rooms. Perhaps those at Kahun were used as storerooms like the ones at Abydos. Nevertheless, it may be assumed that the water basins in the Kahun mansions acted as the centre of activity for a distinct group of people working or living in each unit of the mansions.

Conclusion

What were the functions of these basins? From the time of Petrie's excavations of Kahun in 1890 until the 1980s, many Egyptologists have referred to them as 'baths' or 'libation areas' for 'daily ablutions' (for example: Petrie 1890, 23; Dunham and Janssen 1960, 13, 115; David 1986, 103, 107). Sometimes these 'daily ablutions' are associated with a more religious or ceremonial significance, such as in Islam (Petrie 1891, 6–7; Petrie 1923, 39; Emery *et al* 1979, 48). This theory is improbable. Most of the basins are in centralised locations within industrial, administrative, or domestic units, strongly disfavouring the possibility of using the basin as a 'bath'. Similarly, the appearance of most basins outside of sacrosanct areas also eliminates the possibility of their use for 'libations'.

Arnold has suggested that the basins at Kahun were used to collect rainwater (Arnold 1989, 82). This suggestion is based on the fact that Meketre's model house has drain-spouts that point towards the central basin in the courtyard (Winlock 1955, pls 9–12). This theory has been adopted by some scholars (for example Frey and Knudstad 2007, 39). Although many basins could collect rainwater, this is unlikely the primary function of the basins. Rain is infrequent in Egypt and Nubia. The building of a basin specifically for this purpose only in planned settlements seems trivial. Moreover, similar basins from sites other than Kahun are located in rooms that might have been roofed (possibly Figs. 3, 6, 7, 8, 9).

In his study of Amarna houses, Endruweit demonstrated how water facilities placed in large open rooms cooled entire buildings (1994, 81–8). The presence of any type of water storage facility undoubtedly would have served to cool the surrounding rooms, although it is doubtful that cooling was the primary purpose of the basins, because occasionally they are found in small and enclosed rooms.

Wegner suggested that the water basins may have been employed for short term storage and water use (Wegner 2007, 93–6). This suggestion is the most credible possibility to date for square and rectangular shaped basins. These basins—with the exceptions of those in the 'Campaign Palace' of Uronarti (Fig. 3)—provided water for people who spent their days working and living in the basin's immediate vicinity. The basins could provide water for administrative activities, industry, production (Arnold 2005, 55–60), and personal cooling. Moreover, a number of cups and small bowls are often found around the basins (Dunham and Janssen 1960, 126; Dunham 1967, 57, 161; Emery *et al* 1979, 9, 48; Eigner, 1996, 76); perhaps Egyptians occasionally drank from them too. In general, eating and drinking most often occurred in the court or hall of domestic quarters (von Pilgrim, 1996, 256), the most probable place for a water basin to be located.

In brief, the water basins that are associated with temple administration, town administration, household administration, and domestic activities are square or rectangular and are found in central locations around which people would congregate for long periods of time. Yet, I believe that their elaborate and central locations show that basins had more than a simple utilitarian purpose. Large water basins in elite housing units or administrative areas were also a conspicuous display of status that people were supposed to notice when entering a room. In these situations, water basins are a symbol of power, bureaucracy, and hospitality.

On the other hand, the function of the cruciform basins found in the Nubian fortresses may have been associated with activities specific to that region. The cruciform basins were designed to facilitate an activity that caught liquid rather than provided water. Because of their sloping arms and deep central basin, their structure points to activities like gold-washing. They are quite different from the basins found in domestic or administrative locations.

The water basin was clearly a significant feature to the Egyptians of the Middle Kingdom. They incorporated it purposely into the design of state-planned settlements. There is still much to learn from these ostensibly prosaic architectural features.

Bibliography:

Adams, W. Y. (1966) 'The Vintage of Nubia', *Kush* 14, 262–83.

Adams, M. D. (1992) 'Introductory Report on 1991–92 Field work conducted at the Abydos Settlement Site', *Newsletter of the American Research Center in Egypt* 158, 1–10.

Arnold, Di. (1987) *Der Pyramidenbezirk des Königs Amenemhet III. in Dahschur.* Mainz am Rhein, Verlag Philipp von Zabern.

Arnold, Do. (2005) 'The Architecture of Meketre's Slaughterhouse and Other Early Twelfth Dynasty Wooden Models', in P. Janosi (ed.) *Structure and Significance: Thoughts on Ancient Egyptian Architecture*, 1–65. Vienna, Österreichischen Akademie der Wissenschaften.

Arnold, F. (1989) 'A Study of Egyptian Domestic Buildings', *Varia Aegyptiaca* 5, 75–93.

Arnold, F. (1996) 'Settlement Remains at Lisht-North', in M. Bietak (ed.) *House and Palace in Ancient Egypt,* 13–21. Vienna, Österreichischen Akademie der Wissenschaften..

Arnold, F. (2001) 'Houses', in D. Redford (ed.) *The Oxford Encyclopedia of Ancient Egypt* (Vol. 2), 122–7. Oxford, Oxford University Press.

Arnold, F. (2005) 'Baukonstruktion in der Stadt Kahun: Zu den Aufzeichnungen Ludwig

Borchardts', in P. Janosi (ed.) *Structure and Significance: Thoughts on Ancient Egyptian Architecture,* 77–104.. Vienna, Österreichischen Akademie der Wissenschaften.

Badawy, A. (1966) *A History of Egyptian Architecture* (Vol. 2). Berkeley, University of California Press.

Badawy, A. (1967) 'The Civic Sense of Pharaoh and Urban Development in Ancient Egypt', *Journal of the American Research Center in Egypt* 6, 103–109.

Bietak, M. (1996) 'Zum Raumprogramm ägyptischer Wohnhäuser des Mittleren und des Neuen Reiches', in M. Bietak (ed.) *House and Palace in Ancient Egypt,* 23–43. Vienna, Österreichischen Akademie der Wissenschaften.

Czerny, E. (1999) *Tell el-Dab'a IX: Eine Plansiedlung des frühen Mittleren Reiches.* Vienna, Österreichischen Akademie der Wissenschaften.

David, A. R. (1986) *The Pyramid Builders of Ancient Egypt.* London, Routledge and Kegan Paul.

Dunham, D. (1967) *Second Cataract Forts 2: Uronarti Shalfak Mirgissa.* Boston, Boston Museum of Fine Arts.

Dunham, D. and Janssen, J. (1960) *Second Cataract Forts 1: Semna Kumma.* Boston, Boston Museum of Fine Arts.

Eigner, D. (1996) 'A Palace of the Early 13th Dynasty at Tell el-Dab'a', in M. Bietak (ed.) *House and Palace in Ancient Egypt,* 73–80. Vienna, Österreichischen Akademie der Wissenschaften.

Emery, W. B. *et al* (1979) *The Fortress of Buhen: The Archaeological Report.* London, Egypt Exploration Society.

Endruweit, A. (1994) *Städtischer Wohnbau in Ägypten: Klimagerechte Lehmarchitektur in Amarna.* Berlin, Gebr. Mann Verlag.

Farid, S. (1964) 'Preliminary Report on the Excavations of the Antiquities Department at Tell Basta (Season 1961)', *Annales du Service des Antiquités de l'Égypte* 58, 87–98.

Frey, R. A. and Knudstad, J. E. (2007) 'The Re-examination of Selected Architectural Remains at El-Lahun', *Journal of the Society for the Study of Egyptian Antiquity* 34, 23–65.

Gallorini, C. (1998) 'A reconstruction of Petrie's excavation at the Middle Kingdom Settlement of Kahun', in S. Quirke (ed.) *Lahun Studies,* 42–59. Surrey, Sia Publishing.

Hughes, G. (1963) 'Serra East: The University of Chicago Excavations, 1961–62: A Preliminary Report on the First Season's Work', *Kush,* 11, 121–30.

Kemp, B. (1986) 'Large Middle Kingdom Granary Buildings (and the archaeology of administration)', *Zeitschrift für Ägyptische Sprache und Altertumskunde* 113, 120–36.

Kemp, B. (2006) *Ancient Egypt: Anatomy of a Civilization* (2nd edition). London, Routledge.

Kemp, B. and Merrillees, R. (1980) *Minoan Pottery in Second Millennium Egypt.* Mainz am Rhein, Verlag Philipp von Zabern.

Lehner, M. (2000) 'Fractal House of Pharaoh: Ancient Egypt as a Complex Adaptive System, a Trial Formulation', in T. Kohler *et al* (eds) *Dynamics in Human and Primate Societies,* 275–353. Oxford, Oxford University Press.

Martin, G. T. (1991) *The Hidden Tombs of Memphis.* London, Thames and Hudson.

Newberry, P. (1894) *Beni Hasan Part II.* London, Egypt Exploration Fund.

O'Connor, D. (1997) 'The Elite Houses of Kahun', in J. Phillips (ed.) *Ancient Egypt, the Aegean, and the Near East: Studies in Honour of Martha Rhoads Bell* (Vol. 2), 389–400. San Antonio, van Siclen Books. .

Ogden, J. (2000) 'Metals', in P. T. Nicholson and I. Shaw (eds) *Ancient Egyptian Materials and Technology,* 148–76. Cambridge, Cambridge University Press.

Petrie, W. M. F. (1890) *Kahun, Gurob, and Hawara.* London, Kegan Paul.

Petrie, W. M. F. (1891) *Illahun, Kahun and Gurob.* London, David Nutt.

Petrie, W. M. F. (1923) *Lahun II.* London, British School of Archaeology in Egypt.

Petrie, W. M. F. *et al* (2001) *Sir William Matthew Flinders Petrie: Including Excavation Notebooks, Tomb Cards, Distribution List, Distribution List Index, Ancient Egyptian Glazing, and Ancient Egyptian Glass.* London, Secure Data Services Limited (CD-Rom).

Quirke, S. (2005) *Lahun: A town in Egypt 1800 BC, and the History of its Landscape.* United Kingdom, Golden House Publications.

Smith, S. T. (1991) 'Askut and the Role of the Second Cataract Forts', *Journal of the American Research Center in Egypt* 28, 107–32.

Smith, S. T. (1995) *Askut in Nubia: The Economics and Ideology of Egyptian Imperialism in the Second Millennium B.C.* London, Kegan Paul International.

van Siclen III, C. (1996) 'Remarks on the Middle Kingdom Palace at Tell Basta', in M. Bietak (ed.) *House and Palace in Ancient Egypt*, 239–46. Vienna, Österreichischen Akademie der Wissenschaften.

Vercoutter, J. (1959) 'The Gold of Kush: Two Washing Stations of Faras East', *Kush* 7, 120–3.

von Pilgrim, C. (1996) *Elephantine XVIII: Untersuchungen in der Stadt des Mittleren Reiches und der Zweiten Zwischenzeit.* Mainz, Philipp von Zabern.

von Pilgrim, C. (1997) 'The Town Site on the Island of Elephantine', *Egyptian Archaeology* 10, 16–18.

Wegner, J. (2007) *The Mortuary Temple of Senwosret III at Abydos.* New Haven, Peabody Museum of Natural History of Yale University.

Wheeler, N. and Dunham, D. (1961) 'Diary of the Excavation of Mirgissa Fort', *Kush* 9, 87–179.

Winlock, H. E. (1955) *Models of Daily Life in Ancient Egypt.* Cambridge, Harvard University Press.

Analysis of Black Coatings on a Mummy and Associated Artefact from The Manchester Museum

Natalie C. McCreesh, Andrew P. Gize and A. Rosalie David
KNH Centre, University of Manchester

Abstract

A human mummy (Perenbast), who is still fully wrapped in her coffin, is on display at the Manchester Museum. A thick black coating covers the bandages. In the grave were found also two black coated shabti boxes. As part of a study into the funerary anointing of the body in ancient Egypt, the black coatings of the bandages and one of the shabti boxes were analysed to determine initially whether they were inorganic, organic, or a mixture, and secondly to determine if the black material on the bandages and shabti boxes were identical. Electron microscopy with energy dispersive spectroscopy provide evidence that the coatings of the bandages were organic, whereas the shabti box coating was an organic/inorganic composite.

Introduction

The Manchester Museum has on display a collection of human mummies including a female named Perenbast (Manchester Museum 5053a), a Chantress of Amun of the Twenty-fifth Dynasty. The mummy is fully wrapped and in the original wooden coffin (David 1979, 5). The bandages are covered with a black material (Fig. 1).

An analytical investigation of the mummy was conducted as part of a study into the funerary anointing of the body in ancient Egypt. The aim of the investigation was to identify the black coating, which has previously been hypothesised as either bitumen or a plant resin. It was decided also to compare this coating to that on another item in the tomb group – a shabti box (Manchester Museum 5053e - Fig. 2). These items could have been painted with traditional black paint, usually made from carbonaceous material, often seen on ancient Egyptian funerary goods (Lee and Quirke 2000, 108). The hypothesis is that the black coating on the bandages is compositionally different to the black substance on the funerary items.

The bandages may have been coated with a specific material on purpose. As it was common for the body to be anointed with organic based scented oils, unguents and resins, as part of the funerary ritual (Taylor 2001, 57), it was hypothesised that the coating was more likely to be organic-based.

Figure 1. Perenbast in coffin base. Note the black coating on the bandages, (coffin length 150.7cm x width 32.0cm, view from right side of the coffin, on display in the ancient Egyptian gallery). Courtesy of the Manchester Museum.

Materials and methods

Figure 2. One of two shabti boxes (box height 26.8cm x width 23.0cm). Courtesy of the Manchester Museum.

Samples of less than 1mg were taken for analyses from Perenbast and her associated artefacts. Samples were taken of the black coating and bandage from the foot of the mummy, and from the shabti box. Analyses used environmental scanning electron microscopy (ESEM) and energy dispersive spectroscopy (EDS).

ESEM was chosen over other types of electron microscopy (such as scanning electron microscopy and transmission electron microscopy) as it gives good topographical imaging and is the least destructive technique. The sample is not damaged by any preparation methods that would be required with other types of electron microscopy. Scanning electron microscopy (SEM) produces higher resolution images than ESEM, but can only be used for conductive samples at high voltage. If the sample to be examined is non-conductive, the sample is made conductive by coating with conductive elements such as gold, carbon, gold/palladium and silver. The coating can also interfere with EDS analysis (Robinson and Grey 1996). Transmission electron microscopy (TEM) requires solid samples to be sectioned. It can only produce three-dimensional images by making reconstructions using two-dimensional images, taken at different levels throughout the depth of the sample (Robinson and Grey 1996, 577). Therefore, it is not useful for viewing tomography but does allow analysis of subsurface material.

With both ESEM and SEM the main information is gained from secondary electrons and back scattered primary electrons. Elemental analyses are gained through characteristic X-rays, which are produced when electrons collide with the sample. X-ray analyses can determine the distribution and concentrations of a specific element, or all elements (mass ≥ carbon) and their concentrations at a particular point (Robinson and Grey 1996, 579).

Results

The bandage from the mummy was made from flax (Fig. 3), indicated by the characteristic fibre walls and thickened nodes (Benson *et al* 1979, 120). The coating has a smooth surface. It was hot and fluid when applied, as determined by the smooth texture over the flax and the presence of air bubbles (Figs 4 and 5). After hardening, it was more brittle in areas where it had been applied thinly as it had cracked easily through preferential cooling (Fig. 6). Resin or bitumen is indicated by conchoidal fractures (Fig. 7), as they are characteristic of materials which do not have natural planes of separation (e.g. cleavage) (Watts 1868, 199).

EDS (Fig. 8) detected aluminium, silicon, and oxygen, suggesting clays, and titanium, present in heavy minerals in sediments. These may indicate that clay/mud packing was

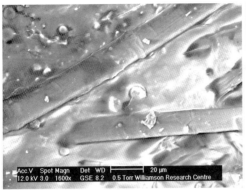

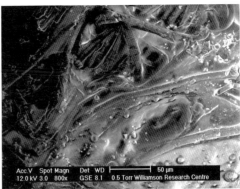

Figure 3. ESEM of bandage from the mummy of Perenbast. The joint nodes along the fibre are characteristic of flax.

Figure 4. Smooth surface of coating over the fibres of the mummy bandage.

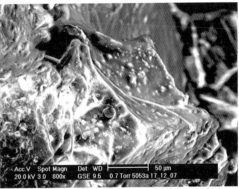

Figure 5. Cracks where the coating has been applied thinly to the mummy bandage.

Figure 6. Air bubbles indicate that the coating had been heated.

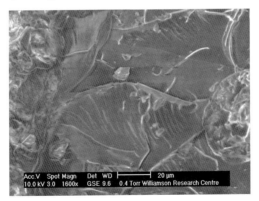

Figure 7. Conchoidal fractures in the coating of the bandages.

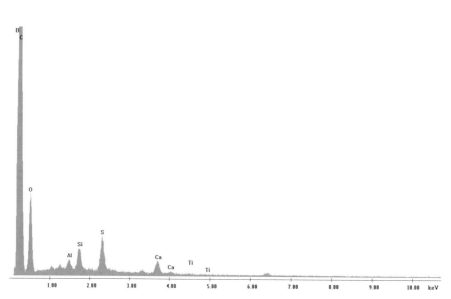

Figure 8. EDX of mummy coating.

used in mummification. Calcium and oxygen indicate carbonates such as limestone, predominantly used in ancient Egyptian statuary. Sulphur may come from sulphates used in mummification.

From the analyses the shabti box can be assessed by the stratigraphy of the layers. The shabti box showed a textured/uneven surface characteristic of wood, from which it was made (visible on the box in areas where there is no coating). The wood was then coated, possibly with gypsum, and a black resin or bitumen. Macroscopically there is a white powder or chalky residue covering the box, however it is not evident if this is below, mixed with, or on top of the black coating. The contrast between the textured surface of

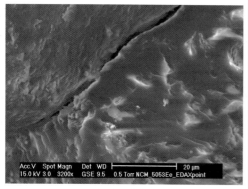

Figure 9. The contrast between the wood base (top left) and the coating (lower right).

Figure 10. Natron particle on the coating of the shabti box (off centre).

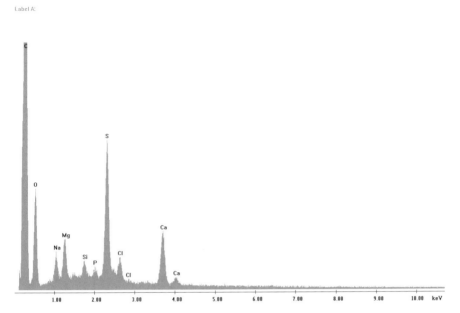

Figure 11. EDS results from shabti box coating.

the wood and the slightly smoother surface of the coating can be seen (Fig. 9). Inclusions of natron salts were found in this layer (Fig. 10), with the top or most recent layer consisting of contaminants of fungi and dust.

EDS (Fig. 11) indicated silicon and oxygen, again suggesting quartz or clays. Calcium and oxygen indicate carbonates (e.g. limestone). Chlorine indicates chlorides such as sodium and magnesium chloride, which together with high sulphur concentrations again could indicate salts such as natron. The high sulphur concentration is partly apportioned to calcium sulphate (gypsum) which was commonly used as a plaster or paint pigment (Green 2001), and may have been applied to create a smooth surface.

Discussion

From the ESEM images it is evident that the texture and formation of the coatings differs between the mummy bandages and the shabti box. It is likely that the coating on the mummy bandages was poured over the body as a hot fluid. In contrast, the shabti box shows a lack of air bubbles and the thick, uneven surface indicates application with a brush. In both instances the substance would have been hot when applied.

The elemental composition of both coatings was surprisingly similar, indicating the use of a resin or bitumen as the main material. Gypsum (used in the making of plaster) may have been added to the shabti box coating as an adhesive or as a lower layer of decoration or structure.

The actual composition of the coating may not have held such importance to the ancient Egyptians, but rather the focus may have been on the colour produced. To the ancient Egyptians colour was extremely significant, with different meaning and symbolism related to each. Black symbolised the Nile mud, a symbol of rebirth (Manniche 1999, 109), so would have been symbolic and possibly vital in a funerary context. Making the body black may have been symbolic to promote rebirth and an afterlife; the funerary items may too have been required to be imbued with the potent magical power of rebirth.

Alternately the application of the black coatings may have held more practical purpose. Bitumen and resins have been identified as products used for mummification (e.g. Buckley and Evershed 2001). Therefore it is possible that the black coating was applied as an extra preservative layer to the mummy and the shabti box, as provisions for the afterlife they would have been required to last for eternity, so any extra preservative measures available may have been employed.

Bibliography

Benson, G. G., Hemingway, S. R. and Leach, F. N. (1979) 'The Analysis of the Wrappings of Mummy 1770', in A. R. David (ed.) *The Manchester Mummy Project: Multidisciplinary Research on Ancient Egyptian Mummified Remains*, 119–32. Manchester, Manchester University Press.

David, A. R. (1979) 'A Catalogue of Egyptian Human Remains and Animal Mummified Remains', in A. R. David (ed.) *The Manchester Mummy Project: Multidisciplinary Research on Ancient Egyptian Mummified Remains*. 1–17. Manchester, Manchester University Press.

Buckley, S. A. and Evershed, R. P. (2001) 'Organic chemistry of embalming agents in Pharaonic and Graeco-Roman mummies', *Nature* 413, 837–41.

Green, L. (2001) 'Colour transformations of ancient Egyptian pigments', in W. V. Davis (ed.) *Colour and Painting in Ancient Egypt*, 43–8. London, British Museum Press.

Lee. L. and Quirke, S. (2000) 'Painting materials', in P. T. Nicholson and I. Shaw (eds) *Ancient Egyptian Materials and Technology*, 104–20. Cambridge, Cambridge University Press.

Manniche, L. (1991) *Sacred Luxuries: Fragrance, aromatherapy and cosmetics in Ancient Egypt*. London, Opus Publishing.

Robinson, G. and Grey, T. (1996) 'Electron microscopy 1–2: Instrumentation and image formation/ Practical procedures', in J. D. Bancroft and A. Stevens (eds) *Theory and Practice of Histological Techniques*, 585–626. London, Churchill Livingstone.

Taylor, J. H. (2001) *Death and the Afterlife in Ancient Egypt*. London, British Museum Press.

Watts, H. (1868) *A Dictionary of Chemistry and the Allied Branches of Other Science*. London, Green, Longman and Roberts.

Animal, Vegetable or Mineral?
Preliminary Results of a Radiological Study of Three Museum Oddities

Lidija M. McKnight

KNH Centre, University of Manchester

Abstract

Three previously unstudied museum specimens of dubious provenance were studied using conventional radiography and computed tomography (CT scanning) in the hope of identifying the nature of their contents. Two displayed the conical form characteristic of mummified birds and the third resembled a small human 'doll'. All three mummies displayed human facial features and two were presented in wooden 'coffins'. Museum records suggested that the mummies could be modern fakes.

Conventional radiology revealed that all three mummies were pseudo-mummies containing no human or animal skeletal material. They all appear to have been given human facial features through the addition of a 'mask' made from a plaster-like substance. The doll-like mummy appears to have been created using mud or clay formed around a central stick used to support the 'body'.

Computed tomography demonstrated that the composition of the layers of bandages used in the mummification of two of the mummies closely resembles that witnessed in ancient Egyptian animal mummies. It is likely that these specimens were pseudo-mummies produced in ancient times to which had been applied a facial mask of plaster at a later date. Radiology has been successful in portraying an insight into these specimens; however the reasons behind this phenomenon remain purely speculative.

Introduction

My PhD research focuses on the potential of radiographic techniques to further our understanding of ancient Egyptian animal mummies. Radiography was chosen as the research method due to its non-destructive and non-invasive nature and because it provides an excellent initial insight into previously unstudied material. In total, 127 mummified animals from four national museum collections have been studied using both conventional radiography and computed tomography (CT scanning). These museums are Bolton Museum and Art Gallery, Manchester Museum, Bristol Museum and Garstang Museum (University of Liverpool). The species identified consisted of cats, dogs, fish, crocodiles, birds, snakes and rodents alongside a number of 'pseudo-mummies' which were found to contain no animal material whatsoever. The majority of mummies in the study group have little in the way of provenance and are believed to belong to the votive mummy category. Votive mummies were made from the remains of animals bred in captivity and ritually slaughtered to supply the enormous demand for devotional objects. Generally, they are crudely mummified and wrapped.

Three previously unstudied specimens from the study group displayed unusual external features; namely the addition of human facial attributes (Fig. 1). Two of the mummies
displayed the conical body shape often given to bird mummies, with the third resembling
a doll in human form. It was decided to study the three specimens during the course of the
project as it was believed that the specimens could represent mummified animals, both
from their size and shape, or alternatively they could have contained isolated human or
animal bones. The conical shaped mummies were presented in wooden coffins with glass
lids.

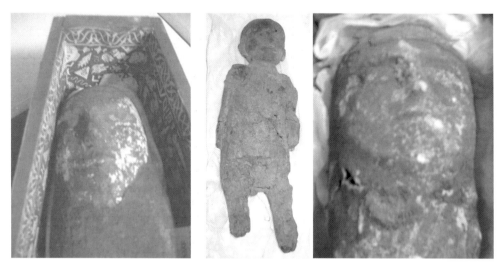

Figure 1. Photographs of (left) MA8.1, (centre) MA8.2 and (right) MA8.3, displaying curious stylised
human facial features.

Methods

Two specimens from the collection held at Bolton Museum and Art Gallery were studied
in December 2004 at York District Hospital (MA8.2 and MA8.3). The third specimen
from Bristol Museum was studied in January 2007 at Manchester Royal Infirmary. All
three were studied using conventional radiography and CT scanning (MA8.1). The two
mummies presented in coffins remained in them for the duration of the radiological study.
The radiation doses and exposure times used varied between objects depending on the
amount necessary to penetrate the material.

Mummified material has proved to be a popular study medium for radiographic techniques as it poses a 'safe' group on which to experiment with radiation doses. Generally,
human mummies have been at the forefront of this research; however mummified animals
also have much to share about the treatment they received during life, death and mummification, and radiography enables these secrets to be unlocked. Until now, most studies
which have utilised CT technology have concentrated on human subjects with only a
limited number of small-scale projects looking at mummified animals (Falke 1997; Pahl
1986). In human mummies, radiographic techniques have demonstrated enormous potential by increasing our understanding of skeletal positioning, wrapping methods, eviscera-

tion, packing of body cavities and inclusions within the mummy bundles themselves. This study hoped to harness the power of radiography to achieve similar success on a large collection of mummified animals for the first time. No previous studies have been identified which have looked at material of this unusual nature.

Before attempting a study of this nature, it is important to discuss the techniques themselves and to be mindful of the limitations which can be experienced as a result. Conventional radiography or plain film X-ray is the simplest research technique available to Egyptologists when looking at a wide variety of remains. It is completely non-destructive and non-invasive and can be carried out relatively easily with little financial outlay. It is possible to use mobile radiography equipment which has made the technique invaluable for use in burial contexts as it is not always necessary to transport the remains from their resting place. If hospital equipment is to be used, it is necessary to enlist the expertise of experienced technical staff to carry out the procedure and to interpret the resulting images.

Conventional radiography does have its disadvantages. Essentially the technique produces a two-dimensional image of a three-dimensional object and in doing so it causes distortion and superimposition of features within the bundle. Anomalies which lie further away from the radiographic film are magnified on the resulting images and it can be difficult to distinguish where items are lying within the bundle as they are superimposed on each other. These factors can be problematic to the interpreter as it can be difficult to determine actual anomalies as opposed to perceived ones (Adams and Alsop 2008).

The technique of computed tomography has revolutionised the medical world since its introduction during the 1970s and is used extensively in the diagnosis of disease and trauma injuries. Essentially the technique enables the body to be viewed as a series of axial slices at thicknesses of as little as 0.5mm. These resulting 'slices' can then be reformatted using computer technology to create a variety of images. They can be viewed as reformations in both the sagittal and coronal plane which are similar to two-dimensional X-rays; however the spatial resolution of these images is not as high as conventional radiographic images due to the loss of definition in the minute spaces between the slices. More importantly the images can be reformatted to produce three-dimensional reconstructions of the object eliminating the problems of superimposition and magnification (Adams and Alsop 2008).

One of the major advantages of CT is that it distinguishes between soft-tissue, skin and bone, enabling a clearer view of the contents of the body or mummy bundle. Mummified tissue presents a number of challenges for CT as the spatial resolution of mummified tissue is similar to bone often making the images difficult to interpret. This problem aside, CT demonstrates the position and composition of structures within the mummy bundle which may not have been clear on conventional X-rays (O'Connor and O'Connor 2005).

The technique of CT requires advanced technology and expensive equipment coupled with experienced staff. Generally, this equipment is based in hospitals or large mobile units so it is often necessary to image archaeological specimens outside of hospital working hours when the valuable machinery is not in use. This can be problematic as it is necessary to transport the specimens to the place of study which can raise issues relating to conservation and ethics.

Figure 2. Sagittal reformation of MA8.2 showing the concave body form, the plaster face mask and the presence of a stick to add support.

Results

The radiographic analysis of the three museum oddities revealed interesting results. All three were found to contain no human or animal skeletal material, making them essentially pseudo-mummies. All three had facial features which appeared to have been modelled from a substance similar to plaster of Paris applied to form a mask over the head of the mummy bundle.

The two mummies which displayed the conical body form (MA8.1 and MA8.3) appeared on the CT images to display similar wrapping techniques as had been previously noted on genuine ancient Egyptian animal mummies. They appear to have been wrapped in stages with a restrictive inner layer, followed by a slightly looser central layer before a final tight layer. This indicates that it is likely that they are ancient specimens which have been modified at some point to incorporate the human facial mask and the addition of the wooden presentation coffin. It is speculated that this modification took place during the Victorian era when it was common for travellers to purchase curios whilst abroad.

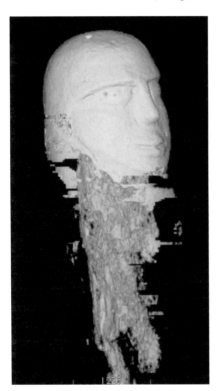

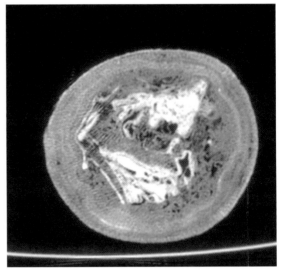

Figure 3a. (left) Volume rendering image of MA8.1 showing the dense central core of the mummy and the plaster face mask. Figure 3b (above) CT axial section showing the distinctive layers of bandaging used to wrap the mummy bundle.

The third specimen that displayed the doll-like form (MA8.2) was perhaps the most intriguing of the three oddities as it had been modelled so closely on the human form (Fig. 2). Its concave stomach and uneven leg length added to its strange appearance. The radiographic analysis revealed interesting results. The specimen had been formed from a mud-like substance containing straw and reeds which could be seen protruding from the exposed fracture to the leg. A central wooden stick could be seen on the images which must have been as a form of support to the body shape as it dried. The plaster mask displaying human facial features can be seen to contain small areas of trapped air within it.

Conclusions and Discussion

The lack of provenance information for the three specimens means any comments made can only be speculative; however the wrapping techniques shown during the CT examination of the two conical shaped mummies (MA8.1 and MA8.3) suggests that they are most probably ancient specimens. To my knowledge, no evidence has been found to suggest that plaster was used in this manner during ancient times which leads me to speculate that the masks have been added in modern times for reasons unknown. The addition of glass-topped presentation coffins in the case of MA8.1 and MA8.3 certainly suggests modern intervention and adds weight to the argument that the objects could have been souvenirs or curios. The origins of the doll-shaped mummy (MA8.2) remain unconfirmed as it cannot be ascertained from the study whether the unusual object is ancient or modern.

Conventional radiography provided the initial insight into the contents of the three oddities, establishing that they contained no skeletal material whatsoever. CT provided a clearer insight into the methods of construction and wrapping of the specimens. Computer software was used to manipulate the CT images which provided the ability to view the specimens in three dimensions whilst at the same time visualising certain components such as the plaster masks (Fig. 3a). Viewing the axial CT sections showed that the bandaging techniques employed on the two conical mummies shared remarkable similarities to ancient specimens (Fig. 3b).

Radiography has provided the initial insight into these specimens; however, further research would be necessary in order to attempt to fully explain what they were intended to be and to provide information on their age and the techniques used in their manufacture. Carbon dating techniques could be used to assess the age of the specimens and biomedical studies could be used to assess the composition of the facial plaster masks. Until then, they remain enigmatic objects of unknown purpose and age.

Key

MA8.1	Bristol Museum Ha6370	
MA8.2	Bolton Museum no number	baby/doll?
MA8.3	Bolton Museum no number	conical doll?

Bibliography

Adams, J. E. and Alsop, C. W. (2008) 'Imaging in Egyptian mummies', in A. R. David (ed.) *Egyptian Mummies and Modern Science*, 21–42. Cambridge, Cambridge University Press.

Falke, T. H. M. (1997) 'Radiology of Ancient Egyptian Mummified Animals', in J. Van Dijk, J. (ed.) *Essays on Ancient Egypt in Honour of Herman Te Velde*, 55–67. Groningen, Styx Publications.

O'Connor, T. and O'Connor, S. (2005) 'Digitising and Image-Processing Radiographs to enhance Interpretation in Avian Palaeopathology', *Documenta Archaeobiologiae* 3, 69–82.

Pahl, W. (1986) 'Radiography of an Egyptian "Cat Mummy". An Example of the Decadence of the Animal Worship in the Late Dynasties?', *OSSA: International Journal of Skeletal Research* 12, 133–40.

The Tutankhamouse Experiment: Investigating Tissue Changes during Mummification

Ryan Metcalfe

KNH Centre, University of Manchester

Abstract

Experimental models have proved invaluable in improving our knowledge of the ancient Egyptians' mummification techniques. Though they have been used for a long time and in a variety of forms, they have almost exclusively been used to verify the recorded methods and determine the finer, practical details of how the process was carried out. Whilst this has provided a wealth of information on the preparation stages and the final result, the intervening stage, where degradation is halted and the soft tissues are stabilised, has remained something of a closed book. It is seemingly presumed that the water is simply drawn from the body, drying it slowly but steadily until it is ready for wrapping and interment.

Whilst this may appear to be the case on a visible level, at the microscopic and molecular level the process is far more complex. The effects of burial in natron on histology and protein preservation were investigated using a model that is described herein with the hope of encouraging others to use experimental mummification in their research. This will not only allow data to be gathered on the process, but will also permit optimisation of experimental protocols without having to use irreplaceable ancient tissue.

Introduction

The majority of Egyptologists have reached consensus on the question of how the ancient Egyptians mummified their dead, placing it in an almost unique position within Egyptology. The method described by Herodotus as the best or most expensive (Herodotus 1996, 115) appears to form the basis of the technique, though it did not, of course, appear immediately in its final form. A great deal of experimentation and improvement was required for optimisation (Taylor 2001, 51). However, this consensus amongst Egyptologists on the eventual method was not reached quickly, thanks primarily to variations in the translation of Herodotus' ethnography of the Egyptians (Sandison 1963). The debate focussed mainly on the use of natron, specifically whether the body was salted like a fish or soaked in a solution like a pickle. Lucas (1932) used a combination of archaeological and pathological evidence, philology, chemistry and experimental mummification to demonstrate that it was almost certainly used as a solid.

Although this was one of, if not the, earliest scientific model designed to test theories about Egyptian mummification, it was certainly not the last. Several other published models have been used to investigate different parts of the process, commonly using the writings of Herodotus as a starting point. Notable examples include the work of Garner (1979; 1985) who studied the effects of different compositions of natron on the preservation of tissue, the effect of reusing the desiccant and the viability of the different methods described famously by Herodotus. The model also included an assessment of preservation for solid natron vs. a solution, reaching the same conclusion as Lucas.

Perhaps the most famous model is that produced by Brier and Wade (1997; 1999), who mummified a human cadaver in the 1990s. Previous models, which used animals for reasons including economy, ease of handling, availability, and suitability for testing the hypotheses were unable to answer questions about the practicalities of the process. In contrast, using a human corpse makes it possible to investigate how long each step took, whether the described tools were viable, what order the internal organs were removed in, and how easily. Although Brier and Wade were able to provide answers for many of these questions, they only had a single body on which to experiment, and therefore were sorely limited in their ability to try different theories. Their results nevertheless provide valuable information about the process which could not have been otherwise obtained. Unfortunately, this experiment was carried out over a decade ago, and has yet to be repeated. Now that it has been performed once, it is possible that repeating the experiment is not seen as necessary. Ethical issues surrounding the use of human cadavers may also be partly responsible for the lack of replication. For example, the number of human bodies donated for medical education and research in the UK has fallen in recent years (Department of Health 2007), to the point where each is a valuable resource that must be put to the best possible use.

Many experimental mummifications focus on the end result, judging the success or failure of the method used on the appearance of the body at the end. In many of these cases, the body is left undisturbed for the length of the dehydration, essentially reducing the drying process to an event with no regard for the changes taking place under the cover of natron. This is not always the case – Salima Ikram's experiments with rabbits, for example, included regular inspection of the corpse (Ikram 2005). During the inspection, the natron bed was also inspected, with lumps broken up and fresh natron used to replace the most hydrated portions, which presents a possible cause for concern. The assumption seems to be that once a body was covered it was left to dry out on its own without any further interference, but how accurate is this? The Brier and Wade experiment showed that approximately a quarter of a ton of natron was required to mummify an adult human (Brier and Wade 1997), which would surely represent a significant expense. It is commonly suggested that anthropogenic mummification was reserved for the most elite members of society (or at least those wealthy enough to afford it), in which case regular checking to ensure the process is working and rectify any problems would not be implausible. Or, to put it another way, if you were chosen to preserve the body of a pharaoh, a god in human form, would you be happy to sit on your hands for over a month just assuming that everything was OK?

This is not to say that regular examination of the corpse was definitely a part of the process, of course. Brier and Wade showed that successful mummification is certainly possible without replacing and remixing the natron bed. It may be that Ikram's rabbits would have been adequately preserved without interference, though replacing the soiled desiccant would almost certainly produce a better result in less time. When Herodotus mentions this phase, he merely says that 'the body is placed in natron, covered entirely over, for seventy days' – a statement that does not rule out inspection, but does not confirm it (Herodotus 1996, 115–6). Diodorus is even less clear, saying that the body is covered with a variety of oils and spices, but neglecting the use of natron altogether (Siculus 1933, 309–13). However, a full discussion of inspection (and of the possibility that Diodorus omitted the use of natron because it was far less common than usually assumed on grounds of expense) is beyond the scope of this paper – it does, however, illustrate that attempts to reproduce mummification techniques can reveal practical difficulties that may not otherwise be considered.

Mummifying tissues

Other experimental mummifications have been carried out for rather different reasons. Unlike those described above, whose primary purpose was the assessment of different techniques for preserving the body, there are a number of experiments where individual tissues have been preserved. These studies are a direct result of the ever increasing application of scientific techniques to the study of mummies because they are used to provide tissue samples that are vital to the early stages of such research. Such samples are used to provide a proof of concept for the wider research, and allow optimisation of the protocols to be used, which can require considerable amounts of tissue. Both of these stages are vital in preventing the wastage of irreplaceable ancient tissue. Examples of these models include the classic study of Zimmerman (1977) on the preservation of cancerous tissue and the more recent work of Terra *et al* (2004), Bastos *et al* (1996) and others.

Many of these models simply dry the tissue using elevated temperatures instead of reproducing anthropogenic techniques. This is a simple method that allows the rapid preparation of tissues for testing hypotheses and optimising techniques, whilst reducing the number of variables that could have an effect on preservation. As the majority of mummies are preserved in a dry state, the results obtained from such tissues are broadly applicable to those studying mummies from a variety of contexts. However, simple desiccation may not be the only method by which tissues are preserved, especially when a chemical desiccant such as natron is used. The use of isolated tissues is also disadvantageous, as the preservation process may well have a different effect on tissue when it is applied directly rather than to a whole body. Nevertheless, these tissues provide a rapid and simple way for researchers to obtain experimental material. Depending on the hypotheses being tested, they may be sufficient in themselves, though a more complete model may well produce more accurate results.

The design of a model is therefore by necessity a compromise. Many different factors must be taken into account. Should it mimic a single technique, or be more broadly applicable? Are isolated tissues sufficient, or would a larger part or even an entire corpse be more suitable? There are rather more practical aspects that need to be taken into consideration as well, such as cost, lab space and the source of the tissue, which in itself can be limited by ethical concerns and experimental design.

The 'Tutankhamouse' experiment

When the author prepared a model, these factors were used to form the design of the experiment. The reasons behind the choices made are presented here in the hope of assisting others who may be tempted to prepare models themselves for their research.

The aim of the project as a whole was to study the effects of Egyptian-style mummification on the preservation of proteins in different tissues. Liver and skin were chosen for two reasons. Firstly, these are the largest organs and as such would provide the most tissue for experimentation. Secondly, part of the project was a comparison of the model with genuine ancient remains. In order to minimise the number of variables that would have to be accounted for, it was decided to use ancient samples from the same geographic and temporal location. The samples that best fulfilled these criteria and provided the largest number were skin and liver samples from mummies excavated at a Ptolemaic and Roman period cemetery at the Dakhleh Oasis, hence the selection of these tissues for the model.

As both internal and peripheral organs were being used, it was decided that an entire body would provide the best results, as this would most closely mimic the processes that genuinely ancient samples would have been exposed to. In order to investigate the changes that occurred during mummification, samples were taken at intervals during the experiment. To avoid disturbing the subjects and affecting the process, a number of different subjects were required. To improve confidence in the results, tempered by the desire to reduce the number of animals required, pairs of subjects were used for each of four time points (5, 10, 20 and 40 days), in addition to fresh controls. Given the number of animals required, space considerations made mice the most appropriate choice.

The decision to use mice was supported by a number of other factors, including the ease of acquisition and handling. The commercial availability of antibodies that react with both human and mouse proteins meant that the same reagents could be used throughout the project, dramatically reducing costs. Limitations were associated with this choice, of course, including the decision not to excerebrate the bodies, as the small size of the bodies made this impractical.

Although frozen mice are available from, for example, pet food suppliers, they were deemed inappropriate for this model as it included histological analysis, and the micromorphology of tissue can be adversely affected by freezing. The mice were therefore obtained from a laboratory colony that was being routinely culled, in order to prevent the sacrifice of mice specifically for this project. One of the most common methods of euthanizing mice, and that used in this case, is gassing by CO_2, which would have no impact on most experimental procedures performed on models using them.

To summarise, in order to minimise the number of animals used and the space required, whilst maximising the returns from the experiment in terms of reliability of results and ease of preparation, it was decided to use 18 mice, split into two groups (one control and one mummified). The decision to use whole mice makes comparisons between the model and ancient remains more straightforward. The mummification itself was a pared-down version of the "best" Egyptian method, concentrating on the removal of the gastro-intestinal tract to reduce the number of bacteria within the sample and dehydration using natron. Removal of the brain was deemed impractical on such small animals, whilst washing with palm wine and the application of resin were dismissed as adding too many variables to the model. Now that data has been collected from the first model however, any additional research could include these steps and judge their effect by comparison to the simpler model.

This model draws heavily on the previous work by Garner (1979) for the methodology employed in the mummification, especially for the natron composition. This was made up from laboratory chemicals in the proportion 50% anhydrous sodium carbonate, 30% sodium bicarbonate, and 10% each of sodium chloride and sodium sulphate. These proportions were chosen in order to provide the best probability for successful mummification, as shown by Garner. Unlike the mummies prepared by Ikram (2005), the bodies were left undisturbed until they were removed for sampling.

Experimental results

Although the experimental protocols used in this project and the detailed results will be presented elsewhere, an overview is included here to show how even a relatively uncomplicated model like this can provide useful information.

Complementary histological techniques including toluidine blue, Masson trichrome and Gram staining were used to provide results to maximise confidence in the final results. Together, they allowed assessment of the tissues' preservation at the microscopic level and the number of bacteria. Immunohistochemistry was used to identify specific proteins.

The differences between the control samples (which were allowed to decompose normally) and the mummified samples were obvious to the naked eye and, somewhat unfortunately, to the nose. Whereas the mummified mice had little or no noticeable odour, the controls had a strong smell of rotting meat after 5 days which became stronger with time. When the containers were opened at 20 and 40 days, flies were drawn to the lab within minutes. This highlights a very important point – when conducting similar experiments, be sure to take into consideration the work and comfort of colleagues. The author was lucky enough to be given access to a disused room for storing and processing his model; others who are not so fortunate may have to consider storing theirs outside the lab, which raises difficulties in itself.

As expected, the controls showed signs of decay (Knight 1997, 28), such as skin slippage and liquefaction of tissues (though bloating was not seen, most likely because of the removal of the digestive tract and the incision) whereas the mummified samples became more emaciated with time. The tissues became harder as they were dehydrated, with the liver becoming quite difficult to cut towards the end of the experiment. The skin, rather than becoming hard as such, became somewhat leathery, and areas with more subcutaneous fat were significantly more supple than others.

The significantly better preservation seen at the macroscopic level was mirrored at the microscopic. Softer tissues were lost quickly from the control samples, with more collagenous parts showing more resistance to decomposition. The growth of bacteria in these samples was rapid and extensive, though the collagenous tissues were again less affected. In contrast, the mummified samples looked almost the same at the beginning and the end of the experiment, with very few if any bacteria seen in these samples. This is a noteworthy result, as it is often stated in reviews of Egyptian mummification that resins were applied at least partially to provide an antibacterial effect. This model shows that bacterial growth is limited during the dehydrating stage of the process, without any resins being necessary. However, once the body has been entombed, a coat of antibacterial resin would be helpful in preventing the growth of bacteria at a later stage.

Interestingly, the microscopic preservation was better than the extent of dehydration would suggest. Even though the bodies retained a large proportion of their water at an early stage, the changes seen in the controls were not seen in the mummified samples. This implies that degradation was retarded by more than simple water loss, though it is impossible to determine exactly what else had an affect with the techniques used for this project.

Protein preservation appears to be affected by a number of variables. Of these, the extent of decomposition is a major factor, as is the nature of the protein itself. Some of the earlier control samples showed preservation of more resistant proteins such as collagen, whose structure makes it inherently less vulnerable, though in later samples there were no positive results. It is hard to say for sure that this was due to the effect of bacterial putrefaction and autolysis on the protein itself, as the tissues to which the protein was specific had been degraded to destruction. For other proteins, although the tissue was easily recognisable, the amount of preserved protein declined over the course of the experiment, even in the otherwise extremely well preserved mummified samples. In these cases, the primary factor for preservation appears to be the protein itself – more soluble proteins would be lost more easily, for example.

Using tissue morphology to determine the likelihood of protein preservation is not therefore a reliable method. It can tell you when a protein is extremely unlikely to be detectable, for example where specific tissues have been completely decomposed, but it cannot tell you when the balance of probability is with a positive result. Its importance as a screening tool and for tissue identification is not to be dismissed, however. Histology represents, in the author's opinion at least, one of the most important techniques in the scientific study of mummies.

Conclusions

There are a wide variety of ways to model mummification, depending on the research question to be answered. Whole bodies and isolated tissues both play a role, and the method used to dry the subjects can be varied to balance requirements of speed of preparation with those of accuracy of reproduction. Although there are a number of choices to be made and compromises reached during the planning stage, this should be taken more as an indication of the flexibility that is possible rather than a reason for concern.

Although the model described here should be sufficient for those wishing to conduct basic biomolecular or chemical research on mummified remains, it was designed specifically to preserve the body as well as possible with a minimum of intervention in order to simplify the interpretation of the results. Now that it is established, it would be a simple task to adjust the underlying methodology to represent either a more complete version of the method described by Herodotus (1996, 115–6), for example by including excerebration or washing steps, or to represent a less ideal situation, such as the mummification of an already partially decomposed body, a possibility explicitly referred to in the literature (Herodotus 1996, 117). For those wishing to investigate the effects of the other methods, the previous work carried out by Garner (1979) would be an excellent starting point.

Even an uncomplicated model such as that presented herein can provide a surprising amount of information regarding the process of mummification and the factors affecting the preservation of tissue at the molecular and micromorphological level. This information can be used to guide research that uses ancient tissue by, for example, indicating which proteins are viable targets and which have such a low preservation potential that they are unlikely to be detectable with today's methods. Therefore, by including a model at the beginning of a project, the wastage of ancient and irreplaceable mummified samples in research with little or no chance of success can be reduced.

Bibliography

Bastos, O. M. *et al* (1996) 'Experimental paleoparasitology: identification of *Trypanosoma cruzi* DNA in desiccated mouse tissue', *Paleopathology Newsletter* 94, 5–8.

Brier, B. and Wade, R. S. (1997) 'The use of natron in human mummification: a modern experiment', *Zeitschrift für Ägyptische Sprache und Altertumskunde* 124, 89–100.

Brier, B. and Wade, R. S. (1999) 'Surgical procedures during ancient Egyptian mummification', *Zeitschrift für Ägyptische Sprache und Altertumskunde* 126, 89–97.

Department of Health (2007) 'More body donations needed to sustain medical education, training and research' [Online] (updated 14 May 2007) Available from http://www.dh.gov.uk/en/AboutUs/MinistersAndDepartmentLeaders/ChiefMedicalOfficer/Features/DH_4120899 (accessed 15 September 2008).

Garner, R. (1979) 'Experimental mummification.', in A. R. David (ed.) *The Manchester Museum Mummy Project* 19–24. Manchester, Manchester University Press.

Garner, R. (1985) 'Experimental mummification of rats', in A. R. David (ed.) *Science in Egyptology*, 11–12. Manchester, Manchester University Press.

Herodotus (1996) *The Histories* (trans. by A. de Selincourt). London, Penguin.

Ikram, S. (2005) 'Manufacturing divinity: the technology of mummification', in S. Ikram (ed.) *Divine Creatures: Animal Mummies in Ancient Egypt*, 16–43. Cairo, American University in Cairo Press.

Knight, B. (1997) *Simpson's Forensic Medicine*. London, Arnold.

Lucas, A. (1932) 'The use of natron in mummification', *Journal of Egyptian Archaeology* 18, 125–40.

Sandison, A. T. (1963) 'The use of natron in mummification in ancient Egypt', *Journal of Near Eastern Studies* 22, 259–67.

Siculus, D. (1933) *Library of History* (trans. C. H. Oldfather). London, Heinemann.

Taylor, J. (2001) *Death and the Afterlife in Ancient Egypt*. London, British Museum Press.

Terra, M. A. B. L. *et al* (2004) 'Detection of *Toxoplasma gondii* DNA by polymerase chain reaction in experimentally desiccated tissues', *Memórias do Instituto Oswaldo Cruz* 99, 185–8.

Zimmerman, M. R. (1977) 'An experimental study of mummification pertinent to the antiquity of cancer', *Cancer* 40, 1358–62.

Re-Materialising Script And Image

Kathryn E. Piquette
Institute of Archaeology, University College London

Textual studies are becoming increasingly attentive to the materiality of the text, recognizing that writing is itself not a transparent medium of language which needs materiality only at its place of application or illustration, but that writing's very materiality influences the range of interpretive responses and receptions of the text.
(Frantz 1998, 791–2)

For more than a decade, the re-materialisation of text and textual meanings has been underway in areas as diverse as digital technology (O'Hara *et al* 2002) and religious studies (Frantz 1998). Within archaeology and anthropology 'materiality' has gained widespread attention (e.g. Pearce 2000; Olsen 2003; Demarrais 2004; Meskell 2005), but as Tim Ingold (2007, 1, 3) argues, these discussions have neglected to address materials in an explicit way. Rather than '…the abstract rumination of philosophers and theorists', Ingold calls for more direct engagement with materials and their properties, transformations and affordances. I am concerned, however, that no matter the view taken on materials or materiality, the traditional 'text:artefact' divide persists and 'writing' and other forms of 'visual culture' (used here with the awareness that although sight may be dominant, engagement is nevertheless multi-sensory, Gosden 2001, esp. 163) continue to be marginalised in reconstructions of past material worlds (see Piquette 2007). Indeed, Ruth Whitehouse (forthcoming) observes that where the main concern of the investigator is the language an inscription symbolises and its meaning (in the sense of linguistic translation and comprehension), it is typically argued that all the other aspects we might study (e.g. archaeological context, material, size, shape, direction, form of writing, etc.) are largely irrelevant.

Within the context of the early Nile Valley, a primary interest among investigators has been to 'identify writing' and interpret its meaning in the sense just mentioned. Such studies tend to overstate the 'readability' of images, and attribute *a priori* linguistic functions based on resemblances to later scripts (e.g. Emery and Sa'ad 1939, 83; Dreyer 1993, 12; 1998; Kahl 2001; etc.). This perspective—a decontextualising approach subject to surprisingly limited critique—has resulted in inadequate study of the material cultural significance of script and image. Likewise, the material implications for associated meanings and social practices, such as creation, use and deposition remain poorly understood. This paper therefore seeks to reassert the essential artefactual nature of this find category and explore ways of re-materialising reconstructions of past image-making.

To support this ontological re-positioning, the significance of materials is considered through a case study on a series of small inscribed, perforated plaques or labels (Figs. 1–2) dating from the Naqada IIIA1 (NIIIA1) through to the Naqada IIIC–early D cultural phases (*c.*3300/3200 BCE–*c.*2800/2770 BCE; Fig. 3). I should emphasise that differentiation between 'writing' and other image types is not always straightforward for this early

Figure 1. Inscribed labels shown in the author's hand to illustrate scale and provoke consideration of the material experience of inscribed objects through manual manipulation and other sensory engagement. Upper: Incised and infilled single-sided label of bone, H 1.4–1.45 cm, W 1.45 cm, Th 0.25 cm; tomb U-j chamber 11; see Dreyer 1998, 124, 125 no. 102 = pl. 31 no. 102). Lower: Incised double-sided label (?) of stone, H 2.25 cm, W 3.8 cm, Th 0.25–0.3 cm; NW of tomb U-j; see Dreyer 1998, 136, 135 no. 191a–b = pl. 35 no. 191a–b). Cemetery U, Abydos, Naqada IIIA1. Author's photograph, used with the permission of the Deutsches Archäologisches Institut, Kairo.

Figure 2. Inscribed labels of varying size, shape and material, exhibiting the incised technique with pigment infilling (but see below), all probably dating from the reign of Djer, Abydos 'Royal' Tombs Cemetery, complex O attributed to Djer. Upper left: Complete single-sided label of bone (*contra* Amélineau 1904) with red paste infilling, subsidiary grave O-22; Amélineau 1904, 57, pl. 15 no. 27. H 2.2 cm, W 2.35 cm, Th 0.17–0.23 cm; Berlin 18066. Upper right: Complete single-sided label of elephant ivory with traces of red paste infilling (the presence of pigment in various cracks may indicate post-excavation addition of infilling), find spot does not seem to be specified by the excavator; Amélineau 1904–5, 396–7, 399–403, 429, pl. 15 no.

19. H 4.25–4.67 cm, W 4.67 cm, Th 0.17–0.35 cm; Berlin 18026. Lower left: Double-sided (non-facing side bears numerical signs) label fragment of hippopotamus ivory, subsidiary grave O-22; Amélineau 1904, 57, pl. 15 no. 26; H 2.6 cm, W 2.3+ cm, Th 0.12–0.23 cm; Berlin 18065. Lower right: Complete label of bone (*contra* Amélineau 1904) with traces of dark grey or black paste infilling, subsidiary grave O-26; Amélineau 1904, 63, pl. 15 no. 28; H 2.2–2.3 cm, W 2.6–2.7 cm, Th 0.3–0.5 cm; Berlin 18067. Author's photograph courtesy of the Ägyptisches Museum und Papyrussammlung, Berlin.

Cultural Phase	Calibrated Dates BCE	Dynasty	Period	Rulers
		2		Hetepsekhemwi
Naqada IIID	from *c.*2900 onwards			Qa'a Semerkhet
Naqada IIIC2	*c.*3000–2900			Anedjib Den
Naqada IIIC1	*c.*3100–3000	1	Early Dynastic	Merneith Djet Djer Neithotep (?) Aha Narmer
Naqada IIIA1–IIIB	*c.*3300/3200–3100	'0'	Proto-Dynastic	Irj-Hor/Ka (?) Owner of Tomb U-j
Naqada IIC–IID2	*c.*3650–3300/3200			
Naqada IA–IIB	*c.*3900–3650		Predynastic	

Figure 3. Chronological table (after Hendrickx 1996, 64; Wilkinson 2001, 27).

evidence and, as discussed elsewhere (Piquette 2007), connotations embodied in the term 'writing' may be inappropriate or indemonstrable based on available evidence (see also Baines 2004, 161). Likewise, at this juncture, my use of the terms 'inscribe' or 'inscription' (or 'graphical image') refers only to the physical act of image-making and its result in a general sense. Taking these as the point of departure for analysis, I focus on the materials and techniques involved in physical expression and then consider their possible impacts on meanings and practice.

Inscribed object worlds and material transformations

Before tackling the case study on the labels it is worth considering the world of inscribed objects surviving from the Late Predynastic and Early Dynastic Periods. In addition to the labels, graphical objects include mudstone palettes, maceheads, flint knives and handles, statues, stelae, clay and stone vessels, cylinder seals, seal impressions and so on. Other less-commonly studied inscribed objects include inscribed furniture elements, boxes, items of personal adornment, gaming pieces, and tools/weapons. Imagery also occurs on architectural elements, although survivals are rare (Petrie 1901, pl. 60). Graphical imagery was also deployed in 'natural' landscapes, for example on the surfaces of living rock (e.g. Darnell 2002).

The materials upon and through which imagery was made include Nile mud and desert marl, bone, elephant and hippopotamus ivory, and various kinds of wood, metal and stone, as well as plastered surfaces and possibly painted textile (see Lucas 1962, 338; also Lee

Figure 4. Left: Globular clay vessel with red decoration including a stylised 'boat' motif, Hu, Naqada II (*c.*3650–*c.*3300/3200 BCE). H 22.9 cm, W (max.) 20.2 cm; BM EA 30920 (© Trustees of the British Museum). Right: Wavy-handled jar (U-j 2/1) bearing a depiction of a horned bovid head on a pike or support applied in black pigment, Abydos Cemetery U, tomb U-j; Naqada IIIA1. H 33.5, Rd 14.6–16.5 max (Dreyer 1998, pl. 18a).

and Quirke 2003, 117–9). Some materials were prepared and used expressly for inscription, such as slabs of stone for stelae or bone, ivory or wooden plaques for labels, while for other items such as containers or implements, inscription was probably a secondary concern. This begs the question of how primary or secondary contexts impacted upon past meaning.

Various materials were also deployed as part of additive techniques. In addition to inlay, coloured substances were applied directly to surfaces and may have included charcoal, burnt ochre, and calcium carbonate or sulphate, among others, although analyses for this period are needed (Lee and Quirke 2003, 107–117). Techniques also involved the removal of material and ranged from pecking, hammering, scratching and incising to carving in raised or sunken relief.

Another image-making technique was impression. Sealing practices illustrate particularly well the mutually-informing relationship of tools, techniques and materials. Rather than involving the addition or subtraction of material, impression entailed the reconfiguration of the surface, such as Nile mud or prepared desert marl when soft. It is worth considering that the method by which a stamp or cylinder was typically deployed would have been incompatible with stone or other hard substance due to the resistance of that substance relative to the degree of manual pressure applied. We might surmise that the relationship between some materials and techniques was dictated by such pragmatic concerns. As Kahl and Engel (2001) have observed for sealing materials and seal types, in some cases material choices were actually related to factors beyond the merely 'functional', a point to which I return below.

Archaeological evidence for where early scriptorial practices took place, such as workshops, is uncommon. Indirect evidence may be found, for example, in a collection of copper tools discovered in a First Dynasty mastaba at North Saqqara (S3471; Emery 1949, 47–8, figs. 23–4) which included tools suitable for engraving and boring (Gale *et al* 2003, 355–6). These give some idea of the tools in use at the time, although caution is required in extrapolating use significance from cemetery contexts vis-à-vis living society (Parker Pearson 2001).

Attitudes towards early scribal practice may be evidenced in another First Dynasty mastaba at Saqqara, S3035 (Emery and Sa'ad 1938). Among finds in the eastern half of Magazine Z, a leather bag was found containing between five and eight perforated wooden plaques (the excavation report lists five, but the Egyptian Museum *Journal d'Entrée* records eight wooden labels/fragments. Beyond mends identified pre-accession, first-hand examination did not reveal further mends. It may be that the excavators counted fragments from different objects as belonging to the same item). Nearby a box containing a flattened role of papyrus (?) was also found. Like the wooden 'labels', however, it also appeared to be uninscribed. While the lack of inscription may be due to poor preservation, it is worth considering the implications of depositing uninscribed objects in the tomb. If we see these objects not as static, but as part of processes unfolding across time and space, their past significance may have lain in a role that was ongoing. Perhaps because they were blank, they were therefore were able to provide the deceased with the potential to create graphical images continuously in the hereafter. Whatever the answer, a key point to highlight is the importance of giving equal consideration to contexts where imagery may be purposefully absent.

Graphical composition

Returning to 'present' imagery, I would like to briefly consider the choices makers confronted in bringing images together to form compositions. In rendering a particular image, choices would have concerned position in relation to previous and subsequent images, as well as available surface. Choices for each image and/or group of images would have also included morphology, direction, view, orientation, and spatial associations.

The effect of particular compositional choices can be illustrated by comparing the decorated wares ('D-Class') of the preceding Naqada II cultural phase with the imagery on Naqada IIIA1 wavy-handled jars. On the former, one finds single or clusters of images extending round the exterior surface of the vessel. Compositions are never entirely visible from a single viewpoint, requiring manipulation of the vessel in making and reception (Fig. 4; see also Wengrow 2006, 102). In contrast, imagery applied to the exteriors of NIIIA1 wavy-handled jars from Abydos Cemetery U (esp. tomb U-j) is fully visible when viewed straight on. If fixed in this position, perhaps in the context of storage or display at the grave side or upon deposition (probably in rows stacked at least two high; Dreyer 1998, 7–9), it would be possible to view the entire composition without rotation. Engagement could have been primarily visual in this context, compared with more dynamic behaviours required in viewing D-Class compositions.

Similarly, sensory engagement with portable objects such as seals or labels would also have involved manipulation while non-portable surfaces required other kinds of bodily

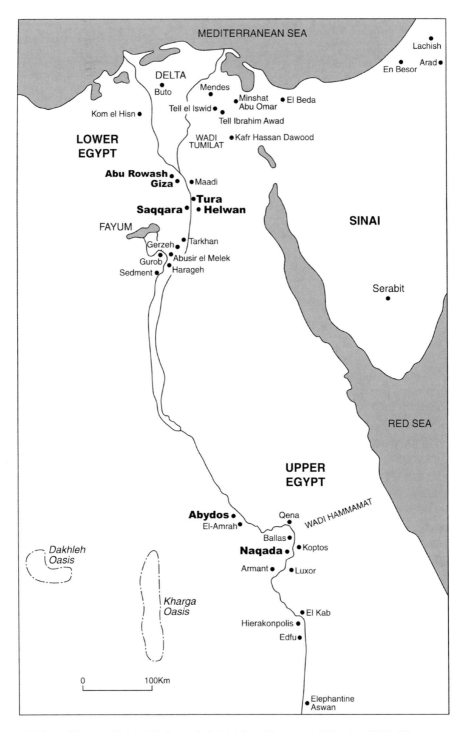

Figure 5. Map of Egypt with label find sites in bold (after Adams and Ciałowicz 1997, 66).

proximity. This latter scenario was probably the case for large stelae, something we might also imagine for the so-called Scorpion macehead where circumambulation may have been required if set on a post or other support for display (a scenario possibly depicted on a bone cylinder in the Ashmolean Museum (E.4714; see also Adams and Ciałowicz 1997, 13, fig. 6)). In the same way that you as reader are manually and visually engaging with these pages in order to read these words, engagements with past graphical symbols involved embodied processes inextricably bound up in the physical parameters of expression.

In this brief survey, I have tried to give some sense of the complex processes involved in physical expression, access and sensory perception of iconography. Turning to the case study on the labels, I now explore the issue of material practice in more detail.

Late Predynastic and Early Dynastic labels: a case study

This study draws on my doctoral research which took an explicitly practice-centred approach as its basis in the study of the inscribed labels (Piquette 2007). These small perforated plaques form one of the largest surviving corpora of scriptorial material from the Nile Valley from the period of *c.*3300/3200 BCE to *c.*2800 BCE (Fig. 3). Over 430 labels and label fragments survive, made of bone, ivory, and wood and possibly two stone examples (further labels and label fragments from the re-excavation of the Abydos 'Royal' tombs await full publication (Günter Dreyer pers. comm.)). These range in size from about 1.0–9.5 cm in height and width, many being quite small, even miniature in scale. It is generally thought that labels were attached to funerary equipment, such as lengths of cloth, sandals, containers of oil and other items. On the basis of later written and linguistic evidence, the labels are understood to communicate information relating to the date, quantity and quality of associated items, as well as place names, personal names, and titles.

Overall, labels and label fragments are encountered at seven cemetery sites in the Nile Valley (Fig. 5), although the vast majority derive from Abydos. The labels can be divided chronologically into two main phases. Of 370 from Abydos, some 200 come from Cemetery U alone, most being found in and around the large multi-chambered tomb U-j. These have been dated to NIIIA1 (*c.*3300/3100 BCE; Hd-12953 (4,470 ± 30 BP) and Hd-12954 (4955 ± 30 BP), both on samples of *Acacia nilotica* (Boehmer *et al* 1993; Görsdorf *et al* 1998)). The remainder date from NIIIC–early D, or the entire First Dynasty. Based on present evidence, label practices cease around the time when the final First Dynasty ruler Qa'a was buried. The nature of the relationship between the two main chronological groupings is difficult to assess given the lack of label finds from NIIIB (for one possible example see Dreyer *et al* 1990, 67–8; see also Wengrow 2006, 206).

Previous research on the labels has centred on their significance in relation to an emerging Egyptian 'state' in its political, administrative, and religious dimensions with a single ruler at its head (e.g. Legge 1906, 252; Kaplony 1963, 292–7; Postgate *et al* 1995, 466; Trigger *et al* 2001, 56, 58; Assmann 2002, 37). Again, where graphical evidence from this period is classified as 'writing', find types such as the labels are examined predominately from philological or palaeographical perspectives (e.g. Scharff 1942; Kaplony 1963; Riley 1985; Helck 1987; Kahl 1994, 2002, 2003, 2004). Where studies offer traditional philological or art-historical treatments, these are often suffused with teleological and progres-sivist notions that, when considered in terms of material and social practice, present two main areas of methodological difficulty. Firstly, the emphasis on discerning philological function and linguistic meaning has effected a dematerialisation of this category of mate-rial culture. As mentioned above, this phenomenon is by no means exclusive to Egyptol-ogy (e.g. Moreland 2001; Whitehouse forthcoming), but the critical evaluation of these issues elsewhere has not yet been systematically directed to scriptorial evidence from the early Nile Valley (nor Mesopotamia, see Matthews 2003, 56–61). Secondly, traditional approaches typically involve the projection of later understandings of Egyptian writing back onto this earlier evidence, effectively flattening the temporal and spatial contexts in which past individuals and social groups attributed meanings to it. In previous research, where the equation of morphological similarity with similarity in meaning is asserted for different time-space contexts, systematic context-based demonstrations of continuities are persistently lacking. Indeed, as recent discourses within sociology, anthropology and archaeological theory emphasise, social practice—how an individual social actor actually practices living in, reproducing and transforming culture around her- or himself—must be seen as ordered across time and space (Giddens 1984; Johnson 1999, 105; Dobres 2000; Wenger 2002). In as far as reconstructions claim to re-present past social practice and meaning, dematerialisation and retrospection are methodologically indefensible. We must therefore develop a framework that engenders a more holistic and contextual reconstruc-tion of past graphical culture.

A framework for re-materialising script and image

To begin re-materialising accounts of the labels, I found the work of Tim Ingold (2007) and James Gibson particularly useful. In his 1979 book *The Ecological Approach to Vis-ual Perception*, Gibson (1979, 16) distinguishes three components of material properties and the inhabited environment:

- Medium: affords movement and perception
- Substances: are relatively resistant to movement and perception
- Surfaces: the interface between the medium and substance

This tri-partite framework is valuable for exploring the labels and their imagery beyond a purely content meaning focus, and for thinking about how each component informs and is informed by perception and engagement.

Medium

Sensory perception of label iconography would have been influenced by various media depending upon environmental factors. Whether indoors or outside, light may have ranged from direct, bright light from the Egyptian sun to dark shadow within the house, workshop, storage area, or tomb, also dependent upon the location of windows and open doorways. Other sources of light may have included oil lamps or candles. Airborne particles such as sand and dust, smoke from cooking fires, lamps, incense, and so on would have also affected visibility and the appearance of surfaces and imagery thereon. Such medium-related factors would have been of concern during plaque shaping, surface preparation and inscription, as well as during subsequent episodes of display, viewing and 'reading' (where intended).

Substance

Gibson's substance refers to the resistant thing in the world we identify through sensory input. We learn to identify substances as paper, cloth, the body, etc. through touch, smell, and even sound, as afforded by the media of air, sunlight, water and so on. All surviving labels are made of highly resistant substances, doubtless a factor in the selection of material types, but also a factor in archaeological preservation. Durability, rigidity and the potential for incision with particular kinds of tools, or the adherence or absorption of applied colour, etc. may have also factored into material choices. Of course meanings and values attributed to substances can also influence selection. The significance of a substance probably varied depending on the social context, perhaps being unimportant in some situations, yet nevertheless informing use and perception on some level.

Surface

The surface is the point at which texture, luminosity and other characteristics allow us to categorise a substance against previous experience. For example, we learn to identify glass through its hard, often-cool and smooth surface. While laboratory analysis of archaeological materials data can tell us a great deal about composition, raw materials procurement and technology from a natural sciences perspective (e.g. Nicholson and Shaw 2003), this does not necessarily reveal how materials and the surfaces they availed in cultural engagement were perceived and attributed meaning in a particular social situation. This therefore requires close study of the relationships between material substances, and the technology and embodied practices through which their surfaces were transformed in order to give physical expression to images.

Although Gibson does not appear to have applied his tri-partite model to the question of graphical imagery, it nevertheless offers a useful starting point for the ways I am interested in exploring early Egyptian script and image. Particularly when married up with notions of practice (e.g. Giddens 1984; Dobres 2000; Wenger 2002), we are well-equipped to begin unpicking the complex networks of material actions which constituted graphical expression and meanings. Further, this vantage point permits script and image to be situated alongside other cultural activities such as stone quarrying, animal butchery, or pottery manufacture, thus engendering an account that is material, dynamic, ongoing, technological, practical, symbolic, embodied and social.

Label materials and techniques

Examination of label materials involves both the substances from which the plaques were made, and those used in additive techniques. A survey shows that the labels were made from at least four materials: bone, ivory and wood, with two examples of stone. Ivory subtypes include hippopotamus and elephant ivory. A range of woods were also employed on

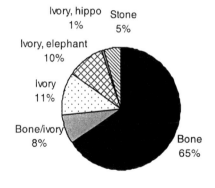

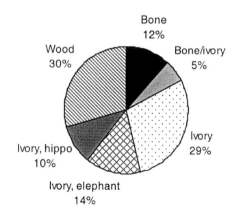

Figure 6. Percentage of materials used in the manufacture of the Naqada IIIA1 labels, all from Cemetery U at Abydos. Bone is the commonest material at 65–73%. The categories 'bone/ivory' and 'ivory' were used where type could not be distinguished with certainty.

Figure 7. Materials used in the manufacture of Naqada IIIC–early D labels, showing the reduction in the use of bone, increase in ivory and the introduction of wood, when compared with the preceding phase (see Fig. 6). The categories 'bone/ivory' and 'ivory' were used where type could not be distinguished with certainty.

the basis of colour, texture, density and other characteristics (bearing in mind the results of preservation). Differentiating sources for bone is difficult, although the use of ungulate metapodia is clearly identifiable in some instances (e.g. Dreyer 1998, pl. 27 no 10; cf. Páral *et al* 2004, pls. 3–4). My first-hand study of almost all accessible examples (over 230), primarily in museum contexts, included non-destructive analysis only. It is my hope that analytical study of labels and other inscribed objects can be undertaken in the future as much remains to be learned about materials.

The NIIIA1 labels were made predominantly of bone, although hippopotamus and elephant ivory are also discernible. Examination showed that each main material type was worked in a particular way. Dreyer (1998, 137) has proposed that some NIIIA1 labels may have been produced from plates of animal bone (see also Kahl 2001, 111). Indeed, many exhibit deep score marks with rough breaks from being snapped off, predominantly at the top and bottom, and very rarely on the right and left sides. Depending on when scoring occurred, this may have influenced plaque and image orientation and location. Interestingly, this method seems to be preferred for bone given that such marks are less common among the ivory labels, although these could have been removed through further surface preparation. Differences in production methods for different materials may relate to pragmatic issues such as shape when materials were acquired and the extent of conversion at that point (e.g. a whole elephant tusk versus off-cuts). Alternatively, choices may have been influenced by values attributed to materials, for example, that ivory was of a greater value than bone and was therefore worked in a more refined manner. The study of other contemporary objects made from these materials will doubtless provide further insight.

In plotting the distribution of materials against the two main temporal groupings, we see that bone and ivory were employed during both, with the possible stone examples

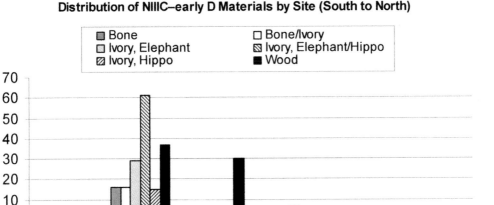

Figure 8. Spatial distribution and quantities of labels by site for the Naqada IIIC–early D phase (material is unknown for the Tura and Giza labels; see Leclant 1961 for Tura). For Naqada IIIA1 material types, all from Abydos, see Fig. 6.

being unique to the NIIIA1 phase. As illustrated in Fig. 6, bone accounts for 65–73% of NIIIA1 labels, contrasting sharply with the 12–17% of NIIIC–early D examples (Fig. 7). Conversely, ivory increases from 22–30% among the NIIIA1 labels to 53–58% among the later group. In as far as preservation is reliable, the use of wood in label manufacture is first introduced during the reign of Narmer (see e.g. Petrie 1901, 19 no. 4, pl. 2 no. 4; pl. 10 no. 1), and continues up to the reign of Qa'a, but remains less common than bone and ivory throughout. Thus, if we accept that NIIIC–early D labels are part of a tradition deriving from the NIIIA1 labels, then it is possible to chart at least two main material changes in label practices. First, there is a change in materials, as seen with the elimination of stone and the introduction of wood. Second, during the NIIIC–early D phase label-makers increase their use of elephant and hippopotamus ivory, while reducing the use of bone.

As mentioned spatial distribution at the level of site shows that the vast majority of labels are encountered at Abydos. Further, materials distribution shows that wooden labels, 71 of which were available for study, are attested at Abydos and North Saqqara only, with a significant proportion deriving from the latter site (Fig. 8). Of the label-yielding tombs dated to the reign of Qa'a, wooden examples are particularly characteristic of Tomb Q at Abydos and Tomb S3504, if not Tomb X, at Saqqara. As for the lack of wooden examples prior to the First Dynasty, this may relate to conventional choices, but poor preservation may also be a factor (very little wood is preserved from label-yielding contexts in Cemetery U (see Dreyer 1993, 34, 36; 1998, 7, 12, 194).

Decoration of label surfaces included subtractive and additive techniques, or a combination. Subtractive techniques usually involved incision of a single thin line to form the outline of an image with varying degrees of detail indicated. Additive techniques included the direct application of colour to the flat surface of the label. In distinguishing

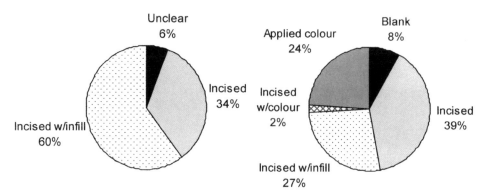

Figure 9. Techniques attested on the Naqada IIIA1 labels and the percentage of each.

Figure 10. Techniques attested on the Naqada IIIC–early D labels and the percentage of each.

directly-applied colour from the thicker, often grainier substances filling many incisions on the labels, the latter is best referred to as 'paste'. Overall four technique types can be distinguished:

    1.   Incision (subtractive)
    2.   Incision with paste infill (subtractive and additive)
    3.   Incision with applied colour (subtractive and additive)
    4.   Applied colour (additive)

Incision is the main technique for three of the four label techniques attested. Alone it is used on 162 labels, comprising approximately one-third of the corpus in each phase (Figs. 9–10). Different incision styles on some NIIIC–early D labels, for example in width, depth and carefulness are suggestive of two episodes of decoration, possibly by different hands (for a similar suggestion for a small number of NIIIA1 labels see Kahl 2001, 211).

Incision with paste infill is attested in both phases, but is the only additive method attested on NIIIA1 examples (Figs. 9–10). Paste infill is visibly different from colour applied directly to the surface (below). The former has a course texture, probably due to the type of binder employed, which may also have served as an adhesive. The identification of coloured substance on the NIIIA1 labels as 'paint' (Wengrow 2006, 202) is probably an oversight. For both phases, whether the difference between incision and incision with paste infill is the result of preservation or past intentions could not be determined. Some instances of infilling may be post-excavation treatments: Petrie (1902, 5) mentions rubbing a white substance into incisions to increase contrast for photography.

Colour is applied to incisions on at least six labels, or 2%, of the NIIIC–early D examples (Fig. 10). Alone, applied colour occurs on at least 57 NIIIC–early D labels, the earliest of which date to the reign of Narmer, if not the beginning of Aha's rule. Once applied, mineral or synthetic colorants and binding media may undergo changes due to the conditions of deposition, degradation over time, post-excavation conservation techniques or other factors (Hodges 1965, 189; Green 2001, 43). In as far as they are preserved then,

Figure 11. Double-sided label fragment of elephant ivory. The incisions forming the internal headgear are infilled with a white substance and the external lines and coil are infilled with red. Abydos 'Royal' Tombs Cemetery, tomb complex T attributed to Den, probably dating from the reign of Den (Petrie 1900, 21, pl. 10 no. 13 = pl. 14 nos. 7–7A) H 2.9–4.0+ cm, W 2.3+ cm, Th 0.3–0.4 cm; JE 34383. Author's photograph courtesy of the Egyptian Museum, Cairo.

pastes among the NIIIA1 labels are restricted to black, bluish-black or grey colour, with a greyish light green attested in one example (Dreyer 1998, 114, 118, 121; Kahl 2001, 111). For NIIIC–early D examples, pastes are black, dark grey, white (not post-excavation), yellow, brown, reddish-brown, red and green. The relatively liquid form of applied pigment exclusive to the NIIIC–early D labels is restricted to black and red, albeit with some variability in hue, while paste occurs in all colours listed. Again, beyond these visual observations, analyses of early Egyptian pigments and binding media are needed for this early period (see Lee and Quirke 2003, 104, 107).

One example of combined techniques which sheds light on the symbolic use of colour is found on a double-sided fragment of elephant ivory found at Abydos in or around Tomb T

Figure 12. Almost complete double-sided incised label of elephant ivory bearing '⌐' along the right side. Abydos 'Royal' Tombs Cemetery, tomb complex Q attributed to Qa'a, Chamber N6N before (*vor*) the entrance, probably dating from the reign of Qa'a. Photograph, Rummel 2007, 74, no. 54; see also Hawass 2002, 7. Drawing, Engel 1997, 446, fig. 218, see also 443–4; Ab K 1442, R 255). H 3.5 cm, W 3.9 cm, Th 0.3–0.4 cm. JE 99161.

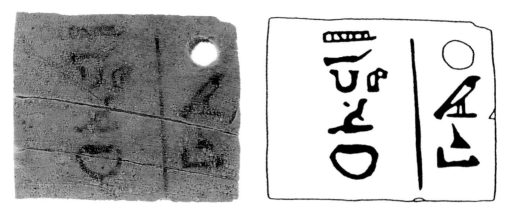

Fig. 13. Almost complete single-sided label of bone with applied black colour, cf. Fig. 12, Abydos 'Royal' Tombs Cemetery, tomb complex Q attributed to Qa'a, chamber N6 in NW corner, probably dated to the reign of Qa'a. Photograph, Dreyer *et al* 1996, pl. 14f, see also 75. Drawing, Engel 1997, 472, fig. 228 Ab K 1459, R 267. H 2.8 cm, W 3.55 cm, Th 0.15–0.2 cm. Currently held in the SCA Magazine, Sohag.

(Fig. 11). For most labels and fragments the question of colour function is difficult to assess in view of differential preservation, but this example shows how colour can be both 'functional' (e.g. creating contrast for enhanced visibility vis-à-vis the surrounding surface) and symbolic. On one side, the upper half of a right-facing human figure is depicted and the headgear worn, traditionally termed the 'double crown', is of particular interest. First-hand examination confirms that the incisions were filled in with traces of coloured paste, the tall bowling pin-shaped crown being infilled with a white substance, and the crown with the protruding coil being infilled with a reddish paste (see Petrie 1900, 21). The earliest depiction of the 'double crown' is possibly attested on Western Desert rock art from the previous reign (Legrain 1903, 221, fig. 7; see also Wilkinson 2001, 192–6), but this label fragment may constitute the earliest evidence for the colour coding of these crowns as later explicitly named in written sources (Sethe 1983, 75, 9 and 98,17).

Overall, a very specific selection of techniques was employed in the elaboration of label surfaces. Comparison with the wider range of contemporary techniques mentioned above raises the question of why label techniques were restricted to three (or four) types. On the basis of the choices evidenced, one could argue for pragmatic explanations. Perhaps the use of less elaborate techniques for label production indicates a desire to minimise time and energy expenditure, possibly a reason why stone never gained acceptance as a label material. At the same time, the use of materials from possibly non-local sources suggests economy was not a primary concern, as does the careful and detailed execution of many labels. Yet, evidence for off cuts and other forms of recycling may indicate that any significance attributed to original sourcing was reduced. Nevertheless, with repeated adherence to these techniques, together with the restricted range of materials and other physical features, these probably came to be integral in what constituted a 'label' as a particular item of material culture. While questions concerning material choices, practices and meanings require further exploration, it is nevertheless possible to gain some understanding when we consider the material variables of substance and surface in combination.

Materially contingent meaning

When we compare materials and technique against reign, an interesting pattern emerges. Starting with the 46 labels and label fragments found in and around Abydos Tomb Q, ascribed to Qa'a, if we group these according to material and then compare image technique, we find the following. A total of 22 bone and ivory labels are incised (or incised and infilled, see above). 24 bone and ivory labels are decorated using applied colour only (see for example Figs. 12–3). Comparison of incised with 'painted' labels shows that all incised examples bear '⌐' along the right side. Where applied colour is used '⌐' is absent ('⌐' does appear on one applied-colour label but this is made of wood—calling to mind the tendency elsewhere for wooden labels to be inscribed using this technique, Piquette 2007). Thus, while the use of bone or ivory (or wood) does not seem to be significant, the choice of technique clearly is.

The meaning of '⌐' cannot be substantiated based on a contextual approach (retrospective interpretations see this as a temporal indicator, perhaps the name of a year), but whatever the interpretation, the key point here is that meaning of ' ⸮ ' was to some extent anchored in the technique and material of its expression, namely incision on ivory or bone. Meanings which did not involve ' ⸮ ' were almost consistently constructed through applied colour rather than incision, and again wood was virtually excluded from this. The choice of materials and technique must have been made with the meaning content of the inscription already in mind, thus indicating the interdependence of symbolic meaning-making on practices involving particular materials, tools, techniques and embodied actions.

Summary

In the foregoing survey and case study I have attempted to demonstrate that 2-dimensional marks, whether classified as 'writing', 'art' or according to some other category, were constituted and perceived through a range of material intentions, actions and transformations. Drawing on Gibson's tri-partite model of material properties, I discussed the value of considering label materials not as mere 'foundations' for imagery but as substances and surfaces whose character and social significance were constructed through embodied and sensory activities in particular environmental circumstances. Indeed, the value of thinking through such factors has become apparent in my work on experimental label-making (Piquette 2007). That material choices actively transformed and constituted meanings was demonstrated in particular for those labels associated with the Abydos tomb complex attributed to Qa'a. Although the role of the labels in relation to other objects deposited in the tomb is archaeologically ambiguous, it is nevertheless apparent that label content meanings were intimately bound up in the method of their material expression—in this case via either incision on or colour applied to surfaces of bone and ivory.

Examples such as this attest to the importance of integrating notions of material practice with philological interpretations. Likewise, as long as graphical activities remain peripheral in discourses on materials and materiality within archaeology, attempts to address the gap in our tool-box of theories concerning objects as material, aesthetic and sensorial (see Gosden 2001, 163) will take us only part way. It is my hope that practice- and materials-centred approaches can be developed further in tandem with philological, epigraphic and palaeographic studies, to enable fuller, more holistic reconstructions of the ways in which people used images in the past to construct and symbolise their material worlds.

Acknowledgements

I would like to thank my supervisors Prof. Stephen Quirke and Prof. Roger Matthews, for their support and encouragement whilst researching this topic for my Ph.D. I am grateful to the two anonymous referees for their comments. My gratitude is also due to Dr. Andrew Gardner for his insightful comments on an earlier draft. Klaus Finneiser at the Ägyptisches Museum and Papyrussammlung, Berlin, the British Museum, Chris Naunton at the Egypt Exploration Society, Prof. Dr. Günter Dreyer and Dr. Eva-Maria Engel also provided their kind assistance. Finally my sincere thanks go to the organisers of CRE 2008, especially Vicky Gashe and Jacky Finch, for giving me the opportunity to present this paper at the symposium. Aspects of this study were supported by the UCL Institute of Archaeology and Graduate School, and the UK Universties Overseas Research Award Scheme.

Bibliography

Adams, B. and Ciałowicz, K. M. (1997) *Protodynastic Egypt*. Princes Risborough, Shire Publications.

Amélineau, E. (1904) *Les Nouvelles Fouilles d'Abydos: 1897–1898*. Paris, Ernest Leroux.

Amélineau, E. (1905) *Les Nouvelles Fouilles d'Abydos: 1897–1898 (Deuxième Partie)*. Paris, Ernest Leroux.

Assmann, J. (2002) *The Mind of Egypt*. New York, Metropolitan Books.

Baines, J. (2004) 'The Earliest Egyptian Writing: Development, context, purpose', in S. D. Houston (ed.) *The First Writing: Script invention as history and process*, 150–189. Cambridge, Cambridge University Press.

Boehmer, R. M., Dreyer, G. and Kromer, B. (1993) 'Einige frühzeitliche 14C-Datierungen aus Abydos and Uruk', *Mitteilungen des Deutschen Archäologischen Instituts, Abteilung Kairo* 49, 63–8.

Darnell, J. C. with the assistance of Darnell, D. and contributions by Darnell, D., Friedman, R. and Hendrickx, S. (2002) *Theban Desert Road Survey in the Egyptian Western Desert I. Gebel Tjauti Rock Inscriptions 1–45 and the Wadi el-Hôl Rock Inscriptions* (Oriental Institute Publication 119). Chicago, The Oriental Institute.

Demarrais, E. (ed.) (2004) *Rethinking Materiality: The engagement of mind with the material world*. Cambridge, McDonald Institute for Archaeological Research.

Dobres, M.-A. (2000) *Technology and Social Agency: Outlining a practice framework for archaeology*. Oxford, Blackwell.

Dreyer, G. (1993) 'A Hundred Years at Abydos', *Egyptian Archaeology* 3, 10–12.

Dreyer, G. (1998) *Umm el-Qaab I: Das prädynastische Königsgrab U-j und seine frühen Schriftzeugnisse*. Mainz am Rhein, Philipp von Zabern.

Dreyer, G., Boessneck, J., von den Driech, A. and Klug, S. (1990) 'Umm el-Qaab: Nachuntersuchungen im frühzeitlichen Königsfriedhof 3./4. Vorbericht', *Mitteilungen des Deutschen Archäologischen Instituts, Abteilung Kairo* 46, 53–89.

Dreyer, G., Hartung, U., Hikade, T. and Müller, V. (1998) 'Umm el-Qaab: Nachuntersuchungen im frühzeitlichen Königsfriedhof 9./10. Vorbericht', *Mitteilungen des Deutschen Archäologischen Instituts, Abteilung Kairo* 54, 78–167.

Emery, W. B. (1949) *Excavations at Saqqara: Great tombs of the First Dynasty*. Cairo, Egypt Exploration Society.

Emery, W. B. and Sa'ad, Z. Y. (1938) *Excavations at Saqqara: The tomb of Hemaka*. Cairo, Government Press.

Emery, W. B. and Sa'ad, Z. Y. (1939) *Excavations at Saqqara (1937–38): Hor-aha*. Cairo, Egypt Exploration Society.

Engel, E.-M. (1997) *Das Grab des Qa'a in Umm el-Qa'a: Architektur und Inventar, I–III*. PhD thesis. Göttingen University.

Frantz, N. P. (1998) 'Material Culture, Understanding, and Meaning: Writing and picturing', *Journal of the American Academy of Religion* 66(4), 791–815.

Gale, R., Gasson, P. and Hepper, N. (2003) 'Wood', in P. Nicholson and I. Shaw (eds) *Ancient Egyptian Materials and Technology*, 353–71. Cairo, American University in Cairo Press.

Gibson, J. J. (1979) *The Ecological Approach to Visual Perception*. Boston, Houghton Mifflin.

Giddens, A. (1984) *The Constitution of Society: Outline of the theory of structuration*. Berkeley, University of California Press.

Görsdorf, J., Dreyer, G. and Hartung, U. (1998) 'New 14C Dating of the Archaic Royal Necropolis Umm El-Qaab at Abydos (Egypt)', *Radiocarbon* 40(1–2), 641.

Gosden, C. (2001) 'Making Sense: Archaeology and aesthetics', *World Archaeology* 33(2), 163–7.

Green, L. (2001) 'Colour Transformations of Ancient Egyptian Pigments', in W. V. Davies (ed.) *Colour and Painting in Ancient Egypt*, 43–8. London, British Museum Press.

Hawass, Z. (2002) *Hidden Treasures of the Egyptian Museum*. Cairo, American University in Cairo Press.

Helck, W. (1987) *Untersuchungen zur Thinitenzeit*. Wiesbaden, Harrassowitz.

Hendrickx, S. (1996) 'The Relative Chronology of the Naqada Culture: Problems and possibilities', in A. J. Spencer (ed.) *Aspects of Early Egypt*, 36–69. London, British Museum Press.

Hodges, H. (1965) *Artefacts*. London, John Baker.

Ingold, T. (2007) 'Materials Against Materiality', *Archaeological Dialogues* 14(1), 1–16.

Johnson, M. (1999) *Archaeology Theory: An introduction*. Oxford, Blackwell.

Kahl, J. (1994) *Das System der ägyptischen Hieroglyphenschrift in der 0.–3. Dynastie*. Wiesbaden, Harrassowitz.

Kahl, J. (2001) 'Hieroglyphic Writing During the Fourth Millennium BC: An analysis of systems', *Archéo-Nil* 11, 102–134.

Kahl, J. (2002) *Frühägyptisches Wörterbuch: Erste Lieferung ꜣ–f*. Wiesbaden, Harrassowitz.

Kahl, J. (2003) *Frühägyptisches Wörterbuch: Zweite Lieferung m–ḥ*. Wiesbaden, Harrassowitz.

Kahl, J. (2004) *Frühägyptisches Wörterbuch: Dritte Lieferung ḥ–ḫ*. Wiesbaden, Harrassowitz.

Kahl, J. and Engel, E.-M. (2001) *Vergraben, verbrannt, verkannt und vergessen: Fund aus dem "Menesgrab"*. Münster, Sazt and Druck.

Kaplony, P. (1963) *Die Inschriften der ägyptischen Frühzeit, I–III*. Wiesbaden, Harrassowitz.

Leclant, J. (1961) 'Fouilles et travaux en Égypte, 1957–1960', *Orientalia* 30, 91–110.

Lee. L. and Quirke, S. (2000). 'Painting materials', in P. T. Nicholson and I. Shaw (eds) *Ancient Egyptian Materials and Technology*, 104–120. Cambridge, Cambridge University Press.

Legge, G. F. (1906) 'The Tablets of Negadah and Abydos', *Proceedings of the Society of Biblical Archaeology* 28, 252–63.

Legrain, G. (1903) 'Notes d'inspection', *Annales du Service des Antiquités de L'Égypte* 4, 193–226.

Lucas, A, (1962) *Ancient Egyptian Materials and Industries*. (4th ed. rev. J. R. Harris) London, Edward Arnold.

Matthews, R. (2003) *The Archaeology of Mesopotamia: Theories and approaches*. London, Routledge.

Meskell, L. (2005) *Archaeologies of Materiality*. Oxford, Blackwell.

Moreland, J. (2001) *Archaeology and Text*. London, Duckworth.

Nicholson, P. and Shaw, I. (eds) (2003) *Ancient Egyptian Materials and Technology*. Cairo, American University in Cairo Press.

O'Hara, K. P., Taylor, A., Newman, W. and Sellen, A. J. (2002) 'Understanding the Materiality of Writing from Multiple Sources', *International Journal of Human-Computer Studies* 56(3), 269–305.

Olsen, B. (2003) 'Material Culture After Text: Re-membering things', *Norwegian Archaeological Review* 36(2), 87–104.

Páral, V., Tichý, F. and Fabis, M. (2004) 'Functional Structure of Metapodial Bones of Cattle', *Acta Veterinaria Brno* 73, 413–20.

Parker Pearson, M. (2001) *The Archaeology of Death and Burial*. Phoenix Mill, Sutton Publishing.

Pearce, S. (ed.) (2000) *Researching Material Culture*. Leicester, School of Archaeological Studies, University of Leicester.

Petrie, W. M. F. (1900) *The Royal Tombs of the Earliest Dynasties: Part I*. London, Egypt Exploration Fund.

Petrie, W. M. F. (1901) *The Royal Tombs of the Earliest Dynasties: Part II*. London, Egypt Exploration Fund.

Petrie, W. M. F. (1902) *Abydos*. London, Egypt Exploration Fund.

Piquette, K. E. (2007) *Writing, 'Art' and Society: A contextual archaeology of the inscribed labels of Late Predynastic-Early Dynastic Egypt*. PhD thesis. University of London.

Postgate, N., Wilkinson, T. A. H. and Wang, T. (1995) 'The Evidence for Early Writing: Utilitarian or ceremonial?', *Antiquity* 69(264), 459–80.

Riley, M. G. (1985) *Paléographie des Signes Hiéroglyphiques sous les deux premières dynasties Égyptiennes*. PhD thesis. University of Paris, Sorbonne.

Rummel, U. (ed.) (2007) *Meeting the Past: 100 Years in Egypt. Deutsches Archäologisches Institut, Kairo 1907–2007, Catalogue of the Special Exhibition in the Cairo Museum (19 November 2007 to 15 January 2008)*. Cairo, Deutsches Archäologisches Institut.

Scharff, A. (1942) *Archäologische Beiträge zur Frage der Entstehung der Hieroglyphenschrift*. München, Verlag der Bayerischen Akademie der Wissenschaften.

Sethe, K. (1983) *Agyptische Lesestücke zum Gebrauch in akademischen Unterricht. Texte des Mittleren Reiche*s. Hidlesheim, Olms.

Trigger, B. T., Kemp, B. J., O'Connor, D. and Lloyd, A. B. (2001) *Ancient Egypt: A social history*. Cambridge, Cambridge University Press.

Wenger, E. (2002) *Communities of Practice: Learning, meaning and identity*. Cambridge, Cambridge University Press.

Wengrow, D. (2006) *The Archaeology of Early Egypt: Social Transformations in North East Africa, 10,000–2650 BC*. Cambridge, Cambridge University Press.

Whitehouse, R. D. Forthcoming. *The Materiality of Writing: A case study from 1st millennium BC Italy*.

Wilkinson, T. A. H. (2001) *Early Dynastic Egypt*. London, Routledge.

A Stylistic Dating Method for Statues of Anubis and other Canine Divinities

Arnaud Quertinmont

Université Libre de Bruxelles / Université Charles-de-Gaulle Lille 3

Introduction

Despite the fact that there were numerous canine divinities in ancient Egypt, representations of Anubis were the most frequent. Imposing respect and humility, this god has always fascinated people, from the Greeks and the Romans to modern man. He plays a pivotal role in the rituals of passage to the Underworld, acting as guardian of the tomb, of the body of the deceased and of the Underworld itself. However, he also has a kindlier aspect, acting as protector during this critical phase for the being in transition - the passage to the afterlife. The role of Anubis should not, however, be limited to the funerary field, but should be widened to incorporate the role of a reincarnator. This function is underlined by the fact that Anubis is, astrologically speaking, identified with the star Sirius (Bradshaw 1957). The date of the rising of this star corresponds to the New Year. Although this can be a time of great danger because it is the end of a cycle, it is also a period of hope. The rising of Sirius indicates that the new cycle (of, for example, the inundation or the solar cycle) will not be long in coming. Another good example of Anubis's associations with the beginning of a new cycle is seen in the representations of Anubis with the lunar disc, i.e. from the Hatshepsut's funerary temple at Deir el Bahari (Naville 1896, pl.55; Ritner 1985). In the inscription which accompanies a similar scene in the temple of Nectanebo I, and that of the divine Emperor Augustus, we can read '*Je suis venu devant le seigneur des dieux voir le fils qu'il aime. J'ai formé ses membres, sa vie et son destin, ils seront rajeunis comme la lune dans le mois*' (Ritner 1985, 151). Through the lunar cycle, during which the moon is 'renewed', Anubis also promises reincarnation to the king, allowing him eternal life in the land of the living and beyond.

The worship of divinities with canine heads goes back to the beginning of Egyptian history. From ancient times, stray dogs (including jackals) travelled through the desolate expanses, searching for food, and sometimes digging up the bodies of the dead in cemeteries (Baines 1993). It may be because of these actions that the Egyptians gave canines the task of guarding and protecting cemeteries and the corpses within them, transforming the negative act of exhuming the corpses into a positive act of divine protection. Thus we encounter gods in full or part canine form as both guardians of mummified corpses (Wepwawet, Duamutef) and as embalmers (Anubis).

If I choose to say 'canine' god and not 'jackal' god, it is with good reason. Canine divinities, such as Anubis, are designated by the appellation *sзb*, which has been translated as 'jackal' (Erman, 1929; Wb., III, 420, 5ff). This interpretation is, to my eyes, more due to convention than to reality. Even if this animal shares common features with representations of Anubis (pointed ears, elongated nose, weak legs, a thick and hanging tail), there are differences between the two: the jackal is covered with fur, which Anubis never is, neither in painting nor in sculpture. In fact, depictions of the Anubien animal seem closer to the family of Egypt's stray dogs, *Canis lupaster*, than to the jackal (Duquesne 2005; 1996). Evidence of mummified dogs from the Anubeion at Saqqara suggests that the ancient Egyptians themselves did not seem to make the clear distinction between various species (Daressy and Gaillard 1905). The work of Animal Mummy Project (http://www.animalmummies.com), where mummies of different types of canine, including dogs, jackals and foxes were found, also supports this conclusion. This evidence supports the idea that *sзb* should not be translated as 'jackal' but as 'savage dog' (Meeks 1998, 77.3341).

Possible research into representations of Anubis

Despite this fascination for the god Anubis, there are few complete works on the subject of his representations, or representations of canine divinities in general. The major texts deal with representations from the Predynastic and the Old Kingdom (Duquesne 2005); the Alexandrian Anubis (Grenier 1977); with particular aspects of the topic (Baines 1993; Fischer 1998; Ischlondsky 1996; Kuhn 1999); or discuss the general topic of animal representations (Arnold 1995; Germond 2001; Gombert 1992–3).

However, using my findings from research undertaken during my studies in history of art and archaeology in Brussels, mainly focussed on representations of Anubis from the Old to the end of the New Kingdom (Quertinmont 2004), I would like to propose a stylistic analysis of the heads of canine divinities dating to the New Kingdom.

The New Kingdom is the only period which provides us with a significant number of representations of canine divinities (in animal or hybrid form), which are relatively well dated and for which the archaeological context is assured. In spite of the recurrence and the importance of canine divinities, and although their sculpture is attested from the Predynastic Period onwards, few significant examples from the ancient periods have been discovered. It is not until the reign of Amenhotep III that we see an increase in the number of zoomorphic statues, as is shown by the hybrid statuary of the temple of Kom el-Heitan (Bryan 1997), as well as the many representations of Sekhmet at the Mut Temple of Karnak (Yoyotte 1980).

By creating a corpus of these various representations, it is possible to determine certain formal features of the canine anatomy which can, in my opinion, serve as chronological markers (Quertinmont 2008). A more technical analysis of these statues also makes it possible for us to learn more about their context. These methods joined together can undoubtedly increase our knowledge of these representations, which are found around the world, and which are often admired only for their aesthetic qualities alone. Apart from this, they can also provide us with much information about the precise conditions at the time of their creation.

Available data

If there is one feature common to Egyptian collections in almost all of the world's museums, it is the presence of a display cabinet dedicated to bronze divinities. All are dated from the Late Period without real justification. Indeed, at present, it is very difficult to define the formal elements which can help us to date bronzes (Ischlondsky 1996; Aubert 2001). Although the majority of canine statues and statuettes belong to precisely this category of objects, I have excluded them from the corpus because of these dating problems and also because of their particular features of production, i.e. the use of moulds and mass production.

The only usable examples for the corpus are in wood and stone, but these are only rarely reproduced in print, mainly to illustrate a chapter or a photographic collection, as in the case of the superb Anubis of Tutankhamen's tomb. These objects are exploited for their aesthetic qualities, but rarely analysed with a specific scientific goal. My work aims at filling this gap. The corpus includes examples of canine heads in wood and stone, from the royal or temple sphere, and excludes private examples made during the New Kingdom. Neither does the corpus include the numerous representations of Anubis found at the base of sarcophagi. The reason for the inclusion of examples from the royal or temple spheres is that these 'official' statues are made according to very precise rules, which were applied in every royal workshop. Because of this, it is easier to determine particular chronological and technical features.

The corpus must be made on very strict criteria of dating and conservation:

1. Each piece must be dated from the New Kingdom.

Some statues must be eliminated because of the lack of a well established dating: i.e. Cairo, Egyptian Museum inv. CGC 38570 (Grenier 1977, pl. I) and Cairo, Egyptian Museum inv. CG 38517 (Davies and Smith 1997, pl. 6).

2. Each piece must be in a good state of preservation.

I have thus rejected the majority of preserved canine statues because of the fact that they are unfortunately fragmentary at the level of the head: either the muzzle is damaged, or it is the only preserved part (Fig. 1, 2).

3. Photographs of each piece must be published both from the front and in profile.

This last condition excludes lots of statues, at least for the moment. Requests have been made to several museums for face and profile photography. Indeed, although three-quarter photography is generally chosen for aesthetic reasons, it deprives us of important information (Fig. 3).

Sadly, at the present stage of my research, the corpus is very small. Only ten heads made between the reigns of Amenhotep III and Ramesses II provide the necessary conditions to be included. Apart from the difficulty in finding examples which meet the above mentioned conditions, there are other reasons why the corpus is so small. It will certainly increase when the considerable numbers of canine figures currently stored in museums' storerooms and in private collections become accessible.

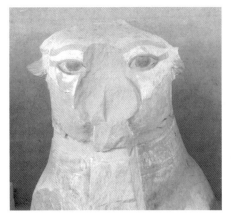

Figure 1. Anubis head.
Limestone (Eighteenth Dynasty, reign of
Amenhotep III). Storeroom of the Funerary
Temple of Merneptah.
© Alain Guilleux with the copyright permis-
sion of Institut suisse de Recherches architec-
turales et archéologiques de l'ancienne Égypte
au Caire.

Figure 2. Muzzle of a dog.
Limestone (New Kingdom). Storeroom of the
Ramesseum.
© Photo Yann Rantier/Mission Archéologique
Française de Thèbes-Ouest.

Figure 3 (left). Anubis statue.
Granodiorite (Eighteenth Dynasty, reign of Amenhotep
III). Karnak.
Copenhague, Glyptothèque NY Carlsberg, inv. ÆIN 33
© Glyptothèque Ny Carlsberg.

Figure 4 (above). Recumbent figure of the jackal Anubis,
on shrine.
Gilded Wood, Gold, Silver, Calcite and Obsidian (Eight-
eenth Dynasty, reign of Tutankhamen)
Tutankhamen's tomb (KV 62).
Cairo, Egyptian Museum, inv. JE 61444
© Jon Bodsworth, The Egyptarchive.

Figure 5 (above). Anubis.
Granodiorite (Eighteenth Dynasty, reign of Amenhotep
III). Deir el-Medina
London, British Museum, inv. EA 64400
© Copyright the Trustees of The British Museum.

Figure 6 (right). Anubis.
Wood (New Kingdom). Origin unknown.
Leiden, Rijksmuseum van Oudheiden, inv. F 1956/4.9
© Rijksmuseum van Oudheden, Leiden.

Figure 7 (below). Double stela of Hatiay.
Limestone (Eighteenth Dynasty). Abydos.
Leiden, Rijksmuseum van Oudheiden, inv. AP.12
© Arnaud Quertinmont.

Analysis of technical features

Creating such a corpus allows us to determine if a canine head comes from an animal or hybrid representation. From my results, it is apparent that two elements must be taken into account:

1. The presence or absence of a wig.

It is obvious that only the hybrid figures have one. Furthermore, a typological comparison of the wigs of hybrid divinities shows that the headdress tends to be worn further and further back with time. This element, when it is present, becomes a dating marker (Gilbert, 1952, 8).

2. The colour of the statue.

In the case of a complete animal representation, more than one option is possible:

a) First, the head can be painted black or covered with bitumen, as in the case of wood i.e. Cairo, Egyptian Museum inv. JE 61444 (Fig. 4).

b) Secondly, the material it is made of can be naturally black, as in the case of granodiorite i.e. London, British Museum, EA 64400 (Bryan 1997, pl. 27 - Fig. 5)

c) Thirdly, it can be sand coloured, as in the case of limestone i.e. Anubis from the Funerary Temple of Merneptah (Fig. 1).

In the case of a hybrid representation:

a) The statue can be entirely black, if in granodiorite i.e. Copenhague, Glyptothèque NY Carlsberg inv. ÆIN 33 (Fig. 3)

b) It can be left in its natural colour, like some wood statues i.e. Leiden, Rijksmuseum van Oudheden inv. F 1956/4.9 (Fig. 6) and Bruxelles, Musées royaux d'Art et d'Histoire inv. E.7688 (Fig. 10)

There is a problem with usable hybrid representations. Only two major statues are, to my knowledge, well preserved: Cairo, Egyptian Museum inv. CGC 38570 (Grenier 1977, pl. I) which was eliminated because of the lack of a well-established date, and a small statue of Hathor and Wepwawet, New York, Metropolitan Museum of Art inv. 17.2.5 (Hayes 1953–9, fig. 18), which is not well published.

In summary, if we have a wooden head coated neither in black nor in bitumen, there is a large probability that it comes from a hybrid representation. In the case of a limestone head, we perhaps have an animal form.

What the method does not help with is the attribution of the representation to a peculiar god. Indeed, even if Anubis's representations are the most frequent, there are other divinities and important canine creatures such as Duamutef, one of Horus's four sons (the

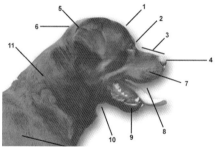

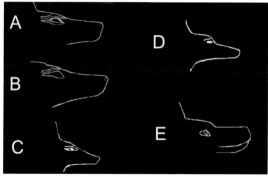

Figure 8. Anatomical figure of the head of a dog:
1. Forehead.
2. Stop.
3. Muzzle.
4. Nose.
5. Skull
6. Base of skull.
7. Moustache.
8. Mouth.
9. Lip.
10. Cheek.
11. Neck
© GNU Free Documentation License

Figure 9. Comparison of the profiles:
A. Amenhotep III (British Museum, inv. EA 64400).
B. Amenhotep III (Musées royaux d'Art et d'Histoire, Bruxelles, inv. E. 7688).
C. Tutankhamen (Cairo, Egyptian Museum, inv. JE 61444).
D. Horemheb (Cairo, Egyptian Museum, inv. JE 32494).
E. Ramesses II (Cairo, Egyptian Museum, inv. JE 31412).
© Arnaud Quertinmont

souls of Nekhen) and especially Wepwawet, the Opener of Ways. The only way to attribute, with certainty, a statue to a god is the presence of his name on the object. The animal iconography of Anubis, just as his functions, can be transferred to the figure of Wepwawet; this is very obvious at Assyut/Lycopolis or on the double stela of Hatiay, Leiden, Rijksmuseum van Oudheiden, inv. AP.12 (Fig. 7). Such a transference of features is in no way shocking or astonishing. Indeed, as Wepwawet has a protective aspect, being the protective god of Assyut, and is also himself a dog, nothing prevents such a transfer. The same situation is found in the attribution of the patronage of necropolises: they can be placed under the protection of Anubis, Sokar or Wepwawet in the same way that the role of the Western Goddesses can be assumed by Isis or Hathor. The totality of the functions are exchanged between the two gods, such as the roles of guard, guide or even of reincarnator, as can be seen in Seti I's temple in Abydos (David 1981). This was not done by accident, especially if we remember that Wepwawet is also regarded as one of Osiris' sons.

Analysis of the dating method

The dating method I propose is based on an element of canine morphology, at the level of the articulation between the muzzle and the forehead (Fig. 8). This zone, named the 'stop' (equivalent to the human 'brow'), is the most characteristic element allowing us to establish a chronology. Indeed, a representative sampling, composed of usable heads of Anubis dating from the New Kingdom (from the reigns of Amenhotep III, Tutankhamen, Horemheb and Ramesses II) leads us to note that the articulation of the 'stop' is accentuated over time. As we can see (Fig. 9), from a rather light depression at the time of Amenhotep III, we pass to a more pronounced brow under the reign of Ramesses II. This evolution of the representation of the 'stop' is clearly visible in statuary made, probably, in royal workshops and thus becomes a dating marker for the representations of canine divinities made in the New Kingdom.

Other elements are also detectable, such as the subtlety and increasingly finely designed features typical of the Amenhotep era, and perhaps also the treatment of the eyes and their position on the face. Unfortunately, full frontal photographs are just as difficult to come by as profile ones.

Concrete applications

The dating markers of the 'stop' and the technical features can be useful to establish contextual information about the statue as well as a more precise dating.

The beautiful wooden canine head preserved in Brussels (Musées royaux d'Art et d'Histoire inv. E.7688) is a very good example of the use of these methods (Fig. 10). The note with this object stated simply that it was a head, perhaps from a hybrid statue, dating from the New Kingdom. The absence of black colour on the head, as well as the small remains of a wig, lean towards interpretation of this head as part of a hybrid statue, which had when intact measured nearly 72 cm in height (calculated with respect to the Egyptian

Figure 10. Head of a canine.
Wood (Eighteenth Dynasty, reign of Amenhotep III). Origin unknown.
Bruxelles, Musées royaux d'Art et d'Histoire, inv. E.7688
© Musées royaux d'Art et d'Histoire de Bruxelles.

canon and proportions). If I examine the 'stop' it clearly indicates a date from the reign of Amenhotep III. Thus, the dating, just as other formal features make this apparently 'common' head, one of the most beautiful, largest and oldest specimens of Egyptian representation of a hybrid canine divinity (Quertinmont 2008).

Another example comes from the canine statue from Leiden (Rijksmuseum van Oudheden inv. F 1956/4.9). This wooden statue (Fig. 6) with unknown provenance is dated from the Eighteenth to the Twentieth Dynasty. There are no remains of bitumen, thus a good example of non-coated hybrid statues. On analysis of the 'stop' it becomes clear that this head dates, at the earliest, to the reign of Ramesses II.

With these two examples, I hope to have shown that a close study of various features and aspects of these heads not only highlights their extraordinary aesthetic qualities, but allows us to restore part of the context they come from, and sometimes even to specify their date and history.

Acknowledgements

I would like to thank the team of the CRE IX and especially Vicky Gashe and Jacky Finch. I'm also grateful to Natacha Massar who has corrected my English.

Bibliography

Arnold, D. (1995) *An Egyptian Bestiary*. New York, The Metropolitan Museum of Art.

Aubert, J.-F. and Aubert, C. (2001) *Bronzes et or égyptiens*. Paris, Cybèle.

Baines, J. (1993) 'Symbolic roles of canine figures on early monuments', *Archéo-Nil* 3, 57–74.

Bradshaw, J. (1957) *The night sky in Egyptian Mythology*. London, Bradshaw.

Bryan, B. (1997) 'The statue program for the mortuary temple of Amenhotep III', in S. Quirke (ed.) *The Temple in Ancient Egypt: New Discoveries and Recent Research*, 57–81. London, British Museum Press.

Daressy, G. and Gaillard, C. (1905) *La faune momifiée de l'antique Égypte*, Cairo, Institut français d'archéologie orientale.

David, A. R. (1981) *A Guide to Religious Ritual at Abydos*. Warminster, Aris and Phillips.

Davies, S. and Smith, H. S. (1997) 'Sacred Animal Temples at Saqqara' , in S. Quirke (ed.) *The Temple in Ancient Egypt: New Discoveries and Recent Research*, 121–31. London, British Museum Press.

Duquesne, T. (1996) *Black and Gold God. Colour Symbolism of the god Anubis, with observations on the phenomenology of colour in Egyptian and comparative religion* (Oxfordshire communications in Egyptology, 5). London, Darengo Publications.

Duquesne, T. (2005) *The Jackal Divinities of Egypt I. From the Archaic Period to Dynasty X* (Oxfordshire Communications in Egyptology 6). London, Darengo Publications.

Erman, A. and Grapow, H. (1929) *Wörterbuch der Ägyptischen Sprache*. Leipzig, Berlin Akademie-Verlag.

Fischer, K. (1998) *Anubis im Dekorationsprogramm der thebanischen Privatgraber*. Unpublished MA thesis, Heidelberg University.

Germond, P. (2001) *Bestiaire Egyptien*. Paris, Thames and Hudson.

Gilbert, P. (1952) *Exposition des objets provenant des fouilles d'El-Kab ou récemment acquis par le département égyptien, 10 mars–26 avril 1952*. Bruxelles, Fondation Egyptologique Reine Elisabeth.

Gombert, F. (1992–3) *La statuaire divine animalière en Egypte des origines jusqu'en 664 av. J.-C.* Unpublished MA thesis, Université Paris IV, La Sorbonne.

Grenier, J.-C. (1977) *Anubis alexandrin et romain*. Leiden, Études préliminaires aux religions orientales dans l'Empire romain.

Hayes, W. C. (1953–9) *The Scepter of Egypt. A Background for the Study of the Egyptian Antiquities in The Metropolitan Museum of Art*. New York, Harry N. Abrams.

Ischlondsky, N. D. (1966) 'A Peculiar Representation of the Jackal-god Anubis', *Journal of Near Eastern Studies* 25, 17–26.

Kuhn, J. (1999) *L'iconographie du chacal dans les tombes de Deir el-Medineh*. Unpublished MA thesis, Université Charles-de-Gaulle, Lille III.

Meeks, D. (1998) *Année Lexicographique. Egypte Ancienne*, 1 (1977). Paris, Cybèle.

Naville, E. (1896) *The Temple of Deir el Bahari, II*. London, Egypt Exploration Fund.

Quertinmont, A. (2004) *Anubis, représentations et fonctions, de l'Ancien à la fin du Nouvel Empire*. Unpublished MA thesis, Université Libre de Bruxelles.

Quertinmont, A. (2008) 'Une tête égyptienne de chien aux Musées royaux d'Art et d'Histoire', *Bulletin des Musées royaux d'Art et d'Histoire* (in press).

Ritner, K. (1985) 'Anubis and the Lunar Disc', *Journal of Egyptian Archaeology* 71, 149–55.

Yoyotte, J. (1980) 'Une monumentale litanie de granit: Les Sekhmet d'Amenophis III et la conjuration permanente de la déesse dangereuse', *Bulletin de la Société Française d'Egyptologie*, 87/88, 46–71.

A Brief Analysis of the Representations of Masculinity within a Case Study of Pre-Amarna Eighteenth Dynasty Funeral Art in Ancient Egypt

Kim Ridealgh
University of Swansea

Introduction

The select number of tombs in the Theban Necropolis that fall into the New Kingdom Pre-Amarna era all share very similar attributes with regard to the artwork portrayed within them, especially when considering the portrayal of the tomb owner. In general, the tomb owner is usually portrayed as much larger in size than the rest of the figures within the funerary scenes, and is shown watching or participating in the activities displayed on the various walls of his tomb (Kanawati 2001, 86). The tomb is essentially a means to display the deceased's world view, arguably a highly masculine view point, and to provide a catalyst for his rebirth into the afterlife.

Much about social hierarchy is reflected within the tomb, highlighting that from birth, the identity of individuals, an amalgamation of age, gender, and social status, had to be constructed in accordance with the norms of the social system they inhabited (Robins 1999, 55). Broadly speaking, the social hierarchy was organised according to the following stratifications: the king, the elite, and the non-elite who formed the greatest part of the population (Baines 1991, 132). The elite group consisted of the literate, male officials who performed the administration of Egypt, together with their families, forming approximately five percent of the population (Robins 2008, 208). Among the elite, men held governmental positions whilst women took care of the household, bore children, made music to accompany temple rituals and occasionally held a position at court. The non-elite would only enter this luxurious world as servants and musicians (Robins 1999, 56 and 2008, 209; Baines 1991, 132).

This paper will focus on the elite male attitude to masculinity as represented in tomb art, following the recent trend of interest in men and masculinity in history. This trend is mostly due to the growing influence of masculine theory in academia, a discipline that evolved to counterbalance the abundant feminist literature that has appeared in the past three decades. Yet, although it provides a counterbalance and perhaps even provides context for the women of the past, masculine theory in no way seeks to undermine the important work of feminist scholars and some feminists even believe that it should be viewed as an off-shoot of feminism (Conkey and Gero 1997). Masculine theory is only beginning to become apparent in Egyptology, with a limited amount of scholars using this approach in their research (Robins 2008; Parkinson 2008), yet within other areas of historical study it is more developed (Smith 1994 and 2000; Rocke 1996; Lees 1994; Sussman 1995). These studies, focusing on various time periods, seek to identify and understand the men of the past and try, in a manner of speaking, to remove the blasé attitude many people have towards the history of men. This view suggests that the history of men is a 'monolithic given, as opposed to femininity's constructed, contested, and therefore discussible nature' (Parkinson 2008, 1). Much of the work based on these theories places the concept of power at the centre of male history, and scholars often investigate how masculine characters and traits (i.e. masculinity) can shape a society's view of men (Connell 1987 and 1995; Kimmel 1987; Brittan 1989; Mac an Ghaill 1996, 97; Bevan 1995, 41).

Yet before a study can begin, a brief introduction to the ancient Egyptian attitude to masculinity is needed. Within Egyptian literature a nuanced presentation of masculine values can be viewed in the Twelfth Dynasty poem the Tale of Sinuhe (see Simpson 1973, 54; Parkinson 1997). Masculinity is a concern of the tale's depiction of social and individual identity, as is the case in many societies where manliness involves procreation, provisioning dependants and protecting one's family. Sinuhe achieves all this but his masculinity is essentially undermined by the fact that he did not complete his social obligations as a member of the male sex in Egypt, being abroad and away from Egypt has unmanned him (Lichtheim 1976, 222). In his life, ultimate success is not just defined as being masculine and potent, with Sinuhe ironically losing his potency during his victory abroad, after which he can return to Egypt and resume his true identity (Parkinson 2008, 11–16).

The celebration of masculinity can be paralleled in the visual idealisation of the male muscular body in representational art. As Meskell (2002, 114) notes, Egyptian art offers an early canonical representation of the 'triangular physique' that is still highly valued in many cultures, in which the male body is glamorised and eroticised. This parallels the way in which kings and heroes are praised for their 'strong arm' or 'brawn' in official texts such as the Tale of Sinuhe, and a man's muscular strength is explicitly an inspiration to a woman's desire in the Late Egyptian Tale of Two Brothers (Parkinson 2008, 10).

This paper will examine tomb art depicted within the Pre-Amarna tombs in the Theban Necropolis, with a particular focus on the tomb of Rekhmire (TT100), a high ranking official from the reign of Thutmose III/Amenhotep II (see PM I², 206–215; Hodel-Hoenes 2000, 140; Whale 1989, 131–2; Wildung 1978, 5). A masculine theoretical approach will be applied in order to determine if the funerary art from the tomb of Rekhmire places the concept of power at the centre of the depictions within the tomb, and examine how masculine characteristics are expressed. Is it possible to gain a comprehensive picture of ancient Egyptian masculinity from the tomb? The tomb is of course a highly male domain and promotes the success of the deceased owner, and whilst religious scenes are not included in this study, other scenes in the tomb will be analysed before a detailed examination of the composition of the scenes, looking in detail at shape, pose, and dress of the figures within the images.

Comments on the role and function of men within the tomb scenes

Banquet Scenes

Banqueting scenes are a common occurrence in pre-Amarna New Kingdom tombs (Hartwig 2004, 98; for examples see TT38(PM I²,70(6)); TT52(PM I²,100(3)); TT69(PM I², 137(4)); TT108(PM I², 225(5)); TT139(PM I², 253(6)); TT249(PM I², 335(4));

TT253(PM I², 337(4))) and possess multivalent imagery mixing themes of sexuality and rebirth with aspects, most commonly, of the Valley Festival but also of other funerary banquets and commemorative feasts held in the tomb (Hartwig 2004, 98; Ikram 2001, 162). The scene generally comprises many participants dispersed over several registers, normally seated on chairs or stools, but occasionally sitting on reed matting (Hartwig 2004, 99). The participants are attended by male or female servants, who adjust locks of hair, apply ointment, serve beverages and bestow lotus flowers and wah collars (Andrews 1996, 119). The symbolism of the banqueting scene has been analysed by Derchain (1975a), Westendorf (1967), Manniche (1987), and Robins (1994 and 1996), who have all focused in larger part on the themes of sexuality and rebirth inherent in the compositions. While eroticism is certainly present, there are likely additional religious and symbolic meanings inherent in banqueting representations. Perhaps a funeral dinner was a customary practise after a loved one died, just like wakes or funerals today.

In comparison to the rest of the scenes considered in this study of the tomb of Rekhmire, the banquet scene includes the highest percentage of female figures (see PM I², 213(18); Davies 1973, pls 64–7). The men in this set of scenes are often shown separated from the women and the male figures present in the scene represent the male elite, their servants and musicians. The musicians and the servants follow a standardised form and are easily recognisable. The elite men in the scenes are often depicted sitting and are dressed in elaborate costumes with decorative jewellery. This elite style of dress provides a stark contrast to the plain manner in which the servants and the musicians are depicted.

Perhaps the presence of women in this scene could be taken as an indication that elite women rarely entered into the male official's sphere except during social events, since women, except for representations of the wife, fail to appear regularly in the other types of funerary scenes in this tomb. It is possible that the banquet scene possesses no affirmative sensual undertones, as suggested by Hartwig (2004, 98), and merely represents a 'snapshot' of elite events and the deceased's desire to continue to hold banquets in the afterlife. However, although the scene may not necessarily represent Rekhmire's sexual vigour, it certainly demonstrates his wealth and lavish lifestyle, an aspect of his publicly projected masculinity.

Fishing and fowling scenes

The fishing and fowling scenes are perhaps the ones to reflect Egyptian ideas of masculinity since they never appear with a woman in the central role in this period and thus can be considered to be purely masculine icons. The scene has been interpreted in four different ways: some believe it represents privileged recreation and the securing of provisions for the dead (Feucht 1992; Assmann 1996); others that it represents a symbolic realm and functioned in an apotropaic manner for the deceased (Wildung 1977; Laboury, 1997), whilst others argue that the imagery is erotically charged and the scene represents rebirth and fertility (Westendorf 1967, 142; Derchain 1975b, 62 and 1976, 8; Manniche 1999, 103 and 2000, 276). Barocas (1982, 429) has even interpreted the scene to reflect the deceased's worthiness of an ancestor cult. However, all interpretations are not mutually exclusive and can be combined along with other commemorative elements in the scene, to illustrate how fishing and fowling scenes functioned on behalf of the deceased within the context of the tomb (Hartwig 2004, 104; Robins 1993, 187; Laboury 1997, 70; Hodel-Hoenes 2000, 23).

In this scene the deceased appears as a very youthful, vibrant character fishing or fowling in the marshes alongside family members. This image changed very little from its introduction in Old Kingdom funerary art (Robins 1997, 22). Perhaps a fifth interpretation of this scene is required, one stressing the masculinity of the scene, since the pose of the deceased mimics the smiting scenes of royal iconography (Robins 1997, 33). The deceased is represented as the protector and provider simultaneously, two characteristics of Egyptian masculinity also expressed within representations of the king. Perhaps in this type of scene, the deceased is able to emulate the masculine qualities of the king that artistic decorum would have prevented him from doing in a more obvious manner. The fishing and fowling scenes in the tomb of Rekhmire are today badly damaged and it is no longer possible to view them in their entirety. Davies (1973, 40), however, suggests that this scene can be reconstructed to follow a very traditional manner with two opposing figures of the deceased upon skips among the marshes (Hartwig 2004, 103; Feucht 1992, 157).

Tribute and professional duty scenes

It seems that the officials who held the titles that linked them to the recording of tribute and diplomatic interactions portrayed this scene in their tomb (Aldred 1970, 106; Hartwig 2004, 73; Vandier 1952, 571; For examples see TT63(PM I², 126(9)); TT78(PM I², 153(8)); TT89(PM I², 182(15)); TT91(PM I² 185(3)); TT118(PM I², 234(1)); TT201(PM I², 305(7))). In its complete form, the tribute icon is composed of Egyptian or Nubian soldiers framing the composition with Asiatic and Nubian tribute-bearers in the middle registers carrying official gifts to the king. Sometimes a large figure of the tomb owner was depicted facing the procession, directing operations (Hartwig 2004, 73). The tribute scenes in the tomb of Rekhmire depict foreigners carrying tribute from their countries to Egypt (PM I², 207(4); Davies 1973, pls 17–23). The depictions of foreigners within this collection of scenes are portrayed as inferior to the Egyptians and they are therefore less masculine both through not being Egyptian and through not being the in a position of authority. Although their dress may be elaborate and their hair well maintained they would have still been viewed as less masculine than their Egyptian counterparts since they lack any power over their own actions.

Similarly the professional duty scenes depict the tomb owner watching over certain tasks, likely to be reminiscent of his official responsibilities during his life. The scenes in Rekhmire's tomb depict life at court, inspection of taxes, filling the storehouses, etc (PM I², 209(5); Davies 1973, pl. 24–5). These scenes are highly dominated by men, not surprising considering that this sphere of Egyptian life would have generally been the sole domain of men. These men are dressed according to their status with Rekhmire dressed in the most elaborate costumes, indicating his authority and prestige.

Offering table scenes

The motif of the deceased seated before an offering table is one of the oldest images in Egyptian art and can be traced as far back as the Early Dynastic Period (Martin 1984). The offering table scene originated in the cylinder seals and elite niche statues of the Early Dynastic Period and was later expanded to include images of family members, offering figures, banqueting and funerary rituals such as the Opening of the Mouth (Martin 1986, 1128). The offering table scene is a common scene motif in tombs of the Eighteenth Dynasty (for examples see TT38(PM I², 70(4)); TT52(PM I², 100(6)); TT69(PM I², 137(7)); TT89(PM I², 182(8)); TT108(PM I², 225(5)); TT139(PM I², 253(6)); TT151(PM I², 261(4)); TT161(PM I², 274(5)); TT175(PM I², 281(4)); TT181(PM I², 288(8)); TT249(PM I², 335(4)); TT253(PM I², 357(7)). The image is composed of depictions of the deceased and wife, sometimes with their mothers or children, receiving gifts from family members, friends or priests. Captions identify actions, gifts and individuals and may include offering lists and prayers (Hartwig 2004, 86). The offering scenes in the tomb of Rekhmire depicts the tomb owner and his wife sitting or standing before an offering table or mound of offerings, sometimes consecrated by one of his sons (PM I², 206–215(1, 17); Davies 1973, pls 9, 63, 75–7). Rekhmire is always more elaborately dressed within the scenes in comparison to his wife and sons, highlighting his superior status and promoting him as the main recipient of any offerings made.

Daily life scenes

The daily life scenes are perhaps the most interesting scenes in this study since they often involve the depiction of a variety of male figures. This genre of scenes encompasses images of winemaking, gardening, agriculture, unguent manufacturing, clap netting, the preparation of fish and fowl and the tending of cattle (Hartwig 2004, 106–7). The men within these scenes are dressed appropriately for the task they perform, with the level of dress providing a marker of social status and an indicator of the level of manual labour performed by an individual. In general the overseers in the scenes are more elaborately dressed then those male figures who must perform the strenuous tasks, such as wine production, who all wear shorter kilts or those working in fields who wear specialised head gear (PM I², 209(8); Davies 1973, pl. 39; and PM I², 210(12); Davies 1973, pls 44–6).

It is not surprising to find that the tomb has a distinct male focus and all scenes in this study, bar the banquet scene, revolve around the male image. Within the funerary art, status is shown within the images by size, and though a scene may contain upwards of fifty male images, the eye is drawn to the largest figure through this contrast in size, which identifies him as the most important individual in the scene. In the tomb as a whole, the deceased appears the largest generally within the offering scenes, in which his representations are often much larger than similar ones depicted within other scenes. Perhaps this is to indicate that the offering scenes are the most important in the tomb, or to indicate the importance of offerings to the deceased, or even perhaps to remind visitors to the tomb to make an offering of remembrance.

Comments on the styles and forms of male figures

Body shapes

In the tomb of Rekhmire the male body is depicted in two very different styles: either in the youthful, muscular, traditional manner (PM I², 207(4); Davies 1973, pl. 16) or as the pot-bellied, ageing figure (PM I², 213(17); Davies 1973, pl. 70). These forms are used in very different ways. The youthful figure is commonly used to represent the male image and can be used for the representation of men from any race or social status. It is the dressing and elaborate nature of this body shape which indicates rank and nationality. This is the most common form of male bodily representation within the chosen tombs, and within Egyptian art in general.

The second body shape shows the male as middle-aged and portly. Once again this figure can be dressed appropriately according to his rank, and appears in the tomb of Rekhmire to depict Rekhmire himself in some offering scenes (PM I^2 206–214(1, 17. 20); Davies 1973, pls 9–10, 95–103, 70–7). It is also used to depict the male harpist in the banquet scenes (PM I^2, 213(18); Davies 1973, pl. 66). In the case of the musician this body shape is used to likely represent his seated position, but in the case of the tomb owner it indicates wealth, social ranking and represents the individual's removal from performing physical labour. This body shape possesses many similarities to the representations of fecundity figures, since both representations possess rounded rolls of stomach fat (Baines 1985, 15). If this body shape is an attempt by the tomb owner to depict himself with the same characteristics as the fecundity figures then the form could be symbolic of fertility and the ability to provide well for oneself.

Poses

The poses of individual figures within the tomb scenes also help to distinguish the status of the elite male as the authority figure. Elite men are depicted in very formal static forms, their poses reminiscent of those seen in traditional royal scenes of the king ruling Egypt. The non-elite, who, especially within the daily life scenes, are depicted in an active, busy manner consumed by their work, heavily contrast this. These main contrasting poses reinforce the divide between the elite and the non-elite.

Dress

As in many cultures, the ancient Egyptians regarded clothes and garments as an important element in a person's life and a signifier of wealth and status (Meskell 2002, 162). Dress allowed the artist to depict a contrast between the elite and the non-elite within the tomb. The elite men, especially the tomb owner, are depicted in elaborate clothing and jewellery, which they can wear due to the fact that they did not need to perform manual labour outside. The non-elite, however, wear no jewellery and only a small kilt or loincloth which would have allowed them to work unrestricted. The level of grooming also highlights the difference between the two classes. Elite men have fine clothes, well-kept hair and manicured nails, contrasting the unkempt depictions of the non-elite to assert their lower status (Robins 2008, 212; Cordin 2000, 174; also see Sweeney and Asher-Greve 2006).

Hair

In many societies hair was, and still is, charged with meaning. Not only can it carry erotic (Derchain 1975b, 55), religious and magical significance but the way it is worn often encodes information about gender, age and social status (Robins 1999, 55; Brown 2000, 181; Fletcher 1994a and 1994b). The depictions of hair in the tomb of Rekhmire are no different and are used to display and reinforce social status/hierarchies among men (Robins 1999, 58). For example, in an offering scene containing an image of Rekhmire and his son, Rekhmire's seniority in the scene is reinforced by his elaborate hair, dress and his ageing, portly body-shape (PM I², 213(17); Davies 1973, pl. 70). Elite men in funerary images usually wear a wig of some kind, but the most prestigious hairstyle is the shoulder length wig, with the hair arranged in strands, curls or braids (Robins 1999, 58). This wig is commonly worn by the deceased in their tombs since it establishes their seniority, whilst the round wig or a shaven head can be used to reveal the junior position of the performer of a ritual in such scenes as the offering scenes (Robins 1999, 60). The round wig seems to be more of an 'all purpose' wig, being depicted on priests, offering bearers and the general lower classes in tombs. Shaven heads are not merely confined to the elite and are also seen on male servants who work indoors, priests, and male musicians who are never shown wearing a wig. Robins (1999, 62) suggests that this may represent the nature of their work being primarily based indoors and, therefore, that they did not require protection from the sun or alternatively a sign of cleanliness; no hair would mean no lice.

However, in many of the scenes from the tomb of Rekhmire, in which many men are represented, there is a vast variance in the types and styles of wigs of the non-elite. This may be an attempt to add variance and depth to the scene by the artist and to display his personal skill at representing male figures. For example, sometimes non-elite men are depicted with their own hair when working out doors either in the fields, the marshes or sometimes in the workshops, such as the leather-makers (PM I², 211(14); Davies 1973, pl. 54). These men are shown with heads of thick, black hair or balding with unkempt hair. The colour of the hair also varies from reddish-brown to grey. The non-elite men can also appear with beards or stubble on their chins (Robins 1999, 62–3).

Extent of masculinity within the tombs

Much of the inspiration of this paper has come from the ground-breaking article by Robins (2008), who argues that the conception of elite masculinity was linked to the erect phallus. Her main argument states that by the New Kingdom it went against social decorum to depict elite men with erect phalli, mimicking the manner in which the gods were often depicted, and so new artistic methods had to be employed to reinforce this notion. Robins claims symbols, such as the sceptre in particular, served as substitutes to the erect phallus, and that they carried the same connotations to the viewer: power and authority (Robins 2008, 215). However, this merely provides a starting point for examining masculinity within ancient Egyptian tomb art. The multivalent nature of the tomb as a catalyst for rebirth and the possibility that the tomb, in its entirety, was designed to promote masculinity and power may also have helped to create and maintain masculine ideology. Symbols, such as the sceptre, merely represent one of the many different key details that were used to amalgamate themes in the various funerary scenes.

This study has shown that the elite social status is not only marked within the scenes through size, but also the grandeur of dress, highlighting the contrast between the elite and the non-elite, and the deceased and other men within the image. Here dress acts as a visual system used to construct and display the social identities of the figures represented. Clothing levels had to be appropriate to age, gender and status of the wearers, as well as hair style, pose and body shape. Robins and others suggest that the repetition and standardising of the various types of male gendered figures helped to reinforce this social decorum (Robins 1999, 69; Weeks 1997, 9; Lustig 1997, 63). It is possible to take this comment even further and suggest that all scenes within the tomb were purposely chosen to display the masculinity of the deceased, with each scene representing a different aspect of the ancient Egyptian concept of masculinity. At least within the confines of the pre-Amarna New Kingdom, strength, authority, wealth, and status are commonly present themes within the tomb art. By utilising this argument the fishing and fowling scenes would then be seen to emulate the smiting scenes of the king, reinforcing the concept of 'might' expressed by the king in the *Tale of Sinuhe*. It is within the 'professional duty' scenes that the authority of the individual is expressed and the wealth of the deceased is demonstrated within the offering scenes.

This paper tackles the design and placement of tomb scenes from a masculine standpoint, with particular focus on one tomb in the Theban Necropolis; further analysis is required for later tombs in the New Kingdom period and tombs in other geographical locations. It is intended to show the growth and development of masculine studies as a credible methodological approach and suggests that there are other directions to approach the study of funerary art. Power and social standing are essential themes expressed in ancient Egyptian funerary art and the deceased has guaranteed the projection of his masculinity through the inclusion and composition of several key funerary scenes within his tomb.

Bibliography

Aldred, C. (1970) 'The Foreign Gifts offered to Pharaoh', *Journal of Egyptian Archaeology* 56, 105–116.

Andrews, C. (1996) *Ancient Egyptian Jewellery*. London, British Museum Press.

Assmann, J. (1996) 'Preservation and Presentation of Self in Ancient Egyptian Portraiture', in P. Manuelian (ed.) *Studies in Honour of William Kelly Simpson*, 1, 55–81. Boston, Museum of Fine Arts.

Baines, J. (1985) *Fecundity Figures: Egyptian Personification and the Iconography of a Genre*. Warminster, Aris and Phillips.

Baines, J. (1991) 'Society, Morality and Religious Practice', in B. Schafer (ed.) *Religion in Ancient Egypt*, 123–200. London, Routledge.

Barocas, C. (1982) 'La decoration des chapelles funeraires egyptiennes', in G. Gnoli and J. Vernant (eds) *La mort, les morts dans les societes ancienne*, 429–40. Cambridge, Cambridge University Press.

Bevan, L. (1995) 'Powerful Pudenda: the Penis in Prehistory', *Journal of Theoretical Archaeology* 3(4), 41–58.

Brittan, A. (1989) *Masculinity and Power*. Oxford, Blackwell.

Brown, S. (2000) 'Hairstyles and Hair Ornaments', in L. Donovan and K. McCorquodale (eds) *Egyptian Art*, 181–9. Guizeh, Prism.

Conkey, M. and Gero, J. (1997) 'Programme into Practice: Gender and Feminism in Archaeology', *Annual Review of Anthropology* 26, 411–37.

Connell, R. (1987) *Gender and Power*. Cambridge, Polity Press.

Connell, R. (1995) *Masculinities*. London, Polity Press.

Cordin, A. (2000) 'Fashion and Clothing', in L. Donovan and K. McCorquodale (eds) *Egyptian Art*, 171–7 Guizeh, Prism.

Davies, N. (1932) *The Tomb of Rekh-Mi-Re at Thebes*. New York, Metropolitan Museum Publication.

Derchain, P. (1975a) 'Le lotus, le mandragore et le persea', *Chronique d'Égypte* 50, 65–86.

Derchain, P. (1975b) 'La perruque et le cristal', *Studien zur Altagyptischen Kultur* 2, 55–74.

Derchain, P. (1976) 'Symbols and Metaphors in Literature and Representations of Private Life', *RAIN: Royal Anthropological News* 15, 7–10.

Feucht, E. (1992) 'Fishing and Fowling with the Spear and Throw-stick Reconsidered', in U. Luft (ed.) *The Intellectual Heritage of Egypt. Studies Presented to Laszlo Kakosy by Friends and Colleagues on the Occasion of his 60th Birthday*, 157–69. Budapest, La Chaire d'Egyptologie (Studia Aegyptiaca, 14).

Fletcher, J. (1994a) 'Cosmetics and Body Care', in G. Vogelsang-Eastwood (ed.) *Clothing of the Pharaohs*, 126–36. Leiden, Brill.

Fletcher, J. (1994b) 'A Tale of Hair, Wigs and Lice', *Egyptian Archaeology: Bulletin of the Egypt Exploration Society* 5, 31–3.

Hartwig, M. (2004) *Tomb Painting and Identity in Ancient Thebes*. Brepols, Fondation Égyptologique Reine Élisabeth.

Hodel-Hoenes, S. (2000) *Life and Death in Ancient Egypt: Scenes from Private Tombs in New Kingdom Thebes*. Ithaca, Cornell University Press.

Ikram, S. (2001) 'Banquets', in D. Redford (ed.) *Oxford Encyclopaedia of Ancient Egypt*, 1, 162–4. Oxford, Oxford University Press.

Kanawati, N. (2001) *The Tomb and Beyond: Burial Customs of Egyptian Officials*. Warminster, Aris and Philips.

Kimmel, M. (1987) *Changing Men: New Directions in Research on Men and Masculinity*. Newbury Park, Ca., Sage Publications.

Laboury, D. (1997) 'Une relecture de la tombe de Nakht', in R. Tefnin (ed.) *La Peinture égyptienne ancienne: Un monde de signes à preserver. Actes de colloque international de Bruxelles, avril 1994*, 49–81. Brussels, Fondation Égyptologique Reine Élisabeth.

Lees, C. (1994) *Medieval Masculinities: Regarding Men in the Middle Ages*. Minneapolis, University of Minnesota Press.

Lichtheim, M. (1976) *Ancient Egyptian Literature, 2: The New Kingdom*. Berkeley, University of California Press.

Lustig, J. (1997) 'Kingship, Gender and Age in Middle Kingdom Tomb Scene and Texts', in J. Lustig (ed.) *Anthropology and Egyptology: A Developing Dialogue*, 43–65. Sheffield, Sheffield Academic Press.

Mac an Ghaill, M. (ed.), (1996) *Understanding Masculinities*. Philadelphia, Open University Press.

Manniche, L. (1987) *Sexual Life in Ancient Egypt*. London and New York, Kegan Paul.

Manniche, L. (1999) *Sacred Luxuries: Fragrance, Aromatherapy and Cosmetics in Ancient Egypt*. New York, Cornell University Press.

Martin, K. (1984) 'Speisetischszene', in W. Helck and E. Otto (eds) *Lexikon der Ägyptologie*, V, 1128–33. Wiesbaden, Harrassowitz.

Martin, K. (1986) 'Vogelfang, -jagd, -netz, -steller', in W. Helck and E. Otto (eds) *Lexikon der Ägyptologie*, VI, 1051–4. Wiesbaden, Harrassowitz.

Meskell, L. (2002) Private Life in New Kingdom Egypt. Princeton and Oxford, Princeton University Press.

Parkinson, R. (1997) *The Tale of Sinuhe and other Middle Kingdom Poems*. Oxford, Clarendon Press.

Parkinson, R. (2008) 'Boasting about Hardness: Constructions of Middle Kingdom Masculinity', in C. Graves-Brown and A. Powell, A. (eds) *'Don your Wig for a Happy Hour'*, *Sex and Gender in Ancient Egypt*, 115–42. Swansea, Welsh Classical Press.

Porter, B. and Moss, R (1960) *Topographical Bibliography of Ancient Egyptian Hieroglyphic Texts, etc. Theban Necropolis, 1: Private Tombs*. Oxford, Clarendon Press.

Robins, G. (1993) *Women in Ancient Egypt*. London, British Museum Press.

Robins, G. (1994) 'Problems in interpreting Egyptian Art', *Discussions in Egyptology* 17, 45–58.

Robins, G.(1996) 'Dress, Undress, and the Representation of Fertility and Potency in New Kingdom Egyptian Art', in N. Kampen (ed.) *Sexuality in Ancient Art: Near East, Egypt, Greece, and Italy*, 27–40. Cambridge, Cambridge University Press.

Robins, G. (1997) *The Art of Ancient Egypt*. London, The British Museum Press.

Robins, G. (1999) 'Hair and the Construction of Identity in Ancient Egypt', *Journal of the American Research Center in Egypt* 36, 55–69.

Robins, G. (2008) 'Male Bodies and the Construction of Masculinity in New Kingdom Egyptian Art', in S. D'Auria (ed.) *Servant of Mut: Studies in Honor of Richard Fazzini*, 208–215. Leiden, Brill.

Rocke, M. (1996) *Forbidden Friendships: Homosexuality and Male Culture in Renaissance Florence*. Oxford, Blackwell.

Simpson, W. (ed.), (1973) *The Literature of Ancient Egypt*. New Haven, Yale University Press.

Smith, B. (1994) *Homosexual Desire in Shakespeare's England: A Cultural Poetics*. Chicago, University of Chicago Press.

Smith, B. (2000) *Shakespeare and Masculinity*. Oxford, Oxford University Press.

Sussman, H. (1995) *Victorian Masculinities: Manhood and Masculine Poetics in early Victorian Literature and Art*. Cambridge, Cambridge University Press.

Sweeney, D. and Asher-Greve, J. (2006) 'On Nakedness, Nudity and Gender in Egyptian and Mesopotamian Art', in S. Schroer (ed.) *Images and Gender*, 126–76. Fribourg, Academic Press Fribourg.

Vandier, J. (1952) *Manuel d'archéologie égyptienne*. Paris, Picard.

Weeks, J. (1997) *Sexuality*. London, Routledge.

Westendorf, W. (1967) 'Bemerkungen zur "Kammer der Wiedergeburt" im Tutanch Amungrab', *Zeitschrift für Ägyptische Sprache* 94, 139–50.

Whale, S. (1989) *The Family in the 18th Dynasty of Egypt: A Study in the Representation of the Family in Private Tombs*. Sydney, Australian Centre for Egyptology.

Wildung, D. (1978) *Ägyptische Malerei: Das Grab des Nacht*. Munich, Piper and Co.

Iconographic Programme and Tomb Architecture: A Focus on Desert-Related Themes

Nico Staring
University of Leiden

Introduction

For a long time the 'scenes of daily life' emanating from the decoration of Old Kingdom elite tombs were considered the source par excellence in the study and understanding of Old Kingdom society. Even though this one-to-one relationship has long been abandoned, the scenes nevertheless present us with one of the most important sources for the study of Old Kingdom elite society. A coherent study of the scenes, integrating all data, has to date proven to be unattainable. The rich dataset thus paradoxically obstructed the examination of data to its full potential. During the last three decades the study of the iconographic programme has shifted towards a more systematic, holistic approach: not only the study of individual scenes, but moreover research into the psychology behind the establishment of these programmes in Old Kingdom elite tombs. Well known in this respect is Harpur's study (1987) focusing on the innovations and developments that altered the composition of scenes. However although this is a useful and extensive work, restrictions connected to a study on paper still make it awkward to use. For this purpose, from the early 1980s onwards, a database has been developed at Leiden University. It includes all data on the Memphite Old Kingdom elite tombs (Van Walsem 1985, 2005). Every published tomb has been included with regard to its decorative content. As a result, it is now possible to study and compare a much larger dataset and produce statistically well founded statements. This *MastaBase* is the main source for the data used for my own research. Without this access, it would not have been feasible to process and examine the same amount of data and eventually arrive at the same complete coverage of the subject introduced below.

Goal of research

This paper aims to explore and illustrate the complexity of the iconographic programme: to examine the degree of consistency or variation in placement through multiple approaches, demonstrating the relationship between a tomb's iconographic programme and its architecture. I will limit myself to the Old Kingdom elite tombs of the Memphite region, stretching from Abu Rawash in the north to Maidum in the south. The iconographic programme includes all decoration applied on the walls of the tomb chapel, both on the interior and the exterior. In the dualism encompassed in the tomb, this accessible part is the opposite of the burial chamber, the substructure. The tomb constitutes both the burial place for the deceased's body and the place where priestly services were carried out and sacrifices made (Bolshakov 1997, 24–5). Notwithstanding the optional decoration in the burial chamber, I will restrict myself to the superstructure, further referred to as the tomb chapel.

The main prerequisite underlying the present research has been illustrated well by Andrey Bolshakov (2006, 37), who remarked that: '*Every Egyptian tomb is unique as concerns its architecture and decoration, and unique is its decoration as regards the selection of represented topics, their treatment and their arrangement*'. Even though the same themes were repeatedly included in successive tombs, there are no examples of two tombs possessing an identical combination of depicted themes. So while there appears to be a set of rules to which a tomb owner, or artist, has to conform, there is also a huge diversity observable, presupposing a certain degree of personal choice.

The huge amount of data makes it impossible to carry out an all-encompassing study. Therefore a selection of four themes has been taken from the large collection of this iconographic programme. These were selected on the basis of their exclusive possession and depiction of desert animals as their main topic. The four sub-themes represent only 2.3% of the total number (172) attested in the Memphite Old Kingdom elite tombs (Van Walsem 2006, Appendix 2). In that respect, only a small percentage of the total iconographic programme is covered. The relatively modest scope of the dataset does not detract from the representativeness of the study. The research is based on a fixed dataset, whose character strengthens the outcome of the analysis on the

- large quantity of data covering a substantial part of the published elite tombs
- wide time span covering the total length of the Old Kingdom
- distribution over all cemeteries of the Memphite region

These four subthemes, displaying mutually unconnected representations, have the desert animals as their shared main subject: the desert hunt, slaughtering, feeding and the offering procession of desert animals (Fig.1). As the selection demonstrates, it is not the objective of the present research to analyze all scenes in which all or part of a desert animal is included. Scenes showing copulating animals and animals carried along in an offering procession as a secondary commodity are omitted. Each theme presents a stage in the meat processing process. These were included in the decoration of the tomb chapel for the eternal provision of meat for the benefit of the cult of the deceased tomb owner. The representational content of the scene will not be discussed here. From the analysis of these themes, the extent to which iconographic themes in general were liable to fixed rules, with regards to their disposition, will be attempted. Thus, these themes are regarded as representing the total iconographic programme.

Theme	Sub-theme	Abbr.	Tombs	Scenes	Registers
Hunt	Desert Hunt	HU/D	16	18	46
Offerings	Procession of desert cattle	OF/Prd	107	140	231
Slaughtering	Desert animals	SL/D	19	24	24
Stock/cattle-breeding	Care of desert cattle	ST/Cd	5	5	10

Figure 1. Studied subthemes and their distribution over tombs, scenes and registers (quantity).

Theoretical framework: definitions and delimitations

This is not the place for an in-depth and all-encompassing discussion on the theoretical framework underlying my research. Nevertheless, in order to understand the approach followed and the methodology applied, at least some theory is required. Through this brief discussion, the reader will receive a full understanding of the scope and objectives of this research.

By dividing the total iconographic programme into themes, and by arranging scenes from different iconographic programmes into these themes, one also de-contextualises the individual data. In order to analyze the context in which scenes were arranged, an opposite approach towards the study of this data is required. This context, i.e. the scene or theme within the larger iconographic programme and the iconographic programme in the context of the tomb's superstructure, will be considered as the external aspects. The study of the representational content of the scene, i.e. the internal dynamics within the scenic representation and interplay between represented activities and text, will be understood as the internal aspects. Both categories consist of data that could be analyzed quantitatively: the data will be converted to numbers and inserted into tables, resulting in an objective analysis.

The orientation of a wall (an external aspect) is an example of such a quantitative datum. A scene can either be applied on an eastern, western, northern or southern wall. The orientation of each single scene will be documented and tabulated. In this table, one counts the number of times a theme is associated with either orientation. The outcome thus gives a clear, objective result for the relationship between theme and orientation. The quantitative data thus could be considered descriptive, while qualitative data are rather interpretative, engaged with the 'meaning' of the representation beyond the apparent observable information. With qualitative data one enters the discussion of *Sinnbild*, referring to the meaning or message integrated in, and communicated through the image (Van Walsem 2005, 71). The meaning of an image is not always apparent through the depiction alone. The context, location and parallels of representation can help in interpreting the scene, but still it is an interpretation proposed by modern scholars from outside the studied culture and not one evidenced or explicated unequivocally from within that culture. In this paper, I will restrict myself to the quantitative aspects only. Before shifting one's attention to the *meaning* of an individual representation, one should first understand the complex coherence of factors responsible for its initial realization and selection.

Within the quantitative data, only the external aspects will be treated. These external aspects, presented in Figure 2, could be considered as factors defining the place of a certain scene or theme inside the architectural entity, i.e. the external factors determining the development of the iconographic programme within the boundaries of tomb architecture, orientation and location. While I speak here of *the* external factors, it should be stressed that these do not necessarily include *all* factors that were of any influence, large scale or small scale, on a certain theme in the tomb chapel. As long as we do not clearly understand the inter-dependability of all factors and of all sources that can be of any influence on the iconographic programme of elite tombs, we cannot be certain when ascribing particular events as the driving force behind changes in these data. The external factors discussed in the present paper at least should offer a point of departure. The results for each external

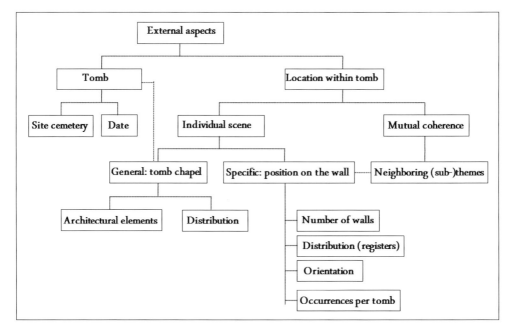

Figure 2. The subdivision and coherence of the identified external factors.

aspect will be presented first, surveying the possibilities of allocating any presumed development. These aspects, related to each individual scene, will be analyzed and eventually describe its disposition inside the architectural unity of the tomb chapel. When the outcome inclines towards a consistency (e.g. in orientation, tomb size, location, etc.) this indicates the existence of 'rules', whereas randomness repudiates a direct correlation and therefore indicates a rather free, personal, choice of the tomb owner with regards to the in- or exclusion, composition and disposition of themes in the iconographic programme and tomb architecture. First of all, one should find a method through which one can allocate any presumed development. The interpretation follows only after establishing such a development.

Analysis

General chronological and geographical distribution

The majority of tombs containing any of the selected four iconographic themes are located in Giza (Fig. 3). A considerable share of the data also originates from Saqqara. These two highly represented sites leave only a small percentage for the remaining Memphite region. Abu Rawash does not contain any of these themes at all. The distribution of tombs over the three dynasties also gives considerable differences. Half of the tombs (49%) date to the Fifth Dynasty and 31% of the examples to the Sixth Dynasty, which leaves only 15% for the beginning of the Old Kingdom. This division corresponds well to the overall chronological distribution of tombs in the Memphite region during the Old Kingdom. The offering procession of desert animals is the only one of the four themes represented

Site	Dyn. 4	Dyn. 5	Dyn. 5/6	Dyn. 6	*Total*
Abusir	-	2	-	-	2
Dahshur	-	1	-	-	1
Giza	14	31	6	14	65
Maidum	3	-	-	-	3
Saqqara	1	24	-	22	47
Total	18	58	6	36	118

Figure 3. Chronological and geographical distribution of tombs.

Theme	Dyn. 4	Dyn. 5	Dyn. 5/6	Dyn. 6	Abusir	Dahshur	Giza	Maidum	Saqqara
HU/D	3	6	1	5	1	-	3	3	8
OF/Prd	16	53	4	28	1	2	55	1	42
SL/D	2	8	-	6	-	-	5	2	9
ST/Cd	-	2	-	3	-	-	-	-	5

Figure 4. Chronological and geographical distribution of themes.

Tomb Type	HU/D	OF/Prd	SL/D	ST/Cd
Single-roomed: cruciform	19%	18%	21%	-
Single-roomed: L-shaped	6%	22%	11%	-
Double-roomed	6%	8%	5%	-
Double-roomed: long corridor	-	10%	5%	-
Multiple-roomed	50%	32%	37%	100%
Other	13%	4%	5%	-
Unknown	6%	6%	16%	-
Total	100%	100%	100%	100%

Figure 5. Distribution of themes over tomb types.

throughout this period and at all sites (Fig. 4). The desert hunt and slaughtering of desert animals are only absent in Dahshur, while the care for desert cattle is restricted to Saqqara, only attested during the Fifth and Sixth Dynasties.

Tomb type and architectural elements

One of the features examined is whether there is any correlation between the size of a tomb chapel and the presence of certain themes. Kanawati (1977, 1) assumed that the costliness of a tomb reflects the tomb owner's wealth. This hypothesis supposes a one-to-one relation between wealth and tomb size. Strudwick (1985, 5) commented that such a thesis must then assume that every tomb owner would put exactly the same proportion of their wealth in their tomb. The autobiographical text in the tomb of Hezi (Saqqara), vizier during the reign of Teti, confirms an anticipated connection between tomb size and social status of the tomb owner, regulated through the king by decree (Silverman 2000, 13). The single-roomed chapel of Hezi illustrates that status, wealth and royal permission do not result, by definition, in a corresponding tomb. There is a difference between royal permission and the ability, through financial potential, of the tomb owner to fulfill the associated expectations. My hypothesis is that the size of a tomb, and thus the disposition of architectural elements within that tomb, was of direct influence on the composition of the decoration. Basically one can assume that the larger the tomb is, the more wall space will be available for the application of decoration. In order to test this hypothesis, the tomb chapels in which the selected themes occur have been divided into five types. The construction of the typology is based on the relative size of the tombs, expressed through the number of rooms: two single-roomed types, two double-roomed types and the large, multi-roomed complexes. Although a much more refined subdivision is possible, the present categorization suffices for answering the present research question. In order to determine the exact location of a scene inside the tomb chapel, irrespective of the tomb type, a set of architectural elements has been distinguished. The rooms will be divided into cult chapel (with false door in the western wall), columned court and *other* room (incorporating all unspecified rooms). Other entities include the façade, entrance portico, doorway and long corridor.

From the results in my database, it appeared that the desert hunt never had a prominent part in the iconographic programme of Old Kingdom elite tombs (Fig. 5). This is slightly different at the initial stage of elite-tomb construction in Maidum. Afterwards the theme is only represented in Saqqara to some extent, as opposed to hardly any examples from Giza. The subsequent inclusion of the theme seems to be closely linked to the size of the tomb chapel: after the Maidum chapels, the theme only occurs in multi-roomed complexes, with just one exception from Saqqara.

The offering procession of desert cattle displays an even, consistent distribution over the different tomb types. One could therefore only conclude that the inclusion of the theme into the iconographic programme has never been dependent on the chapel's size and available wall space.

The relation of stock/cattle breeding with tomb type appears to be a close one, since all examples originate from multi-roomed complexes. Thus, the theme was not only a late addition to the corpus, confined to one site and selected with high exception, it also appeared exclusively in the larger tomb chapels: only when the available wall space allowed, the subject was integrated into the chapel's decoration. These factors add to the sense of exclusiveness of the theme, not only highly dispensable, but also a medium to express uniqueness or originality, for the tomb owner a medium to communicate the message of possessing a unique, original and thus personified tomb, at least with regards to the composition of the iconographic programme.

The slaughtering theme also appears to be independent from tomb size. It is only when one compares the distribution of the theme over time and cemetery-sites that preferences are observable. During the Fourth Dynasty, the theme is restricted to Maidum only, while during the Fifth Dynasty the theme appears predominantly in the multi-roomed chapels, as opposed to a rather even distribution over tomb types during the Sixth Dynasty. With regards to the location, the theme appears most frequently in Saqqara, where it occurs almost exclusively in multi-roomed tombs.

Distribution over the wall: registers

The relative position or distribution of scenes over walls, i.e. wall composition, will be examined on the basis of the division of walls into registers. What, for example, does the predominant placement of a particular scene on the lowest register signify with regards to the theme's relative importance? Generally, scenes positioned at eye-height could be considered to be more 'important' than those applied just below the ceiling, since these possess a higher 'eye-catching value'. Vischak (2007, 446) states that the living audience's ability to see the panels applied on the pillars of rock-cut tombs in Qubbet el-Hawa was of primary concern on their design and distribution. These were applied at eye-height and oriented towards the entrance of the tombs, so that the visitor would not miss them. However, many more factors, left out of the present discussion, could very well be of influence on the eye-catching value.

Relative position	HU/D	OF/Prd	SL/D	ST/Cd
Upper part	14%	5%	8%	64%
Central part	35%	20%	-	22%
Lowerpart	51%	75%	92%	14%

Figure 6. Relative position occupied by themes on tomb walls.

In order to document the relative position of a scene on a wall, the height, measured in registers, should be counted from top-to-bottom and bottom-to-top. Obviously, this is only possible for walls that are completely preserved, since only then the exact height, expressed in the number of registers, is known. The relative position for each individual scene has been catalogued per theme (Fig. 6). The slaughtering of desert animals appeared to possess a clear preference for the lowest register on the wall, to where the majority of scenes are confined. The offering procession also has a preference for the lowest registers, though not necessarily the very lowest. Furthermore, a considerable number of scenes is distributed over a larger range between top and bottom. HU/D and ST/Cd tend towards a position higher up the wall. For ST/Cd this preference is most obvious. Even though the overall trend is the preference of a high position over low, HU/D also has a number of scenes placed on the lowest register.

To recapitulate, the slaughtering and offering procession scenes exhibit the highest eye-catching value. For OF/Prd this is strengthened through a multiple occurrence on the same wall, thus occupying a larger wall surface. This makes it easier to distinguish the subject from all other subjects depicted on the same wall or even complete room.

Wall orientation

There are examples of themes clearly related to a certain direction. In such cases, a connection between theme and physical orientation is emphasised by applying that scene on a wall directed towards the actual location where that activity is thought to have taken place. The desert-related, or more specifically desert animal-related themes obviously have their 'real-life' setting in the desert. The geography of Egypt thus offers two possible

Relative position	HU/D	OF/Prd	SL/D	ST/Cd
East	33%	32%	29%	-
West	33%	23%	13%	60%
North	11%	15%	21%	40%
South	17%	26%	33%	-
Unknown	6%	4%	4%	-
Total	100%	100%	100%	100%

Figure 7. Orientation of walls on which any of the themes are applied.

directions: east and west. One could also argue for a northern and southern orientation, since these surround the tomb, located in the western desert, as well. Considering the preferred east-west axis of mastaba tombs, the east functions normally as the entrance to the tomb. From a practical perspective, this could be the direction from which the animals enter the tomb. In that case, the northern and southern wall would carry these themes. So even though the conception of the west as the most obvious, expected orientation for the walls containing desert-related themes, the posed possibilities expose a more complex and ambiguous interpretation for the use of orientation. Several factors are possibly, though not necessarily to the same degree, responsible for the application of a certain theme on a specific wall. It suffices here to be able to state that scenes of a particular theme do occur on a wall with orientation x. Only when a clear pattern is observable in the orientation, i.e. a majority of scenes occurring on a wall with orientation x, will it be necessary to explain that choice. Otherwise, in case of a diffused result, the choice was clearly not motivated through an ascribed relation between depicted activity and physical orientation.

The east appears to be the most prominently selected orientation for all themes (except for ST/Cd, see Fig.7). The east was selected during all dynasties and at all cemetery-sites. Furthermore, no theme was represented on a western wall during the Fourth Dynasty. The results for the ST/Cd theme differ considerably from all other desert animal-related themes. Perhaps this is due to the fact that it concerns an indoor activity, while all other activities obviously concern outdoor pursuits. Even so, it is impossible to argue, based on the outcome, that any connection existed between the orientation of a wall and the subject of that theme, thus presuming a relationship between wall orientation and actual or ascribed fictional location of that activity. In this case, at least, no strict correlation of desert related subjects and the west existed. The slight preference for the east might be explained through the fact that these themes constitute stages in the meat producing process, which normally would not be situated in the desert (west) but moreover in the inhabited areas (east). When adopting this interpretation, the results for the ST/Cd scenes should be explained otherwise.

Conclusion

In the discussion above, I have presented some of the factors determining the place of iconographic themes in the tomb's superstructure. By analyzing these external factors quantitatively, one arrives at an objective rendering of a supposed relationship between theme and tomb chapel. The degree of consistency with which the scenes were distributed and their likewise development with an increasing available amount of wall surface (through an increase of tomb size) hint at the existence of certain 'rules' connected to the construction of tombs and their associated decoration. However, there are many more factors, 'key indicators' (Alexanian 2006, 1), responsible for the resulting tomb per individual tomb owner, irrespective of their social status and wealth. Vischak (2006, 258) has argued that the context in the iconographic programme is of less importance than the actual presence of the scene. This is only valid if one assumes that it is the social association and status a tomb owner communicates to the outside world through the decoration. This, then, would probably imply less strict rules with regard to the choice of location inside the tomb. Such a thesis complicates the pursued identification of rules. Scenes such as the desert hunt, feeding and, to a lesser extent, slaughtering will probably comply with the 'status communicating' message of the scenes. This hypothesis is based on the fact that the scenes of offering bearers connected to desert animals are much more common than the other three desert animal-related themes. With a presence in 30% of all Memphite tombs in the *MastaBase*, one could speak of a quite regularly included scene, though definitely not indispensable. The others are only seldom attested. In these instances, it is justified to presume that the personal choice of the tomb owner is present, whether it is for status communicating reasons or otherwise.

To return to the main question posed at the beginning of the paper, the selected themes indeed indicate a certain degree of homogeneity with regard to their inclusion and disposition in the tomb chapel. The degree of restrictedness, e.g. to orientation, position on the wall, tomb size, architectural entity, etc., seems to comply with the degree of indispensability or otherwise of the scene. The lower the esteem for the deceased tomb owner, expressed in the absolute number of examples of the concerned theme, the more obvious the relation with the external aspects. None of the results indicate complete randomness nor restrictedness. This might be the result of the proposed research approaches to some degree, but also indicate that the 'rules' nevertheless offered a set of possibilities instead of one choice. Furthermore, it seems as if the thematic content of the tomb chapel's iconographic programme constituted 'basic needs' that could only be supplemented with additional, less indispensable themes when extra wall surface so allowed. The association with a certain orientation, architectural entity, etc. of each theme furthermore regulated the possible inclusion. Thus the inclusion of themes in the iconographic programme of a tomb chapel is indeed subject to certain rules, depending on the degree to which the scene is dispensable or indispensable, but are at the same time also liable to the tomb owner's personal choice.

Acknowledgements

I would like to thank my thesis supervisor, Dr. René van Walsem (University of Leiden), for his stimulating discussions on the subject and comments on the present article, Dr. Nadine Moeller (Oriental Institute, University of Chicago) for her suggestions and correcting my English spelling, and the CRE IX organisers, Vicky Gashe and Jacky Finch, for enabling me to present and publish these aspects of my research.

Bibliography

Alexanian, N. (2006) 'Tomb and social status. The textual evidence', in M. Bárta (ed.) *The Old Kingdom Art and Archaeology. Proceedings of the conference held in Prague, May 31 – June 4, 2004*, 1–8. Prague.

Bolshakov, A. O. (1997) *Man and his Double in Egyptian Ideology of the Old Kingdom* (Ägypten und Altes Testament 37), Wiesbaden, Harrassowitz.

Bolshakov, A. O. (2006) 'Arrangement of Murals as a Principle of Old Kingdom Tomb Decoration', *Internet-Beiträge zur Ägyptologie und Sudanarchäologie* 6, 37–60.

Harpur, Y. (1987) *Decoration in Egyptian tombs of the Old Kingdom*. London, KPI.

Kanawati, N. (1977) *The Egyptian administration in the Old Kingdom: evidence on its economic decline*. Warminster, Aris and Philips.

Silverman, D. P. (2000) 'The Threat Formula and Biographical Text in the Tomb of Hezi at Saqqara', *Journal of the American Research Center in Egypt* 37, 1–13.

Strudwick, N. (1985) *The administration of Egypt in the Old Kingdom: The Highest Titles and Their Holders*. London, KPI.

Vischak, D. (2006) 'Agency in Old Kingdom elite tomb programs: traditions, locations, and variable meanings'. *Internet-Beiträge zur Ägyptologie und Sudanarchäologie* 6, 255–76.

Vischak, D. (2007) 'Identity in/of Elephantine: The Old Kingdom Tombs at Qubbet el Hawa', in Z. Hawass and J. Richards (eds) *The Archaeology and Art of Ancient Egypt: Essays in Honor of David B. O'Connor*, 443–57. Cairo, Supreme Council of Antiquities.

Walsem, R., Van (1985) 'The Mastaba Project at Leiden University', in S. Schoske (ed.) *Akten des vierten Ägyptologenkongress München* 2, 143–54.

Walsem, R., Van (2005) *Iconography of Old Kingdom Elite Tombs. Analysis & Interpretation, Theoretical and Methodological Aspects*. Leiden, Peeters.

Walsem, R., Van (2006) 'Sense and Sensibility. On the Analysis and Interpretation of the Iconography Programmes of Four Old Kingdom Elite Tombs', *Internet-Beiträge zur Ägyptologie und Sudanarchäologie* 6, 277–331.

Predynastic and Protodynastic Mudbrick Settlement Architecture: an Overview and New Interpretation in the Light of Recent Research

Szymon Zdziebłowski,

Adam Mickiewicz University, Poznań

Introduction

Excavation of the early settlement sites in Egypt started on a large scale in the 1980s (e.g. von der Way 1997; van den Brink 1989; Eigner 2003) but since then, no attempt to summarise architectural features has been made. Kemp (2000) has recently summarised mudbrick architecture in Egypt but did not focus much on the earliest stages of its appearance. Among settlement remains, the most interesting category constitute the mudbrick constructions which present a new quality in Predynastic architectural craft. In this paper I would like to answer the following questions:

- when and why did people start to use mudbricks on a large scale in Egypt?
- were bricks a local or foreign (non Egyptian) invention?
- what was the connection between the appearance of complex mudbrick architecture and state formation?

The timeframe of my research includes the Predynastic and Protodynastic Period, and as a geographical range I have chosen the classical borders of Egypt – from the mouth of the Delta up the Nile to Elephantine/Aswan (first cataract region). During my research I have found that no Predynastic mudbrick architecture has been uncovered either in the Western or Eastern Deserts. Nor are there any such remains to be found further south of the first cataract region where at this time A Group settlers existed. It must be stated that the data on the earliest settlements we have collected so far is sparse and final conclusions should be taken as a preliminary.

Mudbrick Types

There are two main types of mudbricks used in the Predynastic and Protodynastic Period. First and the most common is sundried and cuboidal with various dimensions (e.g. 24×12cm, 34×17cm) and of different admixture (Nile silt/clay/straw/sand mixed together). This type of brick was used for house and perimeter wall construction. The second type of mudbrick is called the 'fire-dog' (Hoffman 1980 134). This kind of material is burnt, D shaped or triangular in section and applied mainly to special constructions like kilns and breweries. Fire-dogs vary in dimensions – the longest known can be nearly a metre long.

Structures formed from cuboidal mudbricks

Here I will describe the earliest known examples of the use of this kind of brick. I exclude wattle-and-daub constructions where bricks were used only as a structure's foundations (e.g. Junker 1932, 3–57; Rizkana and Seeher 1989, 51–5, pl. 15, figs 1–3) and focus on buildings/structures which were entirely made of bricks.

It has been mentioned in many publications (e.g. Wengrow 2006, 82) that true mud-brick architecture appeared for the first time in Naqada during the late Naqada II Pe-riod. However, this statement is mainly based on Petrie and Quibell's excavations (Petrie and Quibell 1896) and Baumgartel's later pottery analysis (Baumgartel 1970). In fact, more recent excavations conducted by an Italian team revealed that mudbrick architecture should rather be dated to Naqada III or the First–Second Dynasties (Fattovich *et al* 2007). These facts can be used to show that the chronology of Naqada is unclear, and that while mudbrick architecture can be dated to between the late Naqada II Period and the Early Dy-nastic Period, we should be careful with these dates until further research is carried out.

In fact, it is not until the Protodynastic Period in Upper Egypt that we come across any structures that can be described as complex mudbrick architecture, and the number of these is few. There are some examples from Kom el-Gemuwia (Nekhen) where the remains of a house built partly from bricks has been dated to late Naqada II (Hoffman 1986), and from Hierakonpolis locality HK 29-A where a mudbrick platform and some brick/stone walls dated to the earliest Naqada IID have been found (Friedman 1996). Even during the rest of the Protodynastic Period in Upper Egypt there are just a few known ex-amples: from Elephantine (Kopp 2006) and possibly from Badari (Brunton 1927). These early examples of settlement mudbrick architecture have already been summarised and compared with funerary mudbrick architecture (Zdziebłowski 2008).

It is quite surprising that the earliest known substantial mudbrick settlement construc-tions were traced in the Delta at the site of Tell el-Farkha (Chłodnicki and Ciałowicz *et al* 2006). These can be dated to the Naqada IIC Period and are substantial walls, 1.4m wide, made of regular cuboidal bricks with an average size of 34×17cm. They can be connected with Lower Egyptian cultural deposits, surrounding a brewery complex on the Western Kom. A very similar, thick wall was constructed at the same time on the Cen-tral Kom (Chłodnicki and Ciałowicz, in press). During the Naqada IID2 Period we can observe a drastic change in the use of mudbrick. Both on the Western and Central Koms, settlers started to use a different type of brick in different contexts, for example, for build-ing the first houses. On the Western Kom there is a monumental complex interpreted by excavators as the Naqadan governor's residence (Ciałowicz 2006, 933). On the Central Kom, described as a subsidiary service area (Chłodnicki and Ciałowicz 2007, 149), quite complex structures were present from the beginning of Naqada IID2/IIIA1 – for exam-ple, a multi chambered house was excavated west of wall 455 (Fig. 1). It was *c.*12×8m, and comprised at least 7 rooms surrounding an inner courtyard. Regular silt mudbricks (measuring $30 \times 15 \times 7$cm) were used as the building material. These two buildings are the oldest known houses of this type that have so far been excavated in Egypt. During the Naqada IIIA2 Period, the building on the Western Kom was destroyed by fire and col-lapsed (Ciałowicz 2006, 924). Similar destructive activity was traced on the Central Kom at the same time.

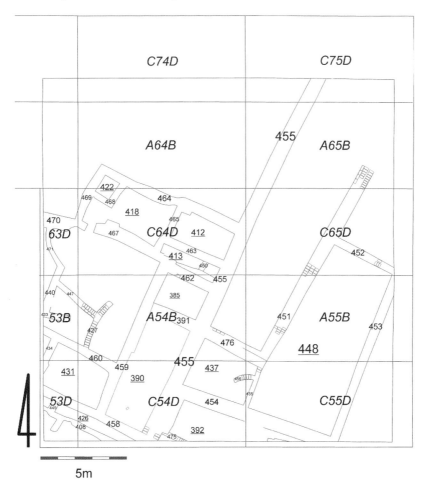

Figure 1. Central Kom at Tell el-Farkha. Mudbrick constructions during Naqada IID2/IIIA1 Period. Drawing by M. Krzepkowski, digitizing by S. Zdziebłowski.

Later (from Naqada IIIB on) new structures were built on both Koms. On the Western Kom a monumental administrative and cult centre appeared (already described in detail elsewhere - e.g. Ciałowicz 2006) and on the Central Kom another settlement. On the Central Kom, a big bulding,15 × 15m square was built east of wall 455 (Fig. 2). It comprised at least 5 rooms (numbers 108, 198, 200, 52, 187) and a square inner courtyard (number 199). The Nile silt bricks used in its construction measured *c.*30 × 15 × 7cm. The walls were not thinner than two bricks laid as headers. Another building appeared west of an open area and was traced west of wall 455. This was not as regular as the complex described previously. Also the walls here were definitely slimmer – *c.*1.5 bricks laid as headers – and the admixture of bricks was different, being comprised of Nile silt and some clay.

The next architectural phase at this site during the Protodynastic Period shows some alterations, mainly west of wall 107 where two courtyards appeared (Fig. 3). In these spaces granaries (silos constructions) were situated.

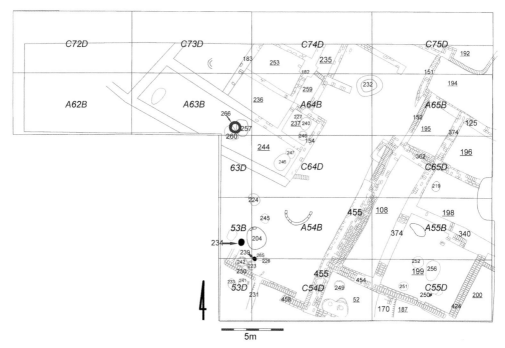

Figure 2. Mudbrick constructions on the Central Kom during Nagada IIIB Period. Drawing by E. Kuciewicz, K. Stawarz and M. Włodarska, digitizing by S. Zdziebłowski. Part of the plan has already been
published (Chłodnicki, Ciałowicz, *et al* 2004).

The only architectural counterparts from the same period (Naqada IID2 to the Protodynastic Period) come from other sites in the Delta, mainly from Buto. The scale of the excavated structures from this site is smaller compared to those at Tell el-Farkha. The structures
at Buto dated to the Early Dynastic Period were much better recognised since their state of
preservation was better (von der Way 1996). It seems that very similar houses with oblong
rooms, comparable to these from the Central Kom at Tell el-Farkha were constructed at
Buto (von der Way 1997). Two granaries, 2.2–2.5m in diameter, were also identified. At
Tell Ibrahim Awad (in the North-Eastern Delta) bricks were also used in a structure of a
different type, presumably a temple or shrine. The earliest phase of this construction can be
dated to Dynasty 0 (phase 5c–6b and 6d) (Eigner 2003, 162–70) and was an oblong building 2.9 m wide and of unknown length. In phase 6b inside the building an L-shaped mudbrick feature was projected into the room. This was made of different kinds of mudbricks
with a high proportion of clay. In phase 6b, adjacent rectangular mudbrick structures were
recorded just south from the shrine with findings that suggest that one of them (R) was a
sacristy or robing room for priests. The data from Tell el-Iswid (S) (again in the North-
Eastern Delta) is sparse. In two small test trenches mudbrick structures dated to Naqada
III or the Early Dynastic Period were found (van den Brink 1989, 58–65). These were
constructed on the north-south axis. Because of the limited excavations, it is impossible to
estimate the plan of the arrangement. All findings (mill and pounding stones, remains of
silos) suggest that these buildings should be associated with domestic activities.

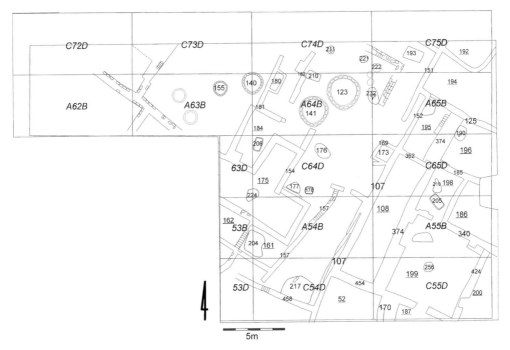

Figure 3. Mudbrick architecture on the Central Kom during Protodynastic Period. Drawing by K. Sta-warz and E. Kuciewicz, digitizing by S. Zdziebłowski. Part of the plan has been already published (Chłodnicki, Ciałowicz *et al* 2004)

Structures made of fire-dogs

This type of brick was use mainly for 1) kiln construction 2) reused in the walls of the houses and 3) constructions called by excavators 'parallel wall structures' (abbreviated to PWS).

Kilns where fire-dogs were present are often interpreted by contemporary researchers as breweries (e.g. Geller 1992). These bricks were used in two ways: to support vessels and to surround whole brewery devices - in other words, they were simply walls (Fig. 4). What is most interesting is that these bricks in fact formed a vault over the whole structures. Vaulted breweries are known from Tell el-Farkha (Chłodnicki and Ciałowicz *et al* 2006) and Abydos (e.g. Peet 1914). Structures from Tell el-Farkha of this type can be dated from Naqada IIB to Naqada IID. At locality 25D in Hierakonpolis, Geller excavated some devices which he called 'breweries', dated to Naqada IIA–B. Here, only a few fire-dogs were found and vessels were supported by mud mixed with pottery sherds. Geller does not describe the arrangement of the bricks, their dimensions or number. In my opinion, these bricks could possibly be from a later context. According to Ciałowicz's (2006, 920) view, structures excavated by Geller (1992) are probably contemporary with those from Tell el-Farkha. Those from Abydos are quite difficult to date but Geller (1992, 23) has suggested a 'time closer to the end of the Predynastic'. At Hierakonpolis, fire-dogs started to be used on a large scale in the mid-Naqada II Period (Takamiya, in press)-just as in Lower Egypt (Tell el-Farkha). Fragments of fire-dogs were also recorded at Tell el-

Iswid (S) and dated similarly (van den Brink 1989, 64). There are a number of sites - Mahasna (Garstang 1902), Ballas (Petrie and Quibell 1896), Naqada (Garstang 1903), Badari (Brunton and Caton-Thompson 1928) - excavated by early researchers where similar kilns or kiln remains were found but it is impossible to date them precisely.

Fire-dogs were also reused in walls used in the construction of houses. Such examples are known from a Tell el-Farkha building dated to Naqada IID2/A1 where they were simply applied together with cuboidal bricks (Fig. 5). Another example was found in the temple at Badari. Brunton (1927, 19) stated that 'the top of the little loose wall is finished off with the long Predynastic fire-bricks used in pottery kilns'.

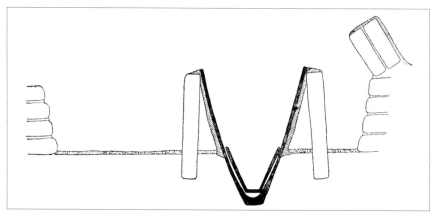

Figure 4. Fire-dogs used in Predynastic kilns in Abydos (after Peet and Loat 1913, 2 fig. 2).

Figure 5. Fire-dogs used together with cuboid bricks, Tell el-Farkha, Central Kom. Photo R. Słaboński.

'Parallel wall structures' (PWS) are constructions known so far in Egypt only from Buto (Fig. 6). PWS have analogies in Near Eastern sites (Faltings 2000, 144, n. 47). We can date them to the Proto- and Early Dynastic Periods. PWS are lines of low walls created in parallel rows. The distance between the walls never exceeded 50cm. The structures are interpreted by the excavator (Faltings *et al* 2000 144, 177) as grain drying devices; on top of the walls, mats and grain was placed and sundried, possibly during a humid season. It is certain that the fire-dogs were reused in this context, because they were burnt but no ash was recorded between PWS. That suggests that in Buto there are still breweries waiting to be excavated.

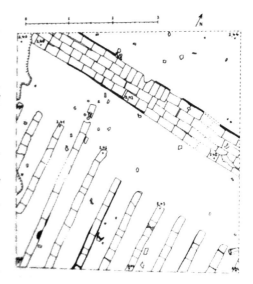

Figure 6. Parallel wall structures in Buto (after Faltings and Köhler 1996, 92).

Conclusions – origins of mudbrick architecture and its significance in the process of state formation

On the basis of archaeological data, it seems that mudbrick architecture appeared both in Upper and Lower Egypt at, more or less, the same time, and that this occurred during the Naqada IIC Period. It is a very important statement, and suggests that we cannot observe the movement of these architectural ideas from the south to the Delta. We do not know about any settlement or sepulchral mudbrick structures in Upper Egypt that predate these from Lower Egypt. This situation was described in more detail elsewhere (Zdziebłowski 2008). From the Naqada IIC Period in Upper Egypt there are examples of mud lined tombs (made of cuboidal sundried bricks) in Hierakonpolis (tomb 100 - Midant-Reynes 2000, 207–10) and in Naqada (tomb 23 - Davis 1983, 20). At this point in my research it is impossible to state with complete certainty where these techniques were first applied in settlements and cemeteries. With regard to breweries constructed of fire-dogs, we are confronted with the same problem, and it is impossible to state where this kind of device originated because throughout Egypt kilns incorporating fire-dogs appeared during the Naqada IIB Period.

The role of Lower Egyptian culture in the process of state formation in Egypt has definitely been underestimated. Their high technological achievement in the field of architecture craftsmanship is one of the most surprising findings. It is true that we cannot see social stratification in the mortuary data in Lower Egypt because burial practices are not always the best indicators of it. What serves as better evidence are the results of the work at Tell el-Farkha, where both walls made of cuboidal, sundried bricks, and breweries constructed entirely of fire-dogs, were dated to the Naqada IIB-D Period. This shows that our knowledge of the archaeological cultures of this period is still limited. It was suggested (Chłodnicki and Ciałowicz *et al* 2006, 77) that such an early appearance of complex architecture 'might be the proof for the early connections between Lower Egyptian and Naqadian culture in that period'. I think, however, that we should look at this problem from a different point of view, which I will try to introduce below.

One question bears consideration here: Why did people begin to use brick on a large scale? It is very probable that one of the most important factors was climate. As Hoffman (1984, 242) has suggested, after 3500 BC a cessation of rainfall (during the terminal phase of the Neolithic Subpluvial) forced people to move towards the Nile valley. Timber started to be a very precious and rare material. This led people to use the abundant mud silt at their disposal. This idea has been recently repeated by Friedman (pers. comm.) and also proven by geological research (Pawlikowski 2004). Another factor – conflict – could have been connected with the beginnings of state formation. Of course, it may yet be too early for such a statement, nevertheless massive walls surrounding breweries in Tell el-Farkha could be interpreted as defensive walls. Due to this assumption, they are said to have been connected with conflicts between protokingdoms within the Nile Valley and Nile Delta.

Researchers often state that Naqadians came down the Nile from Upper Egypt equipped with what might be described as advanced technology (pottery, architecture) and new mortuary practices. Nowadays, this movement is described rather as a more elaborate process than conquest (eg Wengrow 2006, 88–9) but, according to this argument, the Naqadians were still the population eventually responsible for state formation. In fact, looking at the spread of architecture in the early stages of Egyptian civilization, the picture becomes even more complicated. Some scholars have suggested that the direction of cultural change came from the opposite direction, i.e. from Lower to Upper Egypt (eg. Scharff 1927). According to Jiménez-Serrano (2001) *serekh* signs recorded as potmarks in Maadi can be dated to Naqada IIC or even Naqada IIB. The earliest *serekh* signs resemble palace - façade architecture, and are metonymy of power. The important point here is that the examples from Maadi are the oldest known from anywhere in Egypt. The earliest examples from Upper Egypt are not older than Naqada IIIA2 (Jiménez-Serrano 2001, 78). We have previously looked at the Naqada IIC walls from Tell el-Farkha, found surrounding the brewery area. The face of these walls was flat, i.e. – there were no signs of niched architecture. But we need to keep in mind that it was an utility serving area (in this case – brewery) and not a residence. In my opinion, it is quite likely that such structures (niched palace - façade made, of course, of mudbricks) still remain to be found and excavated in Maadi, Buto or Tell el-Farkha. *Serekh*s of early date from Maadi, described by myself, suggest such possibility.

Does the sudden appearance of complex brick usage across Egypt suggest that this invention was introduced to Egypt from abroad? Recent excavations of Tall Hujayrat al-Ghuzlan (Aqaba-Jordan) in some way support the suggestion that mudbrick constructions were first made in Lower Egypt, and that this invention came into Egypt from Transjordan. The site of Tall Hujayrat al-Ghuzlan is a settlement dated between 3900 and 3500 BC cal. (Khalil *et al* 2002) so it is contemporaneous with Lower Egyptian Predynastic culture. Both stone and mudbrick architecture was excavated. Here mudbrick was used mainly in the north-western part of the investigated area, which can be described as a storage building with a number of small rooms measuring 90×90cm and 2×1.5m. There were two kinds of bricks used: $35 \times 25 \times 8$cm and $52 \times 35 \times 22$cm. The number of the artifacts found clearly proves that there are connections to Predynastic Egypt, and especially to the site of Maadi. Exchange between the so-called Southern Levant, or Canaan, and Lower Egyptian culture from Naqada IIC onwards has been proven by Mączyńska (2006). We also cannot disregard parallels in brick dimensions, from Tall Hujayrat al-Ghuzlan and from walls which surrounded the brewery at the Western Kom at Tell el-Farkha, as well as from the other features on Central Kom. We can date them roughly to the final stage of settlement at Tall Hujayrat al-Ghuzlan. It should be kept in mind that the chronology of Tell el-Farkha is based on pottery analysis, while that of Tall Hujayrat al-Ghuzlan is based on carbon dating. These walls were made also of relatively big bricks – their size varied from $40 \times 20 \times 15$cm to $35 \times 17 \times 10$cm. In the next phases (from Naqada IID2 onwards) at Tell el-Farkha smaller, regular bricks were used ($c.30 \times 15 \times 10$cm) and incorporated into constructing, for the first time, houses. In my opinion, the fact that at first bigger bricks were used suggests that the idea of making them came possibly from Transjordan. After the period during which new building material was used, it was adopted to local conditions and slightly changed in dimensions to best suit the necessities.

It should also be remembered that the subject is not limited only to architecture. In a couple of her revisionary articles, Köhler (1995 and in press) suggested that we should start to look at cultural units in Egypt in a different way. In her opinion, 'it is appropriate to call an end to labelling the entire material culture of the north 'Upper Egyptian' when a certain chronological stage is reached, be it Naqada IIC/D or III, because there is no evidence to suggest that the material transformations observable in prehistoric Egypt can be isolated to the north or can be attributed to an ethnic or cultural superposition by the south' (Köhler in press). This assumption is based on pottery (both from settlement or cemetery inventories), graves and lithics analysis. Köhler suggests that both Upper and Lower Egypt developed together 'gradually, organically and from within, each depending on its geographic and ecological settings, each differently influenced by adjacent outside regions, each with in interregional contact with the others' (Köhler, in press). She avoids pointing out which region brought more into the final product, i.e. centralised Egyptian civilization. That gives us some ideas about spreading complex mudbrick architecture over Egypt.

Another interesting innovative point of view about Predynastic cultures was recently presented by Luc Watrin (2002). Similarly to Köhler, he also stresses that previous researchers underestimated Lower Egyptian influence and focuses on Maadi. His work attempts to prove that the Maadi site stretches in chronology to Naqada IA–IIA (Watrin 2002, 55). Watrin suggests that from the beginning of the third millennium BC, the Delta has been strongly influenced by Palestinian cultures. In his opinion, 'the arrival of Palestinian people, mastering advanced technologies such as metallurgy and stone and brick architecture had certainly a major impact on the Nile Delta with its predominantly crude material culture and mediocre daub dwellings' (Watrin 2002, 56).

To conclude, my research suggests that there are three main trends in identifying the beginnings of mudbrick architecture. According to these theories, the architecture might have originated in: a) Upper Egypt, b) Lower Egypt, or c) Palestine/Levant as an outside influence. It is too early to formulate final conclusions but, in my opinion, it seems that mudbrick architecture spread from Lower Egypt further south to the Upper Egyptian Naqada culture. Questions concerning the role of contact between Egypt with Palestine or even Mesopotamia in the development of mudbrick architecture and, strongly connected with this, the formation of the Egyptian state, still remain to be answered.

Acknowledgements

I would like to express my gratitude to Adam Mickiewicz University authorities, Rector Prof. K. Przyszczypkowski, Dean of the Historical Department; Prof. D. Minta; Tworzowska, and the Director of the Institute of Prehistory; Prof. H. Hanna Kóčka-Krenz for their financial support. The research was possible thanks to a scholarship funded by Ministry of Science and Higher Education of the Republic of Poland undertaken at the Polish Centre of Mediterranean Archaeology in Cairo from November 2006 to June 2007. I would like also to express my gratitude to Dr. M. Chłodnicki and Prof. R. Koliński for constant support in my scientific research. I am indebted to Dr. D. Faltings for discussion and for her approval to use images from her article and to Dr. E. Ch. Köhler for sending me her still unpublished article and for her fresh ideas in the field of Egyptian archaeology. Many thanks to Agnieszka Gabor and Bori Németh for their help in translating this paper. Last but not least I am indebted to Vicky Gashe for hosting during the conference in Manchester and her help with editing this paper. Any remaining errors are my own.

Bibliography

Baumgartel, E. J. (1970) *Petrie's Naqada Excavations: A Supplement*. London, Quaritch.

Brunton, G. (1927) *Qau and Badari I*. London, British School of Archaeology.

Brunton, G. and Caton-Thompson, G. (1928) *The Badarian Civilisation and Predynastic Remains near Badari*. London, British School of Archaeology in Egypt.

Chłodnicki, M. and Ciałowicz, K. M., (in press) 'Tell el-Farkha (Ghazala), Season 2008', *Polish Archaeology in the Mediterranean*.

Chłodnicki, M. and Ciałowicz, K. M. (2007) 'Tell el-Farkha (Ghazala), Season 2005', *Polish Archaeology in the Mediterranean* 17, 143–54.

Chłodnicki, M. and Ciałowicz, K. M. with contributions by R. Abłamowicz, K. Cichowski, J. Dębowska-Ludwin, M. A. Jucha, J. Kabaciński, M. Kaczmarek, M. Pawlikowski, G. Pryc, A. Rewekant, M. Skrzypczak, P. Szejnoga, M. Wasilewski (2006) 'Polish Excavations at Tell el-Farkha (Ghazala) in the Nile Delta. Preliminary Report 2004–2005', *Archeologia* 57, 71–128.

Chłodnicki, M. and Ciałowcz, K. M. with contributions by R. Abłamowicz, J. Dębowska, M. Jucha, E. Kirkowski, A. Mączyńska (2004) 'Polish Excavations at Tell el-Farkha (Ghazala) in the Nile Delta. Preliminary Report 2002–3' *Archeologia* 55, 47–73, pls XIV–XIX.

Ciałowicz, K.M. (2006) 'From Residence to Early Temple: the case of Tell el-Farkha', in K. Kroeper, M. Chłodnicki, M. Kobusiewicz (eds) *Archaeology of Early Northeastern Africa*. Poznań, Poznań Archaeological Museum.

Davis, T. (1983) 'Cemetery T at Nagada', *Mitteilungen des Deutschen Archäologischen Instituts, Abteilung Kairo* 39, 17–28.

Eigner, D. (2003) 'Tell Ibrahim Awad: A sequence of Temple Buildings from Dynasty 0 to the Middle Kingdom', in Z. Hawass (ed., in collaboration with L. Pinch Brock), *Egyptology at the dawn of the 21st century, Proceedings of the 8th International Congress of Egyptology, Cairo 2000*, vol. 1, Archaeology, Cairo, 162–70.

Faltings, D., Ballet P., Förster, French P., Ihde Ch., Sahlmann H., Thomalsy J., Thumshirn Ch., Wodzińska, A. (2000) 2. 'Zweiter Vorbericht über die Arbeiten in Buto von 1996–1999', *Mitteilungen des Deutschen Archäologischen Instituts, Abteilung Kairo* 56, 31–179.

Faltings, D. and Köhler, E. Ch. (1996) 'Vorbericht über die Ausgrabungen des DAI in Tell el-Fara´in/Buto 1993 bis 1995', *Mitteilungen des Deutschen Archäologischen Instituts, Abteilung Kairo* 52, 87–114.

Fattovich, R., Malgora, S., Pirelli, R. and Tosi, M. (2007) 'Explorations at South Town by the Naples Oriental Institute (1977–1986)', in H. Hanna (ed.) *The International Conference on the heritage of the Naqada and Qus region, January 22–28, 2007, Preprints*, vol I.

Friedman, R. (1996) 'The Ceremonial Centre at Hierakonpolis Locality HK29A', in A. J. Spencer (ed.) *Aspects of Early Egypt*, London, British Museum Press.

Garstang, J. (1902) 'A Pre-Dynastic Pot-Kiln recently Discovered at Mahasna, Egypt', *Man; Journal of the Royal Anthropological Institute* 2, 38 – 40.

Garstang, J. (1903) *Mahâsna and Bêt Khallâf*, London, Quaritch. Geller, J. (1992) 'From Prehistory to History: Beer in Egypt', in R. Friedman and B. Adams (eds), *The Followers of Horus*, Oxford, Oxbow Monographs. 19–26.

Hoffman, M. A. (1980) 'A rectangular Amratian house from Hierakonpolis and its significance for Predynastic research', *Journal of Near Eastern Studies* 39 (2), 119–38.

Hoffman, M. A. (1984) 'Predynastic cultural ecology and patterns of settlement in Upper Egypt as viewed from Hierakonpolis', in L. Krzyżaniak and M. Kobusiewicz (eds) *Origin and Early Development of Food Producing Cultures in North-Eastern Africa*, Polish Academy of Sciences – Poznań Archaeological Museum, Poznań.

Hoffman, M. A. (1986) 'A preliminary report on 1984 excavations at Hierakonpolis', *Newsletter of the American Research Center in Egypt* 132, 3–14.

Jiménez-Serrano, A. (2001) 'The Origin of the Palace-Façade as Representation of Lower Egyptian Élites', *Göttinger Miszellen* 183, 71–81.

Junker, H. (1932) *Vorläufiger Bericht über die Grabung der Akademie der Wissenschaften in Wien auf der neolitischen Siedlung von Merimde - Benisalâme, 3. Vorbericht, vom 6. November 1931 bis 20. Jänner 1932*. Vienna, Sonderabdruck aus dem Anzeiger der phil.-hist Klasse der Akademie der Wissenschaften in Wien.

Kemp, B. (2000) 'Soil (including mud-brick architecture)', in P. T. Nicholson and I. Shaw (eds) *Ancient Egyptian Materials and Technology*, Cambridge, Cambridge University Press, 78–103.

Khalil, L., Eichmann, R., and Schmidt, K. with contributions by M. M. Atoom, N. Benecke, Th. Hikade, T. Krämer, A. al-Manaseer, B. Müller-Neuhof, R. Neef, G. Nockemann, K. Pfeiffer, D. Rokitta, M. Ronza, M. Tarboush and S. Kerner (2002) 'Archaeological Survey and Excavations at the Wādī al-Yutum and al-Magass area – al-'Aqaba (Aseym): A Preliminary Report on the Third and Fourth Seasons Excavations at Tall Hujayrat al-Ghuzlan in 2002 and 2003 Wadi Al-Yutum', *Annual of the Department of Antiquities of Jordan* 47, 159–82.

Kopp, P. (2006) *Elephantine XXXXII: Die Siedlung der Naqadazeit.* Mainz am Rhein, Philipp von Zabern Verlag.

Köhler, E. Ch. (1995) 'The State of Research on Late Predynastic Egypt: New Evidence for the Development of Pharaonic State?', *Göttinger Miszellen* 147, 79–92.

Köhler, E. Ch. (in press) 'The interaction between and the roles of Upper and Lower Egypt in the formation of the Egyptian State. Another Review', *Proceedings of the International Conference 'Origines', Toulouse, 5th – 8th September 2005.*

Mączyńska, A. (2006) 'Egyptian-Southern Levantine Interaction in the 4th and 3rd Millennium B.C. – A view from Tell el-Farkha', in K. Kroeper, M. Chłodnicki and M. Kobusiewicz (eds) *Archaeology of Northeastern Africa, Proceedings of the International Symposium "Archaeology of the Early Northeastern Africa", Poznań, 14th –17th June 2003.* Poznań, Poznań Archaeological Museum.

Midant-Reynes, B. (2000) *The Prehistory of Egypt. From the first Egyptians to the First Pharaohs* (trans. I. Shaw). Oxford, Blackwell.

Petrie, W. M. F. and Quibell, J. E. (1896) *Naqada and Ballas.* London, Quaritch.

Pawlikowski M. (2004). 'Reasons for the Predynastic - Early Dynastic Transition in Egypt. Geological and Climatic Evidence', in S. Hendrickx, R. Friedman, K. M. Ciałowicz and M. Chłodnicki (eds) *Egypt at its origins. Studies in memory of Barbara Adams, Proceedings of the International Conference "Origin of the State. Predynastic and Early Dynastic Egypt", Krakow, 28th August – 1st September 2002.* Leuven, Peeters.

Peet, T. E. (1914) *The Cemeteries of Abydos, Part II, 1911–1912.* London, Egypt Exploration Fund.

Peet, T. E. and Loat W. L. S. (1913) *The Cemeteries of Abydos. Part III. 1912–1913.* London: Egypt Exploration Fund.

Rizkana I. and Seeher J. (1989) *Maadi III, The Non-Lithic Small Finds and the Structural Remains of the Predynastic Settlement.* Mainz am Rhein. Philipp von Zabern.

Scharff, A (1927) *Grundzüge der ägyptischen Vorgeschichte* (Morgenland 12). Leipzig.

Takamiya. I. H. (in press) 'Firing Installations and Levels of Specialisation: A View from Recent Excavations at Hierakonpolis Locality 11C', in *Proceedings of the International Conference "Origines", Toulouse, 5th – 8th September 2005.*

van den Brink E. C. M., (1989) 'A Transitional Late Predynastic – Early Dynastic Settlement Site in the Northeastern Nile Delta, Egypt', *Mitteilungen des Deutschen Archäologischen Instituts, Abteilung Kairo* 45, 55–108.

von der Way, T. (1996) 'Early Dynastic Architecture at Tell el-Fara'in-Buto', in M. Bietak (ed.) *House and Palace in Ancient Egypt: International Symposium in Cairo, April 8–11, 1992,* 247–52. Vienna, Verlag der Österreichischen Akademie der Wissenschaften.

von der Way, T. (1997) *Buto I. Ergebnisse zum frühen Kontext. Kampagnen der Jahren 1983–1989.* Mainz am Rhein, Verlag Philipp von Zabern. Watrin, L. (2002) 'The Ma'adian Timeframe. A relational Interpretation of Lower Egyptian Proto-history', *Journal of the Ancient Chronology Forum* 9, 38–59.

Wengrow, D. (2006) *The Archaeology of Early Egypt. Social Transformations in North-East Africa, 10,000–2,650 BC.* Cambridge, Cambridge University Press.

Zdziebłowski, S. (2008) 'Some remarks on the earliest settlement mudbrick structures in Egypt', *Göttinger Miszellen* 217, 111–22.

The following paper was presented by Jackie Campbell on behalf of Essam el-Saeed, University of Alexandria. It is published here to commemorate the first video link between a CRE symposium and an Egyptian institution.

A Reassessment of the Landing Place
of Hatshepsut's Fleet in Punt

Essam el-Saeed
University of Alexandria

Introduction

Eminent Egyptologists have suggested that the landing place of Hatshepsut's fleet in the Land of Punt is the Sudanese coast of the Red Sea or the Eritrean coast. This paper, based upon the work and conclusions of Professor Abdel Monem Sayed, supports his thesis that Hatshepsut's fleet landed on the north eastern coast of the Republic of Somalia. The various scholarly proposals have been reviewed along with the textual, artistic, classical and logistical evidence to propose this new location and present a reasoned rationale in support of Sayed.

Previous opinion

The scholarly work of Leclant, Kitchen and Fattovich is renowned. Each considered the geography, embarkation, travel, landing point, and feasibility of Hatshepsut's expedition to Punt.

Leclant, in a short article entitled 'A la quête de Punt' (Leclant 1976, 39–43), opined that the Egyptians reached Punt by sea and that Punt was situated within the region of the valley of Baraka in Eritrea and extended to the valley of Gash and River Atbara. He considered that this location permitted the Egyptians to reach Punt, on occasions inland via the River Nile. Fattovich, in a short essay 'In search of Punt' (Fattovich 1984, 104–8) proposed that Punt was located near the city of Kassala in the upper reaches between Khor Baraka, Khor el-Qash and the River Atbara. Moreover, the port of 'Aqiq' on the Sudanese coast was the landing place of the Egyptians. Kitchen, in 'The Land of Punt' (Kitchen, 1993, 604), proposes a similar location: *'It* [Punt] *occupied an area along the Red Sea coast from (perhaps) north of Port Sudan to northern Eritrea, and extending inland (along with the aromatic flora) perhaps as far as Kassala, and Er-Roseires southward'*. These proposals, each specific in location, are not dissimilar, placing Punt in an area from the Red Sea coast to the vast hinterland, west to the environs of the River Nile.

Reassessing the evidence

Chosen route

A question arising from these scholarly proposals is that if Punt extended to the environs of the Nile in the Sudan, and the Egyptians could obtain its precious products (especially the much-prized ꜥntyw or ꜥntyw-incense) from the region near the Nile waterways (Kassala or similar), what compelled them to risk the journey along the longest route, from the

Red Sea coast across the vast area of the eastern Sudan or Eritrea, towards the Nile?

Expedition objective

The objective of Hatshepsut's mission to Punt and the purpose of this long, dangerous journey was to collect thirty-one valuable incense trees and return them to Egypt for transplanting.

Dangers and hardships

The route from the Red Sea to the hinterland approaching the River Nile environs, would have taken at least twenty-five day's march to cover the 250 miles through dangerous regions, probably inhabited by wild animals and primitive tribes. African regions have long been considered dangerous places, indeed this remains so today. Even at the commencement of the twentieth century AD, foreign merchants could not penetrate for more than two or three days march inland from the shore. Moreover, the procurement of precious articles from the hinterland was dependent on native carriers and guides. The situation has changed little today. If that was the case less than one hundred years ago when expeditions were well equipped with tools, maps, shelter, communication and weapons, the dangers confronting the Hatshepsut's expedition to Punt in those early days must have been immense.

This arduous route, which traversed extensive mountainous and wooded regions would have required all provisions and sustenance to be carried, thereby posing additional hardships. Foremost amongst these was the heavy load requiring some one hundred and eighty men to carry the trees the two hundred and fifty mile route to the Red Sea coast. The representations in Queen Hatshepsut's temple at Deir el-Bahari illustrate some six men for every tree (Naville 1898).

Furthermore, the textual evidence indicates that it was a heavy and arduous task, indeed one of the Puntite carriers is represented looking behind towards his fellow workers and addressing them:

rd.wy rḥw di.k ȝtp n wrḏ.n.ti wrt

'(Mind your) feet, oh comrades, the load is very heavy.'

Sea-shore location

The difficulties of transporting thirty-one frankincense trees, combined with the inherent dangers and obstacles confronting their journey, compels the search for another location for Punt. It is logical that Hatshepsut's expedition to acquire the incense trees would seek a location as close to the sea shore as possible, thereby facilitating ease of transport and minimizing hardship and risk. Indeed, the representation and the texts themselves refer clearly to the proximity of the frankincense trees to the sea shore. The texts of the traffic scene between the Egyptians and the Puntites at Deir el-Bahari reads:

ḥr imȝw n nsw wpwty ḥnꜥ mšꜥ.f
m ḫtyw ȝntyw nw Pwnt ḥr gs.wy wȝḏ-wr

'The erection of the tent of the Royal Messenger, with his army
among the incense terraces of Punt on the two sides (sic.) of the great-green (=sea).'

In addition to this textual evidence clearly locating the proximity of the incense trees to the sea-shore, a representation of resin collection also depicts the sea-shore. A scene from Deir el-Bahari illustrates a living frankincense tree located near the sea shore and a man tapping the tree for its resin into a collecting pot. Hence, an essential prerequisite to locating Punt is to identify an area around the vicinity of the Red Sea where the incense trees grow as close to the sea shore.

Frankincense trees

Prior to addressing the location, the natural habitat and species of frankincense trees needs to be established. What species of frankincense tree did Hatshepsut's expedition transplant? What is the ancient and current distribution of trees around the Red Sea shore? What is the change in distribution of frankincense trees in the Red Sea region in the 3500 years elapsing from the time of Hatshepsut to this day?

Species

The species of incense tree known to the Egyptians as ⸺𓈖𓏌, *ꜥntwy* or *ꜥnty,* was recorded in the Egyptian texts as white incense. Lucas identifies it as frankincense, which is known in Arabic as 'lubban dakar', a fragrant resin from the *Boswellia* species. Today, the tree's natural habitat is Somalia and southern Arabia (Lucas 1926, 111). Frankincense was known to Classical scholars as 'lebanos' (Muller 1855, 264–5), its colour often described as having a greenish tint. This may be why the Egyptians referred to it as ⸺𓈖𓏌, *ꜥntyw wȝḏ,* 'green frankincense' or 'fresh frankincense'.

Hepper studied the distribution of frankincense trees around the coasts of the Red Sea. He identified *Boswellia* species growing near the sea on the north eastern coast of Somalia. It is here that two species of frankincense of high quality may be found; *Boswellia frereana* and *Boswellia bhau-dajiana* the latter synonymous with *Boswellia sacra* (Hepper 1969, 69). Today, *Boswellia frereana* grows in northern Somalia and occasionally is sold on an interchangeable basis with *Boswellia sacra* despite the smell being very different. The historic and current phytogeography supports the conclusion that the north-eastern coast of Somalia was the most probable place from which Hatshepsut's expedition acquired the thirty-one frankincense trees and is therefore the region referred to as Punt.

Habitat

It is difficult to establish any change in habitat of frankincense trees from the time of Hat-shepsut to the modern day. This is in part due to the absence of any detailed geological or phytogeographical study of the Red Sea shores, particularly that of the Somali coast.

The classical authors, however, allow a historical comparative study to be made, based on their descriptions of the incense producing and exporting regions on the African Red Sea shore. Their descriptions, when compared with the present distribution of incense trees in this area, demonstrates a remarkable similarity.

The classical scholars

The *Geography* of Strabo, the *Periplus of the Erythraean Sea*, and the *Natural History* of Pliny date from the first century BC to the first century AD and are highly significant. They describe the geography and flora some 1500 years after the reign of Hatshepsut. This classical evidence, coupled with our subsequent knowledge of habitat and phytogeography affords a picture of the distributional changes of frankincense species during the last 2000 years.

The Classical scholars' descriptions of the incense trade along the Red Sea coast, north and south of Bab-Mandab Strait, are invaluable evidence in tracing the prevalence or otherwise of frankincense trees. Strabo does not refer to the existence of frankincense north or south of the Bab-Mandab Strait, but instead records incense originating from styrax and myrrh. He cites that styrax grew in the regions that extended from Eumenes (near Assab in South Eritera), to Deire (on the northern coast of Tajura Bay, Djabouti). Myrrh however was produced in the region which lay south of Deire (Strabo Book XVI).

Styrax and myrrh, whilst also described as incense, are of different genera to frankincense. Myrrh (*Commiphora molmol*) is found in the form of reddish flakes with a yellowish tint. Styrax (*Styrax officinalis* L) is the balsam obtained from the trunk of the tree and is a brown viscous liquid. Neither fits the description of being white with a greenish tinge, which is consistent with frankincense in the ancient Egyptian texts (Lucas 1926, 111). Some scholars translated the word ꜥntyw-wꜣḏ as 'myrrh', a mistranslation which led to myrrh being confused with frankincense.

Strabo (Book XVI), however, noted a clear distinction between the two plants: *'Frankincense is produced in the region that comes next to the region which produces myrrh'*. This description is corroborated by the present distribution of myrrh and frankincense trees on the northern coast of Somalia. Myrrh trees are more abundant on the northwestern coast line, whilst frankincense is more prolific on the northeastern coast.

Pliny's description is comparable with that of Strabo. He states that the troglodytes brought myrrh to the port of Isis which was ten days rowing from the town of Adulis (Pliny, VI 34). Scholars define the location of the port of Isis as being on the Bay of Assab in south Eritrea (Muller 1855, 264–5).

The most precise and detailed description of the incense producing and exporting regions is given in the *Periplus of the Erythraean Sea*, which substantially supports the descriptions of Strabo and Pliny. The *Periplus* cites that '*myrhit*' was exported from the port of Avalites, presumably the present Zeila, consistent with Strabo describing myrrh being grown (Huntingford 1980, 22). Furthermore, the *Periplus* mentions both myrrh and frankincense among the articles exported from the port that lay on the northern Somali coast next to Avalites.

It also records that the port of Malao (probably Berbera) exported myrrh and a little frankincense, whilst the next port, Mundus (presumed to be Hais), exported frankincense and a type of incense which he called '*mocrutu*' (Huntingford 1980, 24). *Mocrutu* may be the frankincense which the Somalis refer to as '*Moḥor*' (Monem 1960, 373) and is of the genus *Boswellia*. It is recorded as a good-grade frankincense and the tree grows in the plains of northern Somalia, relatively distant from the shore. Finally the *Periplus* says that the port Mosyllum (believed to be Ras Amtara), exports '*mocrutu*' and frankincense.

An important paragraph in the *Periplus* describes the physical features of north eastern Somalia.

> *...sailing along the coast beyond Mosyllum after a two days course, you come to the so-called 'Little Nile River', and a fine spring, and a small laurel-grove, and Cape Elephante. Then the shore recedes into a bay, and has a river called Elephant (Gr. 'Elephas Fiume') and a large laurel-grove called Acannae.* (Huntingford 1980, 26)

This paragraph in the *Periplus* is most significant since the place names conform substantially with the present day Somali names. Cape-Elephante is called Cape Filuk by the Somalis. The word 'filuk' has two syllables, the first being an Arabic word 'fil' meaning elephant. The second syllable is the Somali definite article 'k', shortened from ka, which accompanies singular masculine names. This similarity between the ancient and the modern names of this Cape may well be due to its shape which resembles a recumbent elephant when seen from a distance. Beyond Cape Filuk there is, as mentioned in the *Periplus*, a little bay and small river, each of which the Somalis call 'Gal-Wein' literally translated as 'the great swamp' or 'the great lagoon'.

One of the most significant phrases in the *Periplus* describes the predominance of the frankincense trees on the Somali coast in the first century AD:

> *...where alone (in the region of Elephas and Acannae) is produced the 'far-side' frankincense (of the Somali coast) in great quantity and of the best grade'.*
> (Muller 1855, 264–5)

The geographical description in the *Periplus* clearly states that the north-eastern coast of Somalia was the only area on the African Red Sea coast renowned for producing the best grade of frankincense in great quantities. The same holds true today. The Somali port of Alula exports nearly 60% of the world requirement of frankincense.

Moreover, the *Periplus*, in referring to the existence of frankincense along the north coast of Somalia, implies that the trees did not grow near the sea-shore in any other area except the eastern part. This is reasoned on the basis that the *Periplus* deployed the expression 'is produced' (in Greek: *ginetay*), when referring to the occurence of frankincense in this coastal area (the region of River Elephas and Acannae). However, the *Periplus* employs the phrase 'is exported' (in Greek: *ekhferitay*) referring to its occurrence in the ports of the western Somali coast (Muller 1855, 264–5). Deployment of these two expressions by the same author implies different conditions. It suggests that the expression: 'is produced' (*ginetay*) refers to the growing of frankincense trees on the coastal region. This concurs with the description in the *Periplus* describing the area where trees are located as being bounded by the rivers Elephas and Acannae, close to the sea shore. The *Periplus* further describes frankincense being produced 'in great quantity', a situation which prevails to this day. Such evidence suggests that the distribution of frankincense trees on the African coast of the Red Sea has not changed during the last 2000 years. Since little change has occurred during this period of 2000 years, it is compelling to deduce that little significant change would have occurred over the preceding 1500 years, from the time of Hatshepsut until the first century AD. Consequently it is then reasonable to conclude that the distribution has not changed since the time of Hatshepsut to this day.

In addition to this preliminary evidence derived from the study of the distribution of frankincense trees, the information obtained from physical features and aquatic fauna affords secondary but nevertheless important and complementary evidence. The north-eastern Somali coast differs from the north-western area owing to distinctly variant geological features. The mountain ranges of the eastern coast are nearer to the sea than are the mountains of the western shore. From Ras Amtara eastward these ranges are covered with frankincense trees arranged in terraces (British Admiralty 1944, 462). This compares with the Egyptian term *ktyw ꜥntyw nw Pwnt*, 'the frankincense-terraces of Punt', defining the place from which Hatshepsut's expedition obtained the frankincense trees for transplantation in Egypt.

Two factors suggest the landing place of Hatshepsut's fleet: first, the renown of this area as being the most productive region of the best grade of frankincense during classical times, and secondly, the location of a wide river mouth in this region, the River Gal-Wein, is consistent with the River Elephante or Elephas described by the classical scholars. Scenes depicting the harbour of Punt in the Deir el-Bahari reliefs further confirm the riverine nature of the location. One scene depicting the Egyptian ships entering the Puntites harbour illustrates marine and freshwater fish side by side (Naville 1898, 72–3; Danelius and Steinitz 1967, 15–24).

The freshwater catfish is represented close to the shore near the mouth of the river, however the *panulirus* or spiny lobster, a purely marine species characteristic of the Red Sea and the Gulf of Aden, is represented at a point much further from the river mouth. This may suggest the ancient artist's intention of indicating sea water. This contrast is endorsed in the illustration with a ship with its sail unfurled indicative of a harbour location and the confluence of fresh and salt water sources.

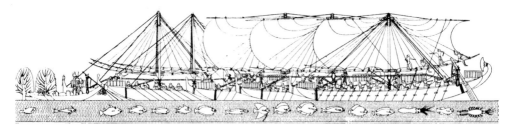

Figure 1. The Egyptian fleet arriving at the harbour of Punt (after Mariette 1877, pl.6).

Conclusion

The work of Professor Abdel Monem Sayed, combined with geographical, classical, phytogeographical and logistical analysis, leads the author to conclude that the landing place of Hatshepsut's fleet on its voyage to Punt was in the north eastern coast of the Republic of Somalia and not on the Sudanese or the Eritrean coast. Textual and artistic interpretation and the accumulation of combined evidence over a period of time reinforced this conclusion.

Acknowledgements

Professor Rosalie David OBE, Director of the KNH Centre for Biomedical Egyptology, The University of Manchester for advice. Dr Jackie Campbell, KNH Centre for Biomedical Egyptology, for presenting the paper on my behalf and drafting for publication. Dr John Campbell for advice and drafting.

Bibliography

Breasted, J. H. (1907) *Ancient Records of Egypt*, 2. Chicago, University of Chicago Press.

British Admiralty (1944) *Red Sea & Gulf of Aden Pilot* (9th ed). London, HMSO.

Danelius, E. and Steinitz, H. (1967) 'The fishes and other aquatic animals on the Punt reliefs at Deir el-Bahari', *Journal of Egyptian Archaeology* 53, 15–24.

Fattovich, R. (1984) 'In search of Punt', *Ligabue Magazine*, III, 5, 104–8.

Hepper, F. N. (1969) 'Arabian and African Frankincense Trees', *Journal of Egyptian Archaeology* 55, 69.

Huntingford, G. W. B. (1980) *The Periplus of the Erythraean Sea*, London, Hakluyt Society.

Kitchen, K. A (1993) 'The Land of Punt', in T. Shaw, P. Sinclair, B. Andah and A Okpoko (eds) *The Archeology of Africa, Food, Metals, and Towns*, 587–608. London, Routledge.

Leclant, J. (1976) 'A la quête de Punt', *Archaeologia*, 39–43.

Lucas, A (1926) *Ancient Egyptian Materials.and Industries.* London, Longmans Green and Co.

Mariette, A, (1877) *Deir-el-Bahari*. Leipzig, Hinrichs.

Muller, K. O. (1855) *Geographi Graeci Minores*, 1. Paris.

Monem, A. H. (1960) *The Somali Republic* (in Arabic). Cairo.

Naville, E. (1898) *The Temple of Deir el-Bahari*, III, London, Egypt Exploration Fund.

Pliny (1950) *Natural History* (trans. H. Rackham) Harvard, Harvard University Press.

Strabo (1930) *Geography of Strabo* (trans. H. L. Jones) London, Heinemann.